P9-ELS-486

What is graphic design?

It is very much more difficult
to talk about a thing than to do it.
Oscar Wilde

2 50

A RotoVision Book
Published and distributed
by RotoVision SA
Route Suisse 9
CH-1295 Mies
Switzerland

RotoVision SA
Sales, Editorial & Production Office
Sheridan House
112/116A Western Road
Hove, East Sussex BN3 1DD, UK
Tel: +44 (0)1273 72 72 68
Fax: +44 (0)1273 72 72 69
Email: sales@rotovision.com
www.rotovision.com

10 9 8 7 6 5 4 3 2
ISBN 2-88046-539-7

Production and separations
by ProVision Pte. Ltd. in Singapore
Tel: +65 6334 7720
Fax: +65 6334 7721

Opposite: Look
The most basic requirement
for understanding graphic
design. Photograph courtesy
of Peter Wood.

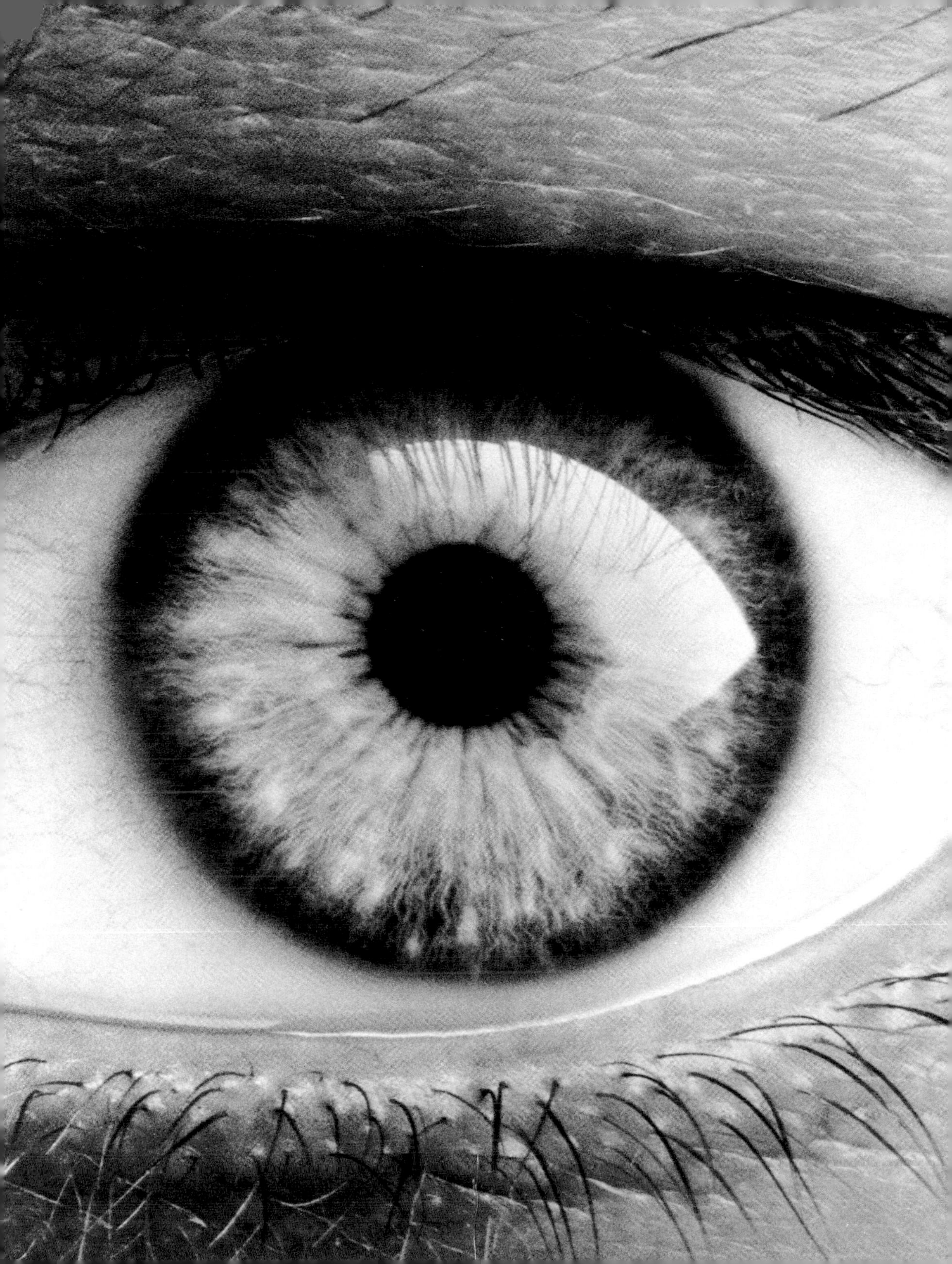

Issues

Anatomy

Portfolios

Etcetera

What is graphic design?

Graphic design is the most universal of all the arts. It is all around us, explaining, decorating, identifying: imposing meaning on the world. It is in the streets, in everything we read, it is on our bodies. We engage with design in road signs, advertisements, magazines, cigarette packets, headache pills, the logo on our t-shirt, the washing label on our jacket. It is not just a modern or capitalistic phenomenon. Streets full of signs, emblems, prices, sale offers, official pronouncements and news would all have been just as familiar to ancient Egyptians, mediaeval Italians or the people of Soviet Russia.

Graphic design performs a number of functions. It sorts and differentiates – it distinguishes one company or organisation or nation from another. It informs – it tells us how to bone a duck or how to register a birth. It acts on our emotions, and helps to shape how we feel about the world around us.

There is an old joke amongst graphic designers: 'Bad graphic design never killed anyone'. This is meant to show that design is inconsequential, ultimately decorative, a question merely of picking one typeface or colour rather than another that would work just as well. Journalists delight in using the adjective 'designer' to stand for a particular kind of cynical consumerism that distracts us with a jazzy visual appearance: fancy bottle-tops, cod-Victorian labels, new logos for unethical companies for example. This has led to phrases like 'designer water', 'designer jeans', even 'designer babies'. Depressingly, graphic designers do sometimes play a small part in producing this tinsel.

Imagine if graphic design was banned, or just simply disappeared overnight. There would be no written word, no newspapers, no magazines, no internet, no science to speak of, books for the wealthy only, cowrie shells for money, a few items of literature, a handful of universities and only the crudest medicine. Everything would have to be painstakingly written by hand. Without design's process and ingredients – structure and organisation, word and image, differentiation – we would have to receive all our information by the spoken word. We would enter another Dark Ages, a thousand years of ignorance, prejudice, superstition and very short lifespans.

Rather than a frivolous extra, the uses and purposes of graphic design are so integral to our modern world – civilisation – that Marshall McLuhan named us "typographic man".

100 DJs revealed
TONG SASHA
JULES OAKEY
The secret life of superstar DJs
Drugs, sex, Ferraris, egos… the lot!
Every Wednesday
LIZ'S BABY
SPECIAL ISSUE!
HARRY POTTER
Star-studded premiere pics
SLIM, TONE
THE 24-HR PARTY DRI
PLAN THAT WORKS
GO ON, GO ON…
WHY YOU SHOULD
INDULGE THIS XMAS
DIET &
The Eat Yourself Slim diet
ORGANIC GARDENING
02078135457
GARDENI
DESIGN
PAY HERE
Triax UK Ltd.
GREAT BRITAIN
C/NO.
MBING · TIM
· PAINTS · LO
Camden
BE RESPONSIBLE
CLEAN IT UP !
BMW
F137 CG
Evans Halshaw

Bilbao and New York
Everything on these pages comes from two cities, gathered using one criterion – it was placed into my hands. Trash that is normally thrown away, it spans almost every conceivable genre of design; pseudo-Victoriana, utopian Modernism, quasi-Mediaeval-mysticism, neo-classical, machine-typography and Renaissance idealism.

600 Pts. / Pta.
3,61 Euros
Bilboko Arte Eder Museoa
Museo de Bellas Artes de Bilbao
Nº 37406
Bilduma iraunkorra

G & J PRINTING CO. N.Y. STOCK FORM NO. 715 PRINTED IN U. S. A.

TELEPHONE MESSAGE

5/26/01 19 Time 10 A M.

MR. Heinz

Room 617

THE FOLLOWING MESSAGE WAS RECEIVED DURING YOUR ABSENCE, FROM

your reservation is confirmed. at 4:00 Pm to JFK, confirmation # 716093. Any change, Please call at 212-501-7400, Spectacular Limo. Thank you and have a Safe trip. Shajiave.

Function versus aesthetics

The father of the term 'graphic design' was an American, William Addison Dwiggins – a very successful designer who produced advertising material in the form of posters, pamphlets and adverts in newspapers and periodicals. In 1922 he wrote: "In the matter of layout forget art at the start and use horse-sense. The printing-designer's whole duty is to make a clear presentation of the message – to get the important statements forward and the minor parts placed so that they will not be overlooked. This calls for an exercise of common sense and a faculty for analysis rather than for art." In this essay, we can see straightaway what the initial ingredients of graphic design were thought to be a century ago, using Dwiggins' terminology: type letters, white spaces, decorations, borders and such accessories and pictures.

Dwiggins saw graphic design as almost entirely concerned with the preparation of the artwork to be printed. One of his alternative terms for graphic design was 'super-printing' (super meaning 'above' or 'before'). But today graphic design and typography are generally understood to be quite distinct. Typography is the arrangement of the mechanical alphabet, type, and by implication is usually focussed on printed reproduction. Graphic design is a broader term and includes typography, as well as other graphic disciplines: image-making and manipulation, the possibilities of which have broadened considerably since Dwiggins' day; logo design and identity schemes; exhibition design; packaging and so on. Much of this work is reproduced by methods other than simply printing on paper: photographic transparencies, digital outputs, coloured vinyl, sodium light, paint, wood and metal, cathode-ray tube and so on.

Dwiggins' ideas about design are concerned with achieving predictable results. Printer-typographer, Francis Meynell, had a more thrilling approach to the role of typography – and therefore graphic design. In 1923 he wrote a piece called 'With twenty-six soldiers of lead I have conquered the world'. "All the heights and depths and breadths of tangible and natural things – landscapes, sunsets, the scent of hay, the hum of bees, the beauty which belongs to eyelids (and is falsely ascribed to eyes); all the immeasurable emotions and motions of the human mind, to which there seems no bound; ugly and terrible and mysterious thoughts and things, as well as beautiful – all are compassed, restrained, ordered in a trifling jumble of letters. Twenty-six signs!"

In contrast to Dwiggins, Meynell emphasises the poetic and aesthetic content of design. This could be because Meynell type-set and printed books – including Shakespeare – whereas Dwiggins dealt with uninspiring commercial messages. But in these two extracts we have the seed of the most fundamental tension that exists within design. One position states that design is essentially a functional activity, with the needs of the paying client foremost. The opposing view regards design as too significant

Lest we take it too seriously, almost all graphic design, sooner or later, is destined to end up in one of these two recepticles.

to be seen in such terms, and that it ought to be used in ways that emphasise and explore its expressive potential: function versus aesthetic possibility. These two ideas are always grinding against one another, both within the field of graphic design and within each individual graphic designer.

Graphic designers constantly struggle with these two models – the model of the artist, and the model of the artisan. The model of the artist is: an individual whose work is concerned with self-discovery. Only she* can know when a piece of art is complete, or what the materials or subject matter for each new piece are to be. The purpose of art, put in the broadest terms by Susan Sontag, is "modifying consciousness and organising new modes of sensibility". This is a purpose that challenges the very idea of purposefulness. Who is the judge? There is no 'client' in art (rarely in modern art as there was in the art of previous centuries), no-one who funds an activity so diffuse and subjective, who might set an objective, a purpose, and call it successful or unsuccessful. And who exactly is the viewer, who can say when it works or when it does not work, or when it fails to do something as difficult to define as "modifying consciousness"?

Art sets out to be unique. Since the artist is not exactly sure of where she wants to get to, the artistic process is experimental, speculative. And it must often fail. When it works, it does so almost by accident. It sets out to be expressive; in Marshall McLuhan's words, each piece of art is a new "sensory mix". It is communication as broad and loose as it can be defined.

Set against this is the model of the artisan: an individual who represents a craft. The artisan is fashioning an object – a book, a bench, an inscription – that must work and be successful, or she will not be paid. She needs to develop methods that are repeatable and reliable.

Her process is purposeful, her aesthetic style expressive within the terms of the purpose. As Stanley Morison put it, typography has "only accidentally aesthetic ends". Communication is focussed within the terms of the commission.

These two models represent the poles between which the graphic designer must choose a position. Is she to produce work that transcends something as mundane as purpose determined by someone else, using a process that aims at uniqueness, and risk failure? Or is she to work using 'horse-sense', with novelty lower on her list, satisfying herself with the reliably successful execution of each task?

*I have used the female pronoun throughout. Almost every book I have ever read uses the male pronoun to represent us all, this book is a minute and deliberate exception.

Definitions

Trying to reduce such a wide-ranging and variable activity into a brief definition, or one portable phrase, is difficult to say the least. One method is to take little bits from other attempts, in the hope that these fragments might add up to some kind of whole.

Christopher Prendergast, attempting to define literature, offered a warning: "A single, generalising description misses too much and is destined to do so, if it is offered as 'the' description". So these two pages, in fact this entire book, is not presented as 'the' definition, but some notes that indicate a definition.

Designer/historian Richard Hollis sees graphic design as constituting "a kind of language with an uncertain grammar and a continuously expanding vocabulary". He goes on to stake out the possible uses. "The primary role of design is identification: to say what something is, or where it came from (inn signs, banners and shields, masons' marks, publishers' and printers' symbols, company logos, packaging labels). Its second function... is for information and instruction, indicating the relationship of one thing to another in direction, position and scale (maps, diagrams, directional signs). Most distinct from this is its third use, presentation and promotion (posters, advertisements), where it aims to catch the eye and make its message memorable."

This kind of definition carves up the purpose in a neat way, but the allocation of categories is very misleading, as most pieces of design perform all of these roles. A poster identifies, instructs and promotes all at the same time. A logo identifies and promotes simultaneously.

The term 'graphic design' was coined in 1922. If things had evolved slightly differently, and Dwiggins had opted for his alternative term,

"Graphic design is the business of making or choosing marks and arranging them on a surface to convey an idea."
Richard Hollis

"Be niggardly with decorations, borders and such accessories. Do not pile up ornament like flowers at a funeral...
Get acquainted with the shapes of the type letters themselves. They are the units out of which the structure is made – unassembled bricks and beams.
Pick good ones and stick to them."
William Addison Dwiggins

"[On first seeing Edward Johnson's letterforms] I was caught unprepared. I did not know that such beauties could exist. I was struck by lightning, as by a sort of enlightenment... and for a brief second seemed to know even as God knows."
Eric Gill

"The type which, through any arbitrary warping of design or excess of 'color', gets in the way of the mental picture to be conveyed, is bad type."
Beatrice Warde

"For modern advertising and for the modern exponent of form the individual element – the artist's 'own touch' – is of absolutely no consequence."
Lazar Markovitch Lissitzky

"The more uninteresting a letter, the more useful it is to the typographer."
Piet Zwart

"...graphic design, in the end, deals with the spectator, and because it is the goal of the designer to be persuasive or at least informative, it follows that the designer's problems are twofold: to anticipate the spectator's reactions and to meet his own aesthetic needs."
Paul Rand

"...once more it was affirmed that typography is not self-expression, but that it is founded in and conditioned by the message it must convey, and that it is a service art and not a fine art, however pure and elemental this discipline is."
Herbert Bayer

"Design can critically engage the mechanics of representation, exposing and revising its ideological biases; design also can remake the grammar of communication by discovering structures and patterns within the material media of visual and verbal writing."
Ellen Lupton/J. Abbott Miller

"Whatever the information transmitted, it must, ethically and culturally, reflect its responsibility to society."
Josef Müller-Brockmann

this book might have been called 'What is super-printing?' Herbert Spencer's version is 'mechanized art'. These terms pick out a useful feature: the relationship of design to machinery. Modernity has brought mass production, and graphic design is mass REproduction. Most design is now digital, more malleable and fluid than Eric Gill, chisel in hand, could have ever imagined. And although much reproduction uses techniques that do not involve ink and paper, it is still mechanically reproduced.

Swiss pioneers like Max Bill and Josef Müller-Brockmann preferred the term 'visual communication' (visuelle kommunikation). It seemed grander, broader and less bound up with printing than 'advertising graphics' (werbegrafik). Certainly it seems more naturally suited to graphic design today, but apart from a few attempts to institute it as a replacement (see page 118), it is not commonly used.

The German word most frequently used to describe design today is 'gestaltung': the forming and shaping of material. 'Gestalt', means a whole, or something complete. Much of a designer's time is spent in preparing materials for manufacture, and here lies a very significant distinction. Is graphic design finished pieces or the process leading to manufacture? One is finished and static, the other is heavy with doubt, hope, choices, potential and action. Is design what you have done, or what you do?

What is a graphic designer?

One way of looking at design is to see it not as finished pieces, but the process itself. Ernst Gombrich, in his seminal book 'The Story of Art', wrote that "there really is no such thing as Art. There are only artists ..." If we say 'there is no such thing as graphic design, only graphic designers', what defines a graphic designer?

Is everyone a designer, as a recent publication by Mieke Gerritzen asserted? It goes on to say (in Dutch-English), "'Everyone is a designer' is a marketing demographic, not a statement about the logic of a practice. While everyone has the same statistical chance of chancing upon a serendipitous moment or two, creating a practice of design still requires linking up hundreds if not thousands of discrete decisions into systems that extend from part to part, from project to project, from year to year."

What are the decisions that make up the practice of design? I suggest there are two fundamental activities that can be found in the practice of every graphic designer. The first I want to call 'making sense'. No designer, however contrary, ever said, 'I want to make this more complicated than it needs to be', or 'I want to leave someone with no idea as to what this is'. The designer's instinct is to simplify and clarify. "Design is the child of the concept of efficiency," says Jorge Frascara. All design has to give shape to its raw material, sequence it, order and sort it, give it a hierarchy. The material forms of design – books, posters, signs, packages, webpages – insist that something needs to be read first, seen first. It follows then that there is an order, something first, and something last. Even the most intricate and florid design is a clear map, indicating with scale, colour and position the issues and subjects that the designer wants the viewer to comprehend.

The second I want to call 'creating difference'. The product, company, or event needs to be unique and easily recognised, picked out and distinguished from thousands of others. The designer wants her work to stand out, not only from the work of other designers, but also from her other work. The compulsion to create difference is unrelenting, the impact and power of visual form that is new is deeply embedded in all designers. Fetishisation of the 'original' drives the constant renewal of the language of design. It sends designers in search of new ways of drawing type and novel combinations of colour. It drives efforts to escape the grid, and lies behind the need to loot art, film, television and the vernacular for ever fresher ways of making typefaces and juxtaposing images and words.

All design, even the newest new work, follows existing patterns, codes, shapes and genres (see page 48). These patterns constitute the fabric of visual language – a language that is constantly being evolved and expanded, but, like any verbal or written utterance, all visual expression has to draw on its grammar if it is to be meaningful.

The graphic designer then is someone who is always making sense of her material, and mediating it through the forms and codes of visual language.

Johann Gutenberg, father of graphic design
Johann was a family nickname. His full name was Friele Gensfleisch zur Laden zum Gutenberg which roughly translates as Freddy Goosefat of Goodcastle. The only form of mechanical, mass reproduction well known in Gutenberg's time was woodcuts. (The Chinese produced prints as early as the 8th century, but development was limited because the wood could only carry so much detail – they consisted almost solely of captioned illustrations.) Gutenberg was a gemcutter and metalworker, with a powerful entrepreneurial urge. At some point in 1440 he revolutionised printing by creating moveable type – individual letters that could be endlessly composed, and recomposed. Along with the type itself came other inventions: the press to print it; rich black, opaque ink, malleable enough to roll onto dozens of tiny letters; the steel punches on which the type was cut with tiny tools (using his gemcutting skills); the alloy – not too soft, not hard enough to shatter – for casting the individual type elements. Gutenberg's multi-invention simultaneously gave birth to the grid (since all modular type elements had to be located and locked into the frame) and typefaces – since lettering now had to be cut for mechanical reproduction. These are two of the primary components of graphic design over 500 years later.

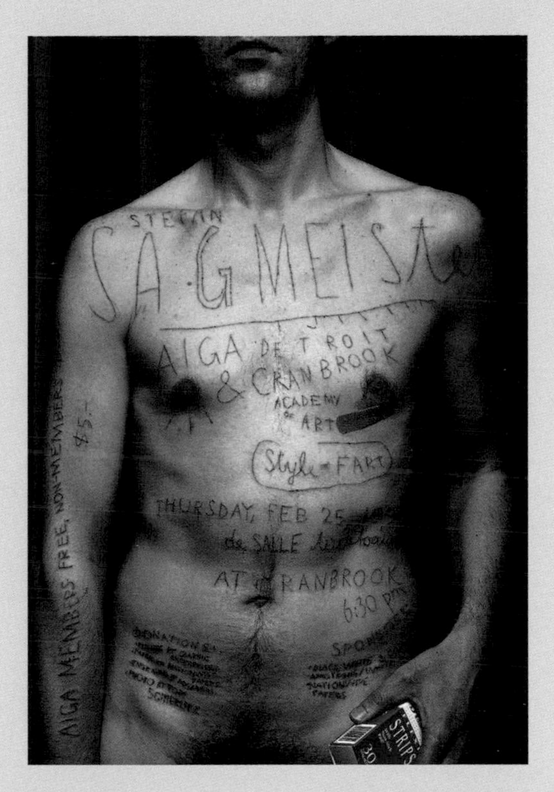

Stefan Sagmeister, child of Gutenberg
Stefan Sagmeister translates as Stephen Talkingmaster. An Austrian working in New York, he is among the most highly regarded designers working today. One of his most notorious pieces is shown above, a poster for a lecture. The text is carved into Sagmeister's own body. He had intended to cut the text himself, but "part of the problem was cutting in reverse, part of the problem was cutting accurately, and part of the problem was cutting". After eight hours of cutting, Sagmeister's body became a piece of graphic design. It was also wracked with pain. Certainly, as an emblem, there is no starker example of 'self expression' Apart from using the mechanical processes of photography and printing, Sagmeister created a piece focussed on himself, made out of himself, in a way that completely steps outside of the constraints of any recognisable genre. This work does, of course, have precedents in the wider culture: tattooing; self-mutilation; self-mutilation as art; adolescents carving lovers' names on their arms. It shows amazing commitment and more than a touch of madness in its struggle for a fresh form of expression.

Before and after
Gutenberg's great work, the '42-line Bible' is below. Sagmeister's 'Lou Reed: Pass Thru Fire, The Collected Lyrics' is opposite. The '42-line Bible', the only work definitively printed by Gutenberg, was printed in Mainz in about 1450. It borrows from the handwritten Bibles of the time, in that it uses their two-column layout and letterforms, a German pen-drawn 'black letter' or gothic script. The swirling plant forms were added later, by hand, for an extra fee. The design mimics the handwritten style, but converts it into graphic design, using a rationalised, uniform typeface, positioned on a grid (shown below).

Beyond a few subtleties of design, Gutenberg follows the genre of the time, and does not assert his own personal aesthetic at all. Inspired by Lou Reed's lyrics, and Reed's recollections of his thoughts at the time of writing, Sagmeister uses a different typestyle for every album. The type is blurred, splashed with tears, raked, overprinted, set like a dictionary, faded out and sprinkled over the page like sugar. Needless to say, the lyrics are often illegible – on the spread below, the type is

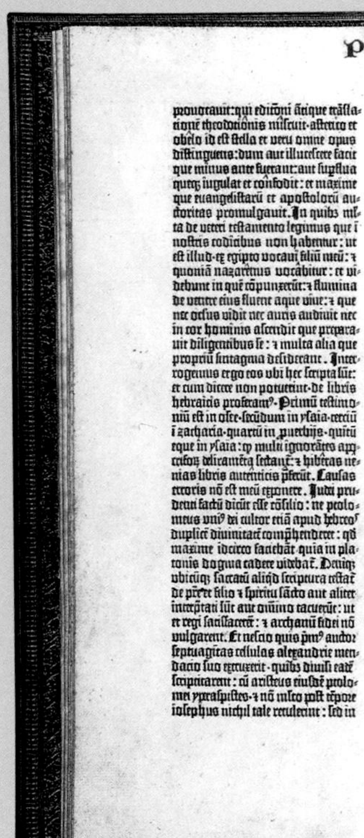

PROLO

prouocauit: qui editõni antique trāsla-
tione theodotionis miscuit, asterico et
obelo id est stella et veru omne opus
distinguens: dum aut illucescere facit
que minus ante fuerant: aut superflua
queq; iugulat et confodit: et maxime
que euangelistarū et apostolorū au-
ctoritas promulgauit. In quibz multa de veteri testamento legimus que ī
nostris codicibus non habentur: ut
est illud, ex egipto vocaui filiū meū: et
quoniā nazareus vocabitur: et vi-
debunt in quē cōpunxerūt: et flumina
de ventre eius fluent aque viue: et que
nec oculus vidit nec auris audiuit nec
in cor hominis ascendit que prepara-
uit diligentibus se: et multa alia que
propriū sintagma desiderant. Inter-
rogemus ergo eos ubi hec scripta sūt:
et cum dicere non potuerint, de libris
hebraicis proferam⁹. Primū testimo-
niū est in osee, secūdum in ysaia, terciū
ī zacharia, quartū in pūerbijs, quītū
eque in ysaia: qd multi ignorātes apo-
crifoꝝ deliramēta sectant: et hibēras ne-
nias libris autenticis pferūt. Causas
erroris nō est meū exponere. Iudei pru-
denti factū dicūt esse cōsilio: ne ptolo-
meus vni⁹ dei cultor etiā apud hebreos
duplicē diuinitatē cōphenderet: qd
maxime idcirco faciebāt quia in pla-
tonis dogma cadere videbat̄. Deniq;
ubicūq; sacratū aliqd scriptura testat̄
de pr̄e et filio et spiritu sācto aut aliter
interp̄tati sūt aut oīno tacuerūt: ut
et regi satisfacerēt: et archanū fidei nō
vulgarent. Et nescio quis p̄im⁹ auctor
septuagīta cellulas alexandrie men-
dacio suo extruxerit, quibz diuisi eadē
scriptitarent: cū aristeus eiusdē ptolo-
mei yperaspistes, et nō multo post tēpore
iosephus nichil tale retulerint: sed in

una basilica congregatos contulisse
scribāt non pphetasse. Aliud ē enī esse
vatem: aliud ē esse interp̄tē. Ibi spirit⁹
ventura p̄dicit: hic erudicio et verborū
copia ea que intelligit transfert. Nisi
forte putādus est tullius economicū
xenofontis et platōnis pitagorā et de-
mostenis pthesifontem afflatus retho-
rico spiritu trāstulisse. Aut aliter de e-
isdem libris per septuagīta interp̄tes,
aliter p apostolos spiritus sanctus te-
stimonia texuit: ut qd illi tacuerūt hij
scriptū esse mentiti sint. Quid igitur?
Damnam⁹ veteres? Minime: sed post
priorū studia in domo dñi quod pos-
sumus laboram⁹. Illi interp̄tati sūt
āte aduentū xp̄i et qd nesciebāt dubijs
protulerūt sententijs: nos post passio-
nem eius non tam pphetiā q̄ histori-
am scribim⁹. Aliter enim audita: aliter visa narrantur. Qd meli⁹ intelligi-
mus meli⁹ et proferim⁹. Audi igitur
emule: obtrectator ausculta. Non da-
mno non reprehendo septuaginta:
sed confidenter cūctis illis apostolos
p̄fero. Per istoꝝ os michi xp̄us sonat
quos ante pphetas inter spiritualia
carismata positos lego: ī quibz ultimū
pene gradū interp̄tes tenēt. Quid liuo-
re torqueris? Quid īperitoꝝ aīos cōtra
me cōcitas? Sicubi ī trāslatiōne tibi vi-
deor errare interroga hebreos: diūsarū
urbiū magistros cōsule. Qd illi habēt de
xp̄o tui codices nō habent. Aliud ē si
cōtra se postea ab aplis usurpata testi-
monia pbauerūt: et emendatiora sunt
exemplaria latina q̄ greca: greca q̄ he-
brea. Uerū hec cōtra inuidos. Nūc te dep̄-
cor desideri carissime: ut qa me tātū op⁹
subire fecisti et a genesi exordiū capere, orō-
nibz iuues: qd possī eodē spū quo scripti
sūt libri ī latinū eos trāsferre sermonē.

GEN ESIS

Incipit liber Bresith quez nos Gene
In principio creauit deus celū et terrā.
et terram. Terra autem erat inanis et
vacua: et tenebre erant sup faciē abissi:
et spiritus dñi ferebatur super aquas.
Dixitq; deus. Fiat lux. Et facta ē lux.
Et vidit deus lucem qd esset bona: et
diuisit lucem a tenebris, appellauitq;
lucem diem et tenebras noctem. Factū
q; est vespere et mane dies unus. Dixit
quoq; deus. Fiat firmamentū in me-
dio aquarū: et diuidat aquas ab a-
quis. Et fecit deus firmamentū: diui-
sitq; aquas que erant sub firmamen-
to ab hijs que erant super firmamen-
tum: et factum est ita. Vocauitq; deus
firmamentū celū: et factum est vespere
et mane dies secundus. Dixit vero deus. Congregentur aque que sub celo
sunt in locum unū et appareat arida.
Et factum est ita. Et vocauit deus ari-
dam terram: cōgregacionesq; aquaꝝ
appellauit maria. Et vidit deus qd esset bonū, et ait. Germinet terra herbā
virentem et facientem semen: et lignū
pomiferū faciens fructum iuxta genus
suū: cuius semen in semetipo sit super
terram. Et factum est ita. Et protulit
terra herbam virentem et facientem semen iuxta genus suū: lignūq; faciens
fructū et habēs unūqdq; sementē scdm
speciē suā. Et vidit deus qd esset bonū:
et factū ē vespere et mane dies tercius.
Dixitq; aūt deus. Fiant luminaria
in firmamēto celi, et diuidāt diem ac
noctē: et sint in signa et tēpora, et dies et
annos: ut luceāt in firmamēto celi et
illuminēt terrā. Et factū est ita. Fecitq;
deus duo luminaria magna: luminare
maius ut p̄esset diei et luminare min⁹
ut p̄esset nocti: et stellas, et posuit eas in
firmamēto celi ut lucerent sup terrā: et
p̄essent diei ac nocti: et diuiderēt lucem
ac tenebras. Et vidit de⁹ qd esset bonū:
et factū ē vespere et mane dies quart⁹.
Dixit etiam deus. Producant aque
reptile anime viuentis et volatile sup
terram: sub firmamēto celi. Creauitq;
deus cete grandia, et omnē animā viuentem atq; motabilem quā produxe-
rant aque in species suas: et omne volatile secundū genus suū. Et vidit deus qd esset bonū: benedixitq; ei dicens.
Crescite et multiplicamini, et replete a-
quas maris: auesq; multiplicentur
super terram. Et factū ē vespere et mane
dies quintus. Dixit quoq; deus. Pro-
ducat terra animā viuentem in gene-
re suo: iumenta et reptilia, et bestias terre secundū species suas. Factū ē ita. Et
fecit deus bestias terre iuxta species suas: iumenta et omne reptile terre in ge-
nere suo. Et vidit deus qd esset bonū:
et ait. Faciam⁹ hominē ad ymaginē et
similitudinē nostrā, et p̄sit piscibz maris,
et volatilibz celi, et bestijs uniūseq; terre:
omniq; reptili qd mouet̄ ī terra. Et creauit deus hominē ad ymaginē et similitudinē suam: ad ymaginem dei creauit illū: masculū et feminā creauit eos.
Benedixitq; illis deus, et ait. Crescite
et multiplicamini et replete terram, et
subicite eam: et dominamini piscibus
maris, et volatilibus celi: et uniuersis
animātibus que mouentur sup terrā.
Dixitq; deus. Ecce dedi vobis omnē
herbam afferentem semen sup terram,
et uniūsa ligna que habēt ī semetipis
sementē generis sui: ut sint vobis ī escā,
et cūctis aīantibus terre, omniq; volucri
celi et uniuersis q̄ mouētur in terra, et ī
quibus ē anima viuēs: ut habeāt ad
vescendū. Et factū est ita. Viditq; deus
cuncta que fecerat: et erāt valde bona.

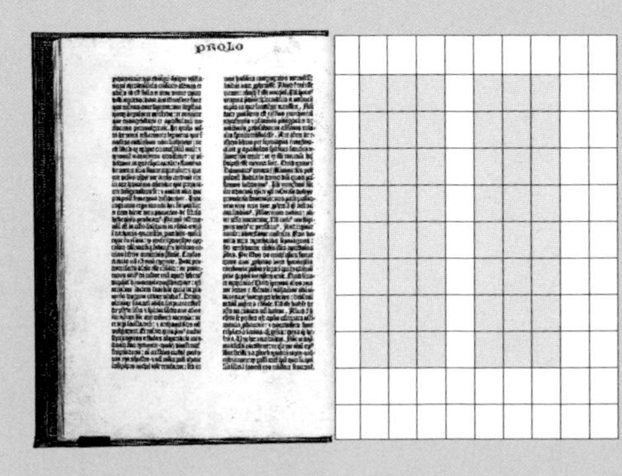

crossed out with thick black bars – but Sagmeister feels it is important, and of more value, to express mood. Together these books represent the two poles within typography, and the presence of the designer. The word of God is treated with a given style – the designer's response detectable only in the subtleties. The words of a singer are treated ironically, usurping expectations of the form, with idiosyncratic expression being foremost.

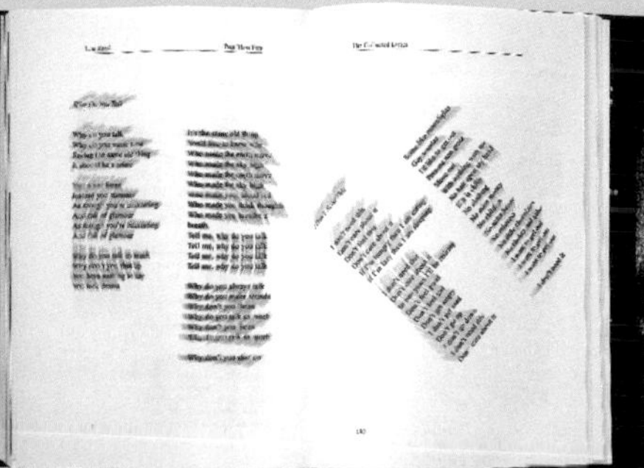

The dilemma of style

What is style? In graphic design, it is the overall effect, the combination of all the particular choices of typefaces, use of space, colour and so on. The best phrase is 'mise-en-page', which translates as 'putting things on the page'.

Designer/writer Lorraine Wild has a way of describing the advent and return of different styles: style>"good design" > mass-market > cliché > embarrassment > "it's over" > fetish > revival > interesting > style > "good design" and so on for ever.

This "Great Wheel of Style" implies that the search for style is a natural cycle. Like the constant need for food, the need for a different style arises naturally a few hours after being satisfied with the last one. This is certainly the external effect of styles becoming voguish, and then old hat. But what is it that motivates designers to seek out fresh styles, or to recycle old ones with added irony, or blend various aspects of different styles? I believe the search is driven by two factors: the need to unify the work, and the wish to infuse it with value.

Style has a function: it limits choices. It excludes certain possibilities, and makes others follow in a chain – it creates a related set of design decisions. In terms of imbuing the design work with value, it has two forms: the personal and the transpersonal. The designer wants her work to be special, her handiwork, but at the same time, she wants to partake of a broader, commonly held set of values. By picking a style she chooses a pattern of decision-making that gives her some latitude for making her work special, but also taps into the values that that style is seen to represent.

When values shift, a new style is needed. William Morris' cod-Mediaevalism drew on radical ideas about the dignity of labour and the value of the individual in the1840s, but would not be regarded as such if a designer employed it today. When Jan Tschichold said "sans serif is the type of the present day", he meant it without irony. He intended "the present day" to mean the modern world. But looking at his words now, we see the futility of trying to peg history down, to freeze human expression into one particular form.

Because different styles can be applied to the same 'content' (see page 68) style can then be separated from the 'content'. All style is self-conscious and unorganic (it never emanates, unbidden, from the content) – it is chosen and imposed by the designer. This is an intolerable idea, the dilemma that any and every style is equal, equally interchangeable, equally meaningful – in effect, meaningless. The search is for the style that seems to mean something, seems to signify real value. The designer wants to avoid the complete and utter irony of all style being meaningless, she wants to infuse her graphic design with an urgency, an authenticity, a contemporaneity.

Style = fart
Stefan Sagmeister often uses his own handwriting instead of a typeface. It avoids the kind of choice that will fix the work too firmly in a particular design genre. Sagmeister is scathing about designers who pursue a style – "style = fart" he says. Handwriting is more direct and immediate, as if he has just drawn on a photograph without going through the stylising contortions of choosing and arranging type. Of course nothing avoids being a style. Here, we are in the murky edges of body art and self-mutilation. It casts Lou Reed as a seer, capable of extreme experiences, a tattooed shaman.

Set the Twilight Reeling

TAKE
ME FOR
WHAT
I AM
A STAR
NEWLY
EMERGING
LONG
SIMMERING
EXPLODES
INSIDE
THE SELF
IS REELING

IN THE POCKET OF THE
IN THE RUSHING
OF THE BLOOD
HEART
IN THE MUSCLE OF MY
SEX
IN THE
MINDFULL
MINDLESS
LOVE
I ACCEPT THE NEW
FOUND MAN
AND SET THE
TWILIGHT
REELING

A SOUL SINGER STANDS ON THE STAGE
THE SPOTLIGHT SHOWS
HIM SWEATING... HE SINKS TO ONE KNEE
SEEMS TO CRY
THE HORNS ARE UNRELENTING
BUT AS THE DRUMS BEAT
HE FINDS HIMSELF
GROWING HARD
IN THE MICROPHONE'S
FACE HE SEES
HER FACE
GROWING
LARGE

AT 5AM THE MOON AND SUN
SIT SET BEFORE MY WINDOW... LIGHT GLANCES
OFF THE BLUE GLASS WE SET... RIGHT BEFORE
THE WINDOW. AND YOU WHO ACCEPT
IN YOUR SOUL AND YOUR HEAD...

WHAT WAS MISUNDERSTOOD... WHAT WAS THOUGHT
OF WITH DREAD... A NEW SELF IS BORNE...
THE OTHER SELF IS DEAD... I ACCEPT THE NEW
FOUND MAN AND
SET THE TWILIGHT REELING

AND THE SWELLING
CRESCENDO NO LONGER
RETARDS
I ACCEPT THE NEW FOUND MAN
AND SET THE TWILIGHT
REELING

AS THE TWILIGHT
SUN BURST GLEAMS
AS THE CHROMIUM MOON IT SETS
AS I LOSE ALL MY REGRETS AND
SET THE TWILIGHT REELING
I ACCEPT THE NEW FOUND MAN
AND SET THE
TWILIGHT REELING

SET
THE
TWILIGHT
REELING

... THE
NEW
ALBUM

LOU
REED

Style as politics

Style represents a set of concerns that can be traced back to a set of political ideas, but this relationship is very approximate at best, and disappears completely as time passes and changes the context.

At one time, the style that is usually called 'Modernism' by designers (very spartan, asymmetric layouts, sans serif type, all forms based on simple geometry) represented progressive politics, a fairer, more rational social order – universal democratic socialism. Contemporary designer April Greiman believes that style no longer has this meaning: "Major capitalism and so-called democracy and all this corporate money that supported design so it had to have one look, one voice, one color, one typeface, all that neutral Swiss greedy stuff, that world is crumbling. We're in a different time. The power structures, the big-bucks people telling people at the bottom of the pyramid what kind of information they could have and when they could have it, is now being totally blown apart by the information revolution and by being truly able to network. There can now be a participatory, interactive kind of information flow." One day Greiman's style too will become disassociated from the vitality and conviction that it exudes now. It was ever thus.

All styles that become ubiquitous ossify: 'can' and 'could' turn into 'must' and 'should'. They become pre-programmed and once mapped out, they are no longer variable. And, crucially, they are seen to represent 'power' – all that is now past, and somehow bankrupt. Styles that are well-worn do not accommodate latecomers eager to bring fresh energy to new contexts.

"The problem for design is that it almost dare not open its eyes to what is really going on, to its complicity, and to its manifest failure to face up to its own responsibilities and argue that design might be anything other than a servant of commercial interests" (Rudy VanderLans).

The problem here is that design is a servant, a servant of its content. It is typefaces, images and the arrangement of these: it is nothing without a content to articulate.

Critic Robert Hughes believes that "art does not act directly on politics... all it can do is provide examples and models of dissent. And the 'newness' of its language carries no guarantees of its effectiveness, even there."

Only so much revolution can be channelled into a typeface. And then it can be repurposed. Look at the fate of Futura, a typeface designed by Paul Renner to herald a new democratic age. Does it signify this when used on a packet of dog biscuits? It is much harder to live out political conviction than to design in a given style. The idea that politics can be summoned up or signalled in style, is ultimately lazy and even futile. Michael Bierut says: "The biggest challenge that faces a designer isn't the quest for novelty, but coming to grips with the fact that much of what we do has little content". The creation of content is not graphic design, any more than acting is the same as writing a play, or dancing is writing music.

A revolution in empathy

No graphic style is more politically progressive than any other, but there is a set of intentions that marks some work out as politically progressive. This is apparent in the work of Frank Philippin, who has studied the effects of common eye disorders – macular degeneration, diabetic retinopathy and retinitis pigmentosa among others – affecting about one in every 25 people. He then redesigned sample packaging like milk and analgesic tablets, and tested the results extensively. The pack shown here (reproduced at 80 per cent of its real size) was chosen by users as a perfect blend of branding and information. Philippin echoes those past designers who sought to establish a demotic, a basic universal standard: "For me, the issue of clear, legible information... became an ethical one... if there is one goal in the designer's approach to typography, it should be clarity."

The implementation of human rights issues in European law will change design habits. Those with less than perfect sight will have a legislative right to information in a form they can read. The Royal National Institute for the Blind already advocates 14-point in a sans serif font as a minimum requirement for all type. How will typographers respond to this challenge? Will they see it as a restriction of their personal expression? Or will they rise to it, and see that typography that deals with the physical needs of millions of people is politically radical: the politics of empathy?

780881 791167

TESCO

Paracetamol

16 Tablets (500 mg)
for the relief of mild to moderate pain
and symptoms of colds, flu, headache,
period pains, toothache and sore throats

Price: 56p / Use by: March 2001
Read the enclosed leaflet carefully

Store in a dry place below 25°C
and protect from light
Manufactured and packaged by
Philippin Laboratories, London, UK
for Tesco Supermarkets

Dosage: Adults and children over
12 years: 1-2 tablets up to 4 times a day
Children 6-12 years: 1/2 to 1 tablet up
to 4 times a day

Oral use, swallow with a glass of water

Do not give to children under 6 years
If symptoms persist, consult doctor

Warning:
Keep out of the reach of children
Do not take if you are allergic to any
of the ingredients or if you have a
kidney or liver disease
Do not take with any other
Paracetamol-containing products
Immediately seek medical advice in the
event of an overdose

Tablet contains: Paracetamol B.P. 500 mg,
Potato Starch, Maize Starch, Talc,
Povidone, Stearic Acid, Sodium Starch,
Glycollate, Nipasept (E214, E216, E218),
Magnesium Stearate

Is design the same as advertising?

What exactly is the difference between graphic design and advertising? Anyone that practises either one knows there is a gulf between them; we do it every day of the week, and yet we cannot say definitely where the variations lie. Eminent British designer, David Stuart, sees no distinction: "They are not separate disciplines. In fact, a flick through a British Design & Art Direction Annual will show you they have adopted each other's clothes for some time now. The only difference is that some designers and consultancies are, for a large part, talking to business, and ad agencies to consumers. Designers tend to whisper, ad agencies tend to shout." It is confusing. After all, on the surface they seem to do more or less exactly the same things: both employ type and images, both produce print and websites, both use logos.

Writer Steven Heller points out that the two are inextricably intertwined, not least because graphic designers have always produced ads. The influential Swiss designers of the 1950s used the phrases 'graphic design' and 'advertising' interchangeably. These designers were happy to produce ads, developing many of their most innovative techniques in the process.

Heller demands a more honest and careful appraisal of the relationship between graphic design and advertising. He describes the relationship as that of a mother and child, advertising having the privileged role as mother. But just when we seem to be getting somewhere interesting, a division of the disciplines with one generative of the other, his essay ('Mother and Child') ends with these words: "Advertising and graphic design are equally concerned with selling, communicating, and entertaining... to appreciate one, the other is imperative". And with this he takes us back into the fog. Richard Hollis sees design as primarily concerned with form, and advertising with intention – a sort of specialised part of design: "If advertising is the message, graphic design is the form". In 'Design is Advertising', an essay for Eye magazine, critic Rick Poynor paints a depressing picture, deliberately melting the two disciplines into a nasty, corrosive conglomerate, which soaks into "everything" so insidiously that "you cannot escape it and there is nowhere it cannot be found". There are distinctions that set the two disciplines apart, otherwise we would not have two terms, recognised by dictionaries, practitioners and the Inland Revenue.

To put it crudely, advertising is the promotion of a product or brand, and it is purely that, whilst, generally speaking, design is the organisation and articulation of many of the products and brands themselves.

Advertising and design are unquestionably of the same family, much as poetry and fiction are both literature. But they are perhaps best looked at not as mother and child, but as Siamese twins. They can be seen as one entity, even as one flesh, but each has a personality of its own.

A conker, noticed after
a visit to the Tate.
Minds open from 10am.

Previous page:
Tate Gallery
Using the ideas of Surrealism and the bricollage of Marcel Duchamp. Art director Paul Belford, copywriter Nigel Roberts, photographer Michael Liam Cumiskey.

Right: Playstation
A picture made of the logo, the world seen through the eyes of the brand. Art director Paul Belford, copywriter Nigel Roberts.

Opposite: Waterstone's
The book as testament. Art director Paul Belford, copywriter Nigel Roberts, photographer Laurie Haskell.

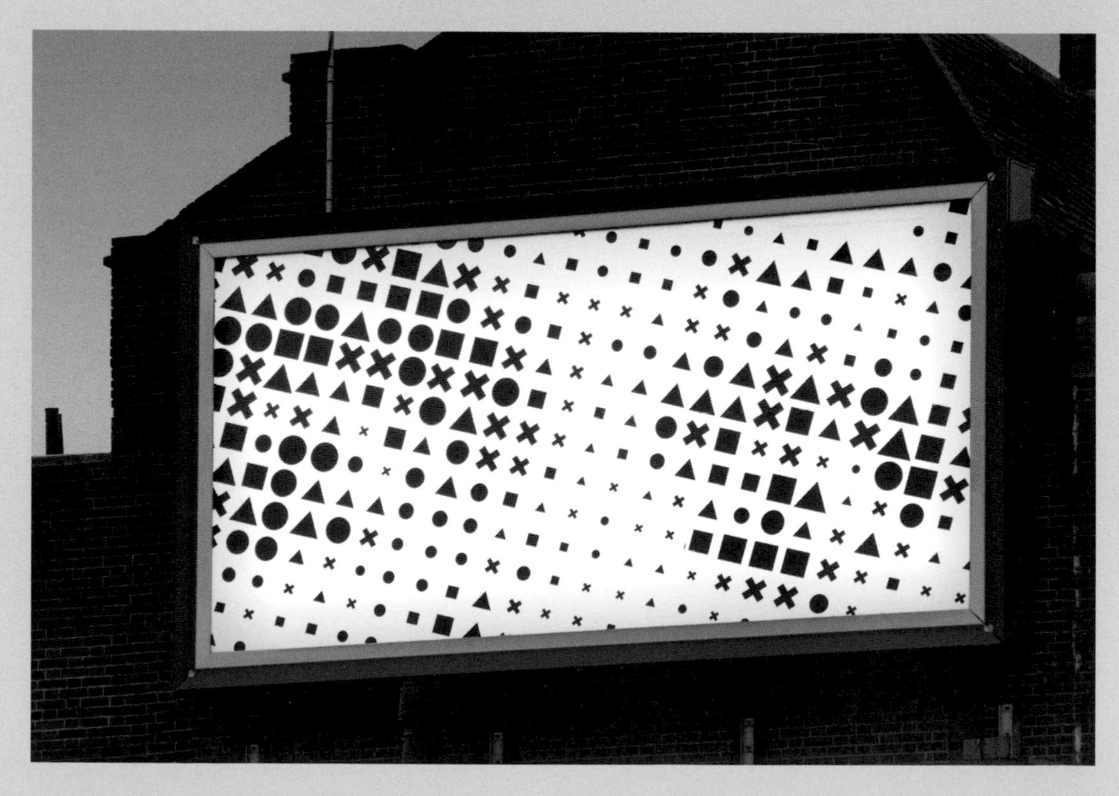

Form

Advertising is usually manifested as billboards, television and cinema ads, newspaper and magazine ads, direct mail. Design is manifested as small-scale posters (underneath billboards), television and cinema intro-sequences, books, newspaper and magazine editorial design, explanatory selling materials. A few crossovers do not obey these generalisations, but they are a tiny percentage of variation from the conventional distinctions.

Material

No one keeps ads. No one buys ads in and of themselves. It is a sweeping generalisation, but design is the articulation of the material that is bought, touched, coveted. Design is the product. In the case of newspapers and magazines, advertising is placed within the framework graphic design. It borrows the paper and printing techniques that the design determines. Management and choice of materials is a fundamental point of design.

Time

All advertising has to work fast. A split second, one or two seconds, 30 seconds at most. Because it intrudes and inserts itself, it has to say its piece quickly. Design has a different relationship to time. Some designs do have to operate as quickly as ads, like logos or posters, but a logo is not seen only once, for a limited 'campaign', but thousands of times, often over decades. Woody Pirtle, who designed the logo for the World Cup in America, was told it was expected to be seen a trillion times. Some logos last for decades. Most other manifestations of design – books, instructional material, signage, packaging – need time to be digested, or will be returned to over time.

Message

Advertising focusses on the product benefit. Design has very varied messages; only a few areas of design focus on the product benefit – packaging, posters for events – concerning themselves with other elements too. Most graphic design deals with diffuse and complex messages, as varied as the content it purveys.

Paul Belford is joint creative director at Ogilvy & Mather, London, with writing partner, Nigel Roberts. Many art directors are happy for typographers to translate their sketches, but Belford takes a designer's interest in the detail of every ad, carrying every project through from concept to completing the artwork himself.

Quentin Newark: Is there a distinction between design and advertising?
Paul Belford: It can be one and the same thing. When it comes to art directing printwork, you become a graphic designer.
So the role of the art director is the same as the role of the designer?
There is a huge overlap, although we produce the content as well, and designers don't always do that. That's quite a big difference, and quite a big benefit for us.
Historically all of the great designers produced ads; the terms graphic design and advertising were synonymous. Many used to work in advertising agencies, making any difference almost impossible to pick out.
There seems to have been a divergence, in the naming of the disciplines at least, about 30 or 40 years ago. This came perhaps with the advent of the "big idea", the first intellectual approach to communicating an idea about a product. [The 'big idea' is a term that covers advertising and magazine design. It began in the late 1950s, and had its heyday in the 1960s. It is typified by the Volkswagen Beetle ads produced by Bill Bernbach at the agency Dolye Dane Bernbach – legendary within advertising. These placed a picture above a headline and fairly brief explanatory text, with a logo in the bottom right-hand corner. The picture and headline often used Surrealist principles – especially those of René Magritte – in being unexpected. Perhaps the most famous is a Beetle with the word 'lemon' underneath it. 'Lemon' is a derogatory term in America, the Beetle in question had a blemish, and had been rejected. It was revolutionary to be ironic about the product at that time.]
The intelligence behind the Volkswagen ads really began modern advertising. That is something that belongs to advertising and not graphic design, the idea of how to intellectually dramatise a product. Graphic design comes into it of course, it's not just a veneer – it's in how you organise the ad.
If we take that as modern advertising's beginning, how has the advertising of today changed?
The best ads from that period are still good today, that's the beauty of strong ideas. But it became formulaic: a picture, a headline and three columns of copy. These ads relied on a lot of copy to communicate their idea. Today it has become more visual. In recent years, there has been more collaboration between art directors and artists and designers to create something visually new. We have just made an ad with Gillian Wearing, and there is a constant pressure to be fresh, because the work has to be noticed.
I have noticed a profound difference in advertising in the last few years – what was once tongue-in-cheek irony about a product has become almost openly cynical. Some ads almost defy you to want the product – 'why would a person like you want this?' Is the industry picking up on a

general cynicism about advertising?
I think it's just a phase, not a revolutionary shift. Advertising reflects and draws on the wider culture, but it will change. Actually, I am rather bored with it already.
I have come up with a kind of a formula of distinctions between advertising and graphic design (see page 25).
I think I could tackle the same things as a designer, but I would do them them in a different way, using advertising techniques.
What are they? Playing up the Unique Selling Point (USP)?
That method is used less and less, as products become more commodified, and therefore similar. One good example of this is cars. You have to invent a difference – the more similar the products get, the more you use non-USP positioning and pure visual methods, ie graphic design, to differentiate.
But it is still about 'benefit' isn't it?
It is still mostly about that.
We can characterise advertising as being "mostly about the benefit of the product", that is a centre, a tendency, but I think it's impossible to characterise graphic design in the same way. You cannot characterise the communication behind a newspaper layout, stamp or logo. There is no centre to graphic design.
Your distinction about time is interesting, the fact that advertising has to barge in, that it leads you towards simplicity. As a constraint, this is no bad thing, I think.
There is, I hate to confess, one way in which advertising and design are growing closer: an increasing concentration on brand – management of all the manifestations of how an organisation expresses itself. I think branding is changing graphic design. It used to be an intuitive part of what designers did, but now it's subsuming all design into schemes, a strict hierarchy with the logo at the top.
It's wrong if it's used as a straitjacket. Advertising shouldn't be restricted or predetermined, nor should architecture or graphic design. The only way that branding can work well is when it's understood and directed by the top guy, then everyone has the confidence to let it work. We have endless problems when we have to deal with nervous middle-managers.
Do you think this would get easier if people had a better understanding of the processes of advertising?
I have always been slightly disappointed with the acknowledgement advertising gets in magazines like Eye, Baseline and Idea in Japan. They just don't go near it, and interesting stuff is happening.
Advertising is certainly a very powerful cultural force. It is often enormously creatively inspiring and inventive. Perhaps as the current fad for ridding design of all commercial impurity fades, advertisers will broaden their idea of what they call visual culture...

Is design the same as art?

Graphic design was once called 'commercial art'. In looking for a simple distinction, this term instantly provides it: commercial purpose.

"Consider the two radical positions in the arts today. One recommends the breaking down of distinctions between genres; the arts would eventuate in one art, consisting of many different kinds of behaviour going on at the same time, a vast behavioural magma or synesthesia. The other position recommends the maintaining and clarifying of barriers between the arts, by the intensification of what each art distinctively is," says Susan Sontag.

There has been much wilful blurring of categories, by both critics and designers, in order for designers to earn, "the same degree of self-expressive freedom, and perhaps the concomitant status, enjoyed by artists" (Rick Poynor). But this is an intended blurring, and in order to merge, there have to be two distinct entities in the first place.

A constant magnet is the attraction of the artistic avant-garde – the attitude and set of ideas that set a small group outside the 'mainstream', and make their work constantly novel and risky. It also needs to be free of commercial compromise, and it helps if the political ideas are extreme. This 'cutting-edge' formula has underpinned much design criticism, and the pronouncements of many designers.

The differences between art and design are felt most strongly in the area of intention. Design has a client who provides the intention for the work, the aims and the outcome by which it must be judged. (I am excluding all art before about 1900, when art's clients were every bit as proscriptive as design's clients. But its materials and forms – oil paintings and sculptures – make it easy to distinguish from mass reproduction.) There is a minute amount of design work where the designer herself is the client, a kind of 'acte gratuit'. But this self-publishing does not alter design's recognisable conventions.

These pages show examples of artworks that sit on the fence. They use the language of design, and its methods, and put any attempt to distinguish between art and design – using a vague idea like 'intention' – under real pressure.

But if the language of art and design is growing closer, the intentions remain separable. It is not just the presence of a client connecting design's content to its readership like a thread, it is that design has become, over centuries, efficient at delivering an unambiguous message.

Art is connotative, associative, implicative; it revels in ambiguity. Its function and its form are inseparable. Art is "certainly now, mainly, a form of thinking" (Susan Sontag). Design is precise, denotative, explicit. It is a mediation, a structure, a method. It connects to its content like dance attaches to music, or cooking to food.

Designer/artist Karl Gerstner says that we must set the initial question – is design art? – in different terms: "Are the problems set by commercial art such that they can be solved by artistic means? Is it a field of human activity in which artistic work and artistic results are possible?" This rewrites the question: 'Can design be as powerful, complex, emotive and enduring as the best art can be?' The answer to this question is an unequivocal yes.

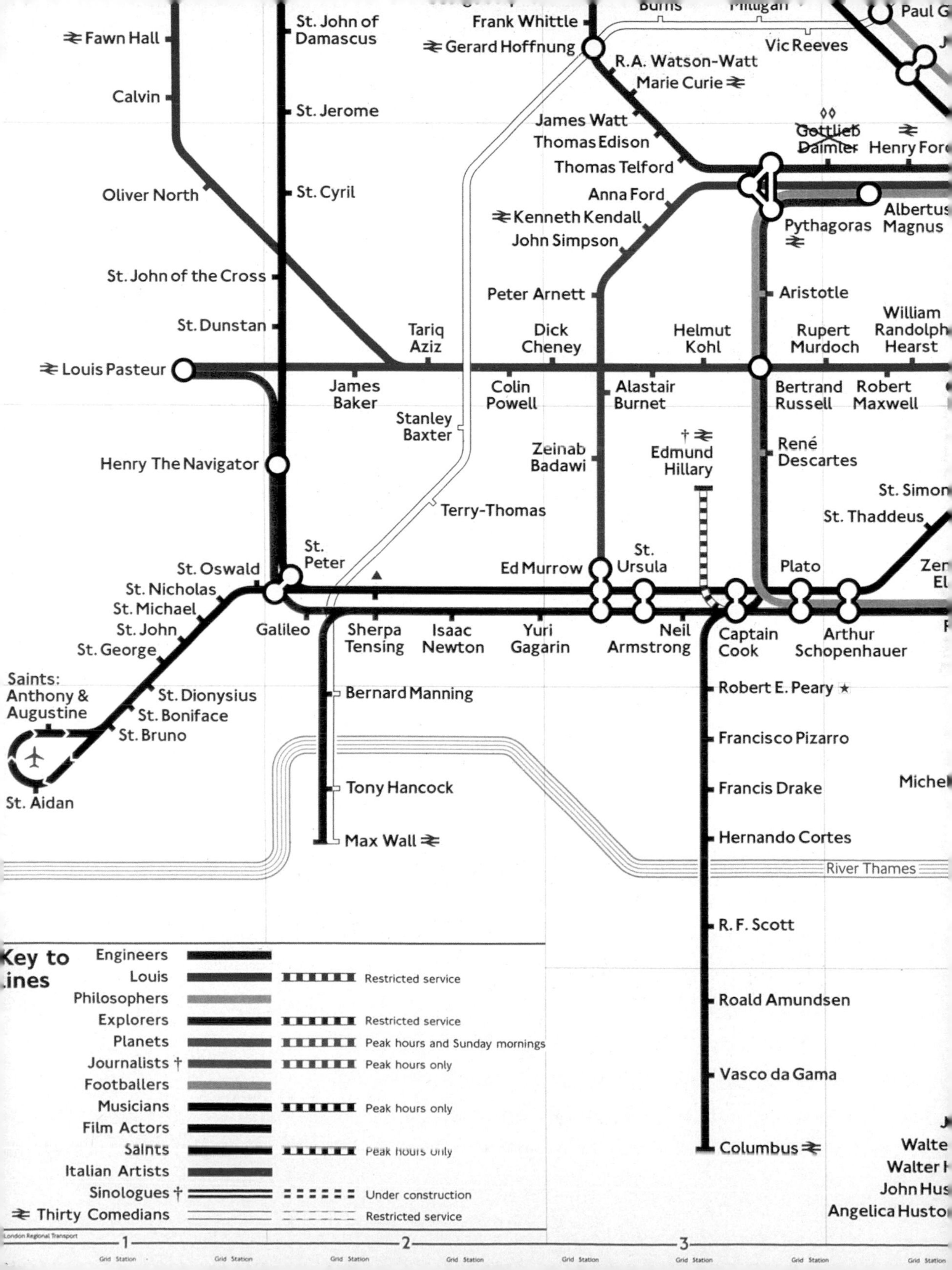

Fawn Hall
Calvin
Oliver North
St. John of Damascus
St. Jerome
St. Cyril
St. John of the Cross
St. Dunstan
Louis Pasteur
Henry The Navigator
Frank Whittle
Gerard Hoffnung
Vic Reeves
R.A. Watson-Watt
Marie Curie
James Watt
Thomas Edison
Thomas Telford
Gottlieb Daimler
Henry Ford
Anna Ford
Kenneth Kendall
John Simpson
Peter Arnett
Pythagoras
Albertus Magnus
Aristotle
Tariq Aziz
Dick Cheney
Helmut Kohl
Rupert Murdoch
William Randolph Hearst
James Baker
Colin Powell
Alastair Burnet
Bertrand Russell
Robert Maxwell
Stanley Baxter
Zeinab Badawi
Edmund Hillary
René Descartes
Terry-Thomas
St. Simon
St. Thaddeus
St. Oswald
St. Peter
St. Nicholas
St. Michael
St. John
St. George
Ed Murrow
St. Ursula
Plato
Galileo
Sherpa Tensing
Isaac Newton
Yuri Gagarin
Neil Armstrong
Captain Cook
Arthur Schopenhauer
Saints: Anthony & Augustine
St. Dionysius
St. Boniface
St. Bruno
St. Aidan
Bernard Manning
Tony Hancock
Max Wall
Robert E. Peary
Francisco Pizarro
Francis Drake
Hernando Cortes
River Thames
R. F. Scott
Roald Amundsen
Vasco da Gama
Columbus
Key to Lines
Engineers
Louis
Restricted service
Philosophers
Explorers
Restricted service
Planets
Peak hours and Sunday mornings
Journalists †
Peak hours only
Footballers
Musicians
Peak hours only
Film Actors
Saints
Peak hours only
Italian Artists
Sinologues †
Under construction
Thirty Comedians
Restricted service
London Regional Transport
1
2
3

Simon Patterson
Previous page and above: 'The Great Bear' 1992, lithograph on paper, 108.5 x 134 cm.
Overleaf: 'JP 233 in CSO Blue', both courtesy of the Lisson Gallery. Patterson says: "There is no code to be cracked in my work. meanings may not be obvious, you may not get a joke, but nothing is really cryptic – I'm not interested in mystification. I like disrupting something people take as read... I'm not nilhilistic. What interests me is juxtaposing different paths of knowledge to form more than the sum of their parts". The playful humour of works like 'The Last Supper Arranged to the Flatback Four Formation (Jesus Christ in Goal)' give way to the quiet horror of 'JP 233 in CSO Blue' which uses a diagram of the huge US Airforce airfield bomb, the JP 233, and its dozens of constituent bomblets and mines, and renders it ludicrous with names sucked up at random. These weird hybrids of real diagrams and real names show how deeply implanted and apparently trustworthy these diagrams, categories and name lists have become. Even when they are mixed to be meaningless, we are compelled to read meaning into them.

Richard Prince
'Adult Comedy Action Drama', published by Scalo. You are looking at a printed photograph of Prince's book which has a printed photograph of printed photographs. This layering lies at the heart of what Prince's work examines. Like many artists since Marcel Duchamp, he asserts himself as an artist through the act of selecting. Duchamp said that in the future all an artist would have to do to make a piece of art is to point his finger, and Prince simply points his camera. What his work does is to use existing images, words, or strings of words, and represent them. He does not try to create fresh meaning, he does not take a moral position with the material, there is no narrative, nothing to be understood. He draws attention to his presence as the selector, and the automatic responses raised by what he shows you. By reproducing imagery Prince is citing it as an instance, a component, in a vast interlaced structure of representation and meaning, which can just as easily be seen as gratuitous and empty.

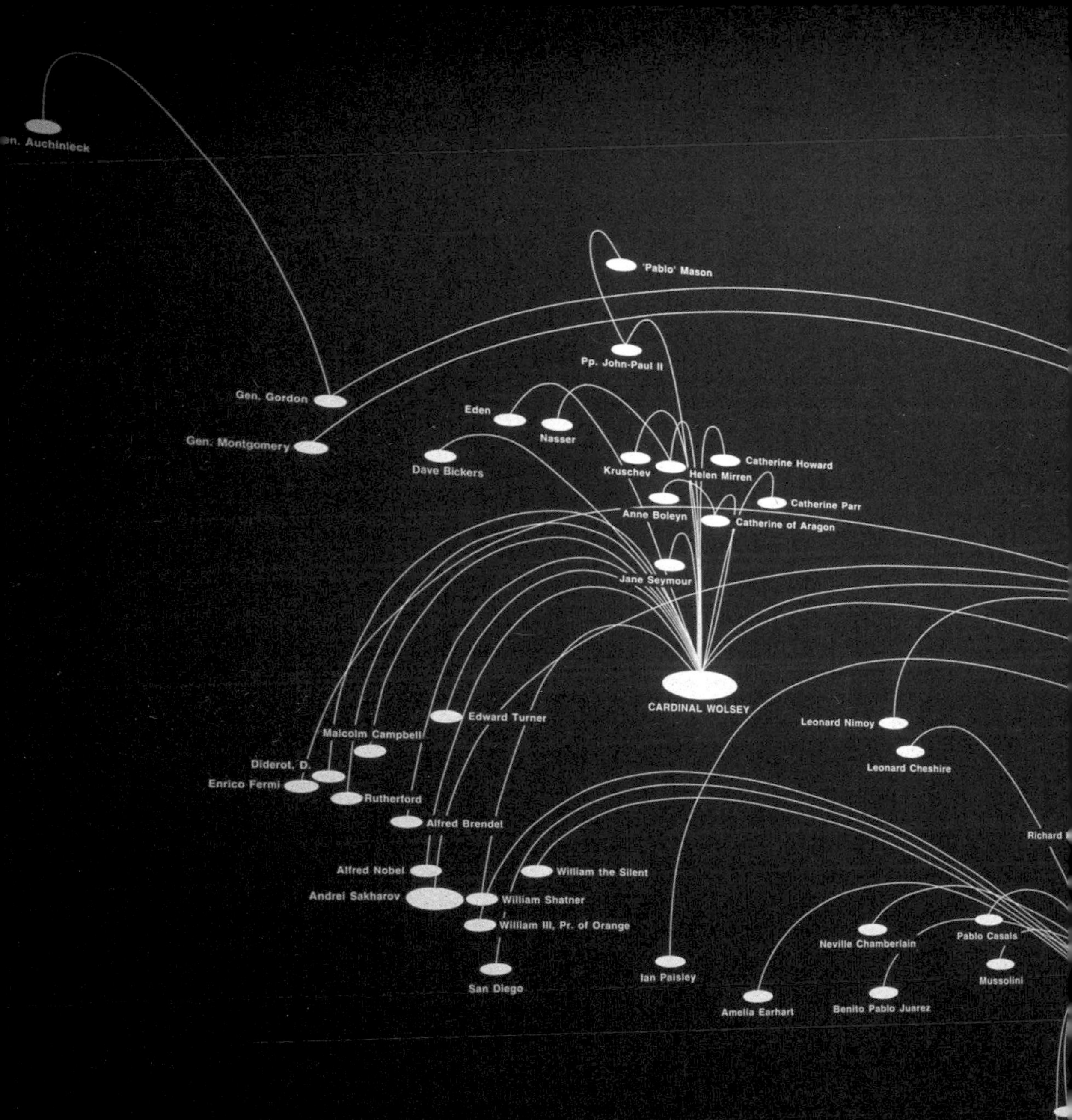

en. Auchinleck
'Pablo' Mason
Pp. John-Paul II
Gen. Gordon
Gen. Montgomery
Eden
Nasser
Dave Bickers
Kruschev
Helen Mirren
Catherine Howard
Anne Boleyn
Catherine Parr
Catherine of Aragon
Jane Seymour
CARDINAL WOLSEY
Edward Turner
Malcolm Campbell
Leonard Nimoy
Leonard Cheshire
Diderot, D.
Enrico Fermi
Rutherford
Alfred Brendel
Richard
Alfred Nobel
William the Silent
Andrei Sakharov
William Shatner
William III, Pr. of Orange
Neville Chamberlain
Pablo Casals
San Diego
Ian Paisley
Mussolini
Amelia Earhart
Benito Pablo Juarez
San Antonio
To D

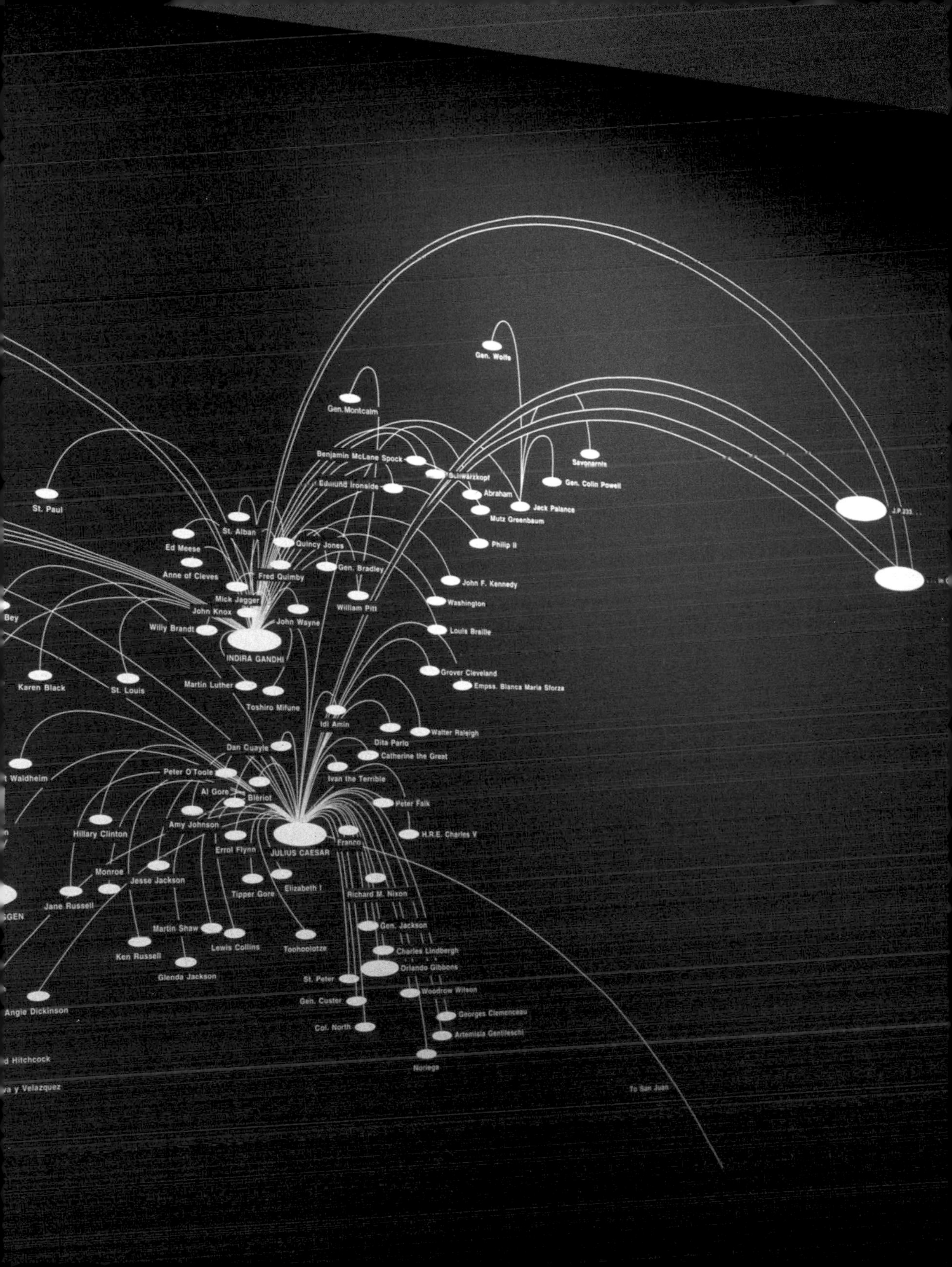
Gen. Wolfe
Gen. Montcalm
Benjamin McLane Spock
Abraham
Gen. Colin Powell
Jack Palance
Mutz Grenbaum
St. Paul
St. Alban
Ed Meese
Quincy Jones
Philip II
Anne of Cleves
Fred Quimby
Gen. Bradley
John F. Kennedy
Mick Jagger
William Pitt
Washington
John Knox
John Wayne
Willy Brandt
Louis Braille
INDIRA GANDHI
Grover Cleveland
Empss. Bianca Maria Sforza
Karen Black
St. Louis
Martin Luther
Toshiro Mifune
Idi Amin
Walter Raleigh
Dita Parlo
Dan Cuayle
Catherine the Great
Peter O'Toole
Ivan the Terrible
Al Gore
Blériot
Peter Falk
Hillary Clinton
Amy Johnson
H.R.E. Charles V
Errol Flynn
JULIUS CAESAR
Franco
Monroe
Jesse Jackson
Tipper Gore
Elizabeth I
Richard M. Nixon
Jane Russell
Martin Shaw
Gen. Jackson
Lewis Collins
Ken Russell
Charles Lindbergh
Orlando Gibbons
Glenda Jackson
St. Peter
Woodrow Wilson
Gen. Custer
Angie Dickinson
Georges Clemenceau
Col. North
Artemisia Gentileschi
Noriega
To San Juan

How design evolves

Design is as much an instrinsic a part of the culture as any activity. This kind of book (in fact any book on any subject) runs a risk in plucking it out and presenting it as autonomous or special. There is a temptation to write about the development of design and present it as sequential, with one era leading naturally to the next; a catalogue of internal developments. But what would drive the evolution? Like everything in the broader culture, design is shaped by forces that pull and push it into new forms.

The first of these must be physical, mechanical. Since all design is produced by technology, its development is inseparable from technological development. A few examples ought to suffice to make the point: Johann Gutenberg invented most of the features of typography that still exist today in one magical act when he devised moveable metal type and the printing press. Illustrations integrated into the design were possible before photography, but had to be inserted into the flatbed of the printing press as a separate entity – a metal or wooden block with the type around it.

Lithography was a laborious printing method based on the properties of wax-repelling waterbased inks. Designs were drawn full-size on large flat stones or rubber sheets, in progressive stages, one for each colour. Most often used for advertising posters, this process enabled images and text to appear together. The lettering was drawn by the artist and so was aesthetically incorporated into the overall design. Lucian Bernhard, Edward McKnight Kauffer and AM Cassandre produced superlative examples of this technique.

The phrase 'typo-photography' was first used in an article in the British and Colonial Printer journal as early as 1888. Techniques had been

Above:
The first graphic design?
This handstruck coin from Apollonia, Greece, 450BC, reproduced actual size, has a right to be called the first ever graphic design. It was made using a machine, a metal die, in all respects identical to the dies Gutenberg used. Thousands of copies were made. The emblems are prototypical logos. The Medusa was used by many Greek cities, and stood for civic virility; the anchor and crayfish for the fishermen who gave Apollonia its wealth.

Opposite:
Historic typography
The American Declaration of Independence, one of the most famous documents in the world, printed on the night of 4 July 1776 by John Dunlap in Philadelphia. The speed of printing may explain its extreme simplicity, and the spindly lines of Caslon. This was the piece of typography that precipitated America into war with Britain, and eventual independence – a sequence fundamental in shaping the modern world. Its text has an emotional clarity missing from modern political texts. Knowing they faced war and possible obliteration, the signatories wrote: "We mutually pledge to each other our Lives, our Fortunes, and our sacred Honor".

IN CONGRESS, JULY 4, 1776.

A DECLARATION

BY THE REPRESENTATIVES OF THE UNITED STATES OF AMERICA, IN GENERAL CONGRESS ASSEMBLED.

WHEN in the Course of human Events, it becomes necessary for one People to dissolve the Political Bands which have connected them with another, and to assume among the Powers of the Earth, the separate and equal Station to which the Laws of Nature and of Nature's God entitle them, a decent Respect to the Opinions of Mankind requires that they should declare the causes which impel them to the Separation.

WE hold these Truths to be self-evident, that all Men are created equal, that they are endowed by their Creator with certain unalienable Rights, that among these are Life, Liberty, and the Pursuit of Happiness--That to secure these Rights, Governments are instituted among Men, deriving their just Powers from the Consent of the Governed, that whenever any Form of Government becomes destructive of these Ends, it is the Right of the People to alter or to abolish it, and to institute new Government, laying its Foundation on such Principles, and organizing its Powers in such Form, as to them shall seem most likely to effect their Safety and Happiness. Prudence, indeed, will dictate that Governments long established should not be changed for light and transient Causes; and accordingly all Experience hath shewn, that Mankind are more disposed to suffer, while Evils are sufferable, than to right themselves by abolishing the Forms to which they are accustomed. But when a long Train of Abuses and Usurpations, pursuing invariably the same Object, evinces a Design to reduce them under absolute Despotism, it is their Right, it is their Duty, to throw off such Government, and to provide new Guards for their future Security. Such has been the patient Sufferance of these Colonies; and such is now the Necessity which constrains them to alter their former Systems of Government. The History of the present King of Great-Britain is a History of repeated Injuries and Usurpations, all having in direct Object the Establishment of an absolute Tyranny over these States. To prove this, let Facts be submitted to a candid World.

HE has refused his Assent to Laws, the most wholesome and necessary for the public Good.

HE has forbidden his Governors to pass Laws of immediate and pressing Importance, unless suspended in their Operation till his Assent should be obtained; and when so suspended, he has utterly neglected to attend to them.

HE has refused to pass other Laws for the Accommodation of large Districts of People, unless those People would relinquish the Right of Representation in the Legislature, a Right inestimable to them, and formidable to Tyrants only.

HE has called together Legislative Bodies at Places unusual, uncomfortable, and distant from the Depository of their public Records, for the sole Purpose of fatiguing them into Compliance with his Measures.

HE has dissolved Representative Houses repeatedly, for opposing with manly Firmness his Invasions on the Rights of the People.

HE has refused for a long Time, after such Dissolutions, to cause others to be elected; whereby the Legislative Powers, incapable of Annihilation, have returned to the People at large for their exercise; the State remaining in the mean time exposed to all the Dangers of Invasion from without, and Convulsions within.

HE has endeavoured to prevent the Population of these States; for that Purpose obstructing the Laws for Naturalization of Foreigners; refusing to pass others to encourage their Migrations hither, and raising the Conditions of new Appropriations of Lands.

HE has obstructed the Administration of Justice, by refusing his Assent to Laws for establishing Judiciary Powers.

HE has made Judges dependent on his Will alone, for the Tenure of their Offices, and the Amount and Payment of their Salaries.

HE has erected a Multitude of new Offices, and sent hither Swarms of Officers to harrass our People, and eat out their Substance.

HE has kept among us, in Times of Peace, Standing Armies, without the consent of our Legislatures.

HE has affected to render the Military independent of and superior to the Civil Power.

HE has combined with others to subject us to a Jurisdiction foreign to our Constitution, and unacknowledged by our Laws; giving his Assent to their Acts of pretended Legislation:

FOR quartering large Bodies of Armed Troops among us:

FOR protecting them, by a mock Trial, from Punishment for any Murders which they should commit on the Inhabitants of these States:

FOR cutting off our Trade with all Parts of the World:

FOR imposing Taxes on us without our Consent:

FOR depriving us, in many Cases, of the Benefits of Trial by Jury:

FOR transporting us beyond Seas to be tried for pretended Offences:

FOR abolishing the free System of English Laws in a neighbouring Province, establishing therein an arbitrary Government, and enlarging its Boundaries, so as to render it at once an Example and fit Instrument for introducing the same absolute Rule into these Colonies:

FOR taking away our Charters, abolishing our most valuable Laws, and altering fundamentally the Forms of our Governments:

FOR suspending our own Legislatures, and declaring themselves invested with Power to legislate for us in all Cases whatsoever.

HE has abdicated Government here, by declaring us out of his Protection and waging War against us.

HE has plundered our Seas, ravaged our Coasts, burnt our Towns, and destroyed the Lives of our People.

HE is, at this Time, transporting large Armies of foreign Mercenaries to compleat the Works of Death, Desolation, and Tyranny, already begun with circumstances of Cruelty and Perfidy, scarcely paralleled in the most barbarous Ages, and totally unworthy the Head of a civilized Nation.

HE has constrained our fellow Citizens taken Captive on the high Seas to bear Arms against their Country, to become the Executioners of their Friends and Brethren, or to fall themselves by their Hands.

HE has excited domestic Insurrections amongst us, and has endeavoured to bring on the Inhabitants of our Frontiers, the merciless Indian Savages, whose known Rule of Warfare, is an undistinguished Destruction, of all Ages, Sexes and Conditions.

IN every stage of these Oppressions we have Petitioned for Redress in the most humble Terms: Our repeated Petitions have been answered only by repeated Injury. A Prince, whose Character is thus marked by every act which may define a Tyrant, is unfit to be the Ruler of a free People.

NOR have we been wanting in Attentions to our British Brethren. We have warned them from Time to Time of Attempts by their Legislature to extend an unwarrantable Jurisdiction over us. We have reminded them of the Circumstances of our Emigration and Settlement here. We have appealed to their native Justice and Magnanimity, and we have conjured them by the Ties of our common Kindred to disavow these Usurpations, which, would inevitably interrupt our Connections and Correspondence. They too have been deaf to the Voice of Justice and of Consanguinity. We must, therefore, acquiesce in the Necessity, which denounces our Separation, and hold them, as we hold the rest of Mankind, Enemies in War, in Peace, Friends.

WE, therefore, the Representatives of the UNITED STATES OF AMERICA, in GENERAL CONGRESS, Assembled, appealing to the Supreme Judge of the World for the Rectitude of our Intentions, do, in the Name, and by Authority of the good People of these Colonies, solemnly Publish and Declare, That these United Colonies are, and of Right ought to be, FREE AND INDEPENDENT STATES; that they are absolved from all Allegiance to the British Crown, and that all political Connection between them and the State of Great-Britain, is and ought to be totally dissolved; and that as FREE AND INDEPENDENT STATES, they have full Power to levy War, conclude Peace, contract Alliances, establish Commerce, and to do all other Acts and Things which INDEPENDENT STATES may of right do. And for the support of this Declaration, with a firm Reliance on the Protection of divine Providence, we mutually pledge to each other our Lives, our Fortunes, and our sacred Honor.

Signed by ORDER *and in* BEHALF *of the* CONGRESS,

JOHN HANCOCK, PRESIDENT.

ATTEST.
CHARLES THOMSON, SECRETARY.

38

PHILADELPHIA: PRINTED BY JOHN DUNLAP.

VAUXH
HAVE YOU SEEN THE IN
IS FIXED
TUESDAY
JERUSA
A VIEW OF THIS BEAUTIF
IS NOW
SPLENDID NEW COACH
COMET!
In 24 Hours
LIVERPOOL
EVERY MORNING AT 9.
Bull & Mouth
Theatre Royal Drury Lan
GREAT ATTRACTION FOR T
NIGHT ONLY!!!
MR.
HARLE
MONDAY MAY 4
Theatre Royal Drury Lane.
GREAT ATTRACTION FOR THIS
NIGHT ONLY!!!
MR.
HARLEY
THIS EVENING!
THE SLAVE
"PITY AND PROTECT THE SLAVE"
AFTER THE OPERA
Grand Concert
FRENCH PLAYS
MADLLE JENY
VERTPRE
THAT HER
BENEFIT
IS FIXED—TUESDAY
MAY 10
THAMES
TUNNEL.
MR. MATHEWS
AT HOME
MONDAY
WEDNESDAY AND
FRIDAY.
ADELPHI THEATRE
READ THE
MIRROR!
PRICE 2D.
Mr PARRY
FAREWELL
SATURDAY
JUNE
IF YOU
Kings Theatre
NEW
MUSICAL FUN
UNDER THE IMMEDIATE PA
THEIR MAJESTIE
FRIDA
JUNE 26TH
A GRAN
CONCE
PAGANINI
WILL PLAY
A SOLO
MISS SALLY
WARD,
SNAP.
THE DESTRUCTION OF
POMPEII EVERY EVN
HARLEY
SLAVE

CROWDE
FLEAS?
ENGLISH OPERAHOUSE
TRIUMPHANT SUCCESS OF NATIVE TALE
NOURJAHAD!
MOUNTAIN SYLPH
AND
HERMANN!
EVERY
KING ARTHUR EVERY EVENING THIS WEEK
YOUR HAT
IS VERY SHABBY?
IMMEDIATELY
15 STRAND.
HATS
17s
ADELPHI THEATRE
EXTRAORDINARY HIT.
THE LAST DAYS OF
POMPEII!
LARLACHE
MARINO
FALIERO
SHAVING
MADE EASY!
BY THE USE OF
MECHIS
PATENT STROP
LAST PERFORMANCE
J.B.CRAMER
MADAME
VESTRIS
having recovered from her
severe indisposition will appear
THIS EVENING!
THE POWERFUL
AND MAGNIFICENT STEAM SHIP
FAVORITE
LEAVE ON TUESDAY NEXT FOR
OSTEND.
CARRYING HIS MAJESTY'S MAILS.
SPREAD EAGLE
PARIS
LANE.
SPECTACLE
ARTHUR
ST JAMES'S THEATRE
BRAHAM
OBERON
ENCHANTED HORN!
TOM THUMB
ICE!
YOUNG PARRY AS
"NOODLE"
EVERY EVENING!
STOP!
WOMAN
Tame Tigers
THE SECRET
IN STATU QUO
The Volunteers
OTELLO.
ADELPHI.
ROBERT MACAIRE
TOM & JERRY
THE CHRISTENING!!
!!!!!!
EVERY EVENING
GUSTAVUS THE THIRD!
MASK'D BALL.
16 WELSH GOATS,
10 COWS, 13 HOGS
3 YOUNG HEIFERS,
SALE.
FRENCH
Olympic
MONDAY NEXT
POSTILLION
WATERMAN
FRA DIAVOLO
FOR ONE WEEK ONLY
THEATRE ROYAL WINDSOR
CHESTER
ROYAL GEORGE.
FOR SALE!
TWO LECTURES
will be delivered in
THE
BULL
MOUTH!!!
TO BE LET
SOLD
A
FEMALE
DONKEY
HORSES!
COWS.
On Friday next
NEW ENGLISH OPERA-HOUSE
SHADOW ON THE WALL
READ !!!
JIM CROW
EVENING

devised to convert photographs into lines or dots of tone on metal plates so they could be incorporated into printed designs. At first photographs were treated as illustrations, the same way they had been used for hundreds of years, with type surrounding isolated blocks. It was the social ferment of the First World War that produced experimental designers like Filippo Tommaso Marinetti and Kurt Schwitters, and the Russians El Lissitzky and Alexander Rodchenko who worked on mass-produced books and pamphlets containing inflammatory revolutionary material. They created a fusion between starkly modern photographic images and the jumble of typefaces that lay in trays at the printers. The image cut out of its block joined the type as part of a unified surface.

To make the point more overtly, the technological, physical possibilities available to the designer set the way in which she creates her design. Physical means suggest the form.

The second main force that shaped design, linked to the first, is commerce. Without a growing mercantile bourgeois to buy his books, and the prospect of generous profits, Johann Gutenberg would not have borrowed the money it took to develop letterpress printing. The development of different typefaces took place so that they were significantly distinctive to signify a particular printing house. The first typefaces were a form of branding. Their proliferation today is not driven by a benevolent interest in the expressive character of new letterforms, but by individuals and companies who want to make profit by selling them.

The creation of new forms of packaging was the result of technical developments in the preservation and sealing of food, driven by the profit motive. The staggeringly rapid growth of

Previous pages: Commercial typography
Looking for all the world like a computer screen with too many windows open, this image gives some indication of how nearly every blank wall might have looked in the early 19th century. The reason for the rapid growth of different typefaces at this time is clear enough, and it also challenges the popular modern phrase condemning the 'increasing commercialisation of our public space'. Increasing? This remarkable image 'Dream of a Flyposter' by John Orlando Parry, is reproduced courtesy of the Dunhill Museum and Archive, London.

Below and opposite: Codifying design
This represents the curriculum at the Bauhaus, Germany in 1923. It continues to exert control over all design courses today, with its introductory 'vorlehre' followed by a segregated study of methods and materials. At the heart lies an understanding of 'bau' (building), hence the bauhaus. Its founder Walter Gropius was of the synaesthetic persuasion, and saw the purpose of all the design disciplines as the dissolving of any barriers to creating seemingly complete buildings.

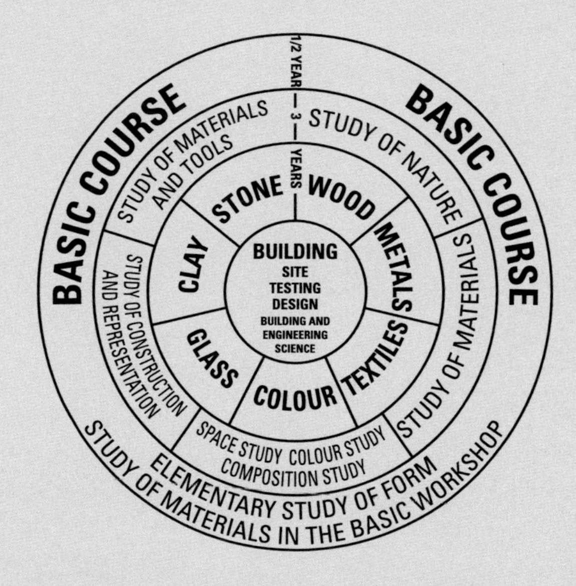

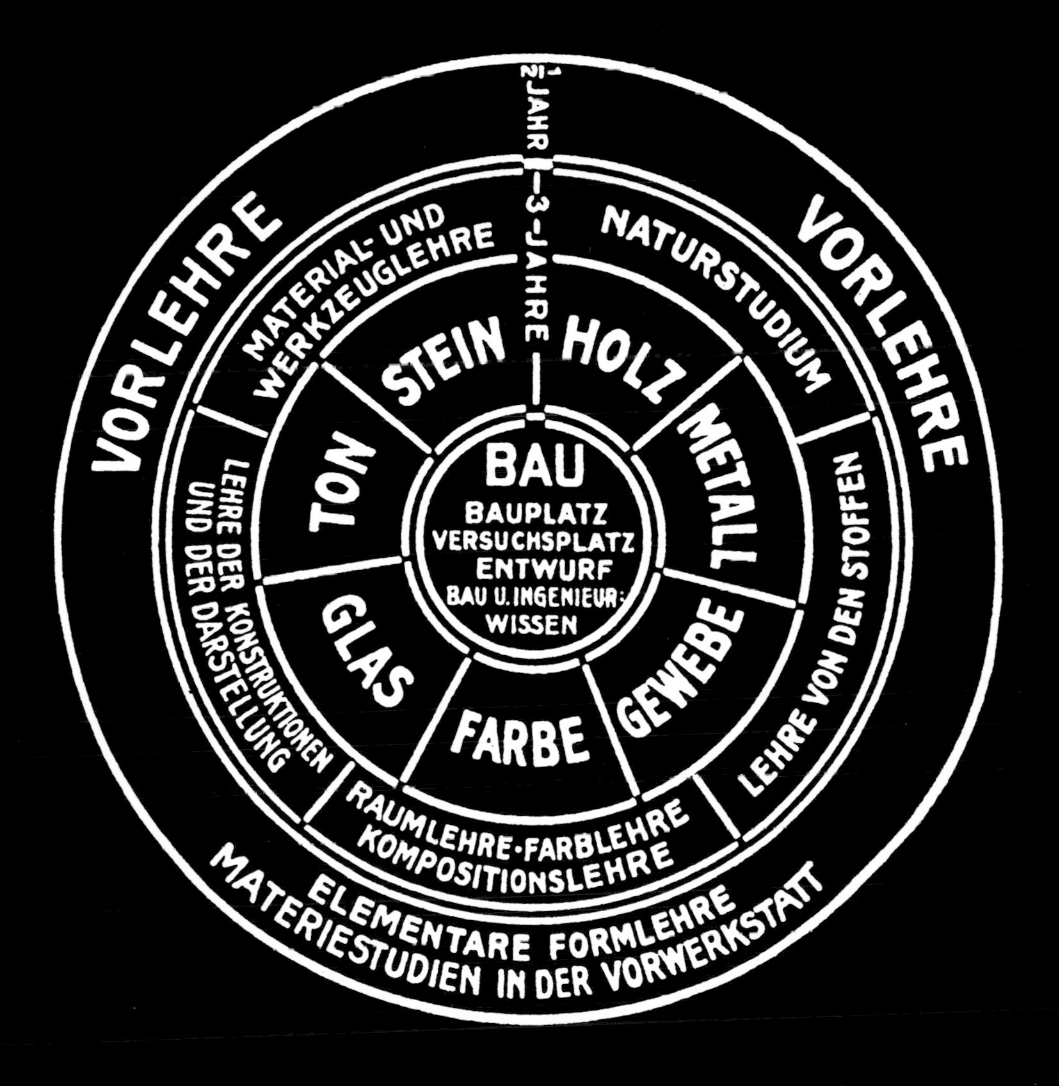
VORLEHRE
VORLEHRE
½ JAHR
3 JAHRE
MATERIAL- UND WERKZEUGLEHRE
NATURSTUDIUM
STEIN
HOLZ
TON
METALL
GLAS
GEWEBE
FARBE
BAU
BAUPLATZ
VERSUCHSPLATZ
ENTWURF
BAU U. INGENIEUR-WISSEN
LEHRE DER KONSTRUKTIONEN UND DER DARSTELLUNG
LEHRE VON DEN STOFFEN
RAUMLEHRE · FARBLEHRE
KOMPOSITIONSLEHRE
ELEMENTARE FORMLEHRE
MATERIESTUDIEN IN DER VORWERKSTATT

websites is due, at least in part, to the interest of hundreds of thousands of companies in exploiting the commercial potential of the new medium and the commercial benefits of hosting and transmitting the communications that result.

These two, mechanics and commerce, present another force: standardisation. Although it has been under theoretical assault in recent years – as representing all that is oppressive and inhuman in society – standardisation has great benefits. Common forms of measuring, common ingredients, terminology and processes are all aspects of mass production, and basic to the efficiency of every modern society.

Key figures in design's history have set about arriving at basic standards. Jan Tschichold in 'The New Typography', published in 1928, wrote that "large differences in weight are better than small. The closer in size different types are to each other, the weaker will be the result. A limit to the number of types used – normally three to not more than five – is always to be recommended." However limiting and coercive this kind of thinking might seem to us now, it derives from the the world of machinery, the natural inclination of the engineer to regulations and predictability. "Standards seemed to embody a collective wisdom, as against the wilful arbitrariness of individual expression" (Robin Kinross).

Although these forces mutate and evolve the material practice of design, at another level – the right fusion of aesthetic quality and utility – the problems are the same as they have always been. The art critic, Robert Hughes, wrote of art that "there is no progress, only fluctuations of intensity". What he meant was that the problems an artist confronts remain the same, whenever and wherever the artist sets about her task, except for a few peculiarly fertile periods that intensify the need for art and its potential subject matter (like the turmoil of the early or mid-20th century). The same is true of design.

Architecture is a bedfellow of graphic design. Like design, architecture is always created for a client, and can be judged functionally and aesthetically, and yet the influential critic Ernst Gombrich saw fit to call architecture an arm of art, and wove it in alongside painting and sculpture in his bestselling 'The Story of Art'. In other words, he demoted graphic design to a lower status. Design history and theory have really just begun, they are infants, and it will be some time before they can attain the sophisticated theoretical analysis that accompanies related fields, such as art and architecture. But if design continues to proliferate at the rate it has in the last few years, and our attempts to explain it continue to deepen our understanding of it as a cultural phenomenon, perhaps the next Gombrich might treat graphic design with the same degree of respect.

Left: Commodification
This remarkable website (www.72-hour-logo-design.com) offers a logo designed for you within 72 hours. You type in your brief and contact details and pay by credit card. Standard terms and conditions apply. This is design as a regularised commodity, a purchase of little consequence. Surprisingly the logos are very good – well drawn, varied, appropriate to the activities of the clients. A company could do a lot worse, and pay a lot more. If all efforts to commodify design are as competent, it will thrive.

Right: Unified art form
Frames from the title sequence for the film Seven, by Kyle Cooper and Imaginary Forces. This is design at its most emotionally charged and expressive. It fulfils its basic function in that it names the film and the director and the actors and the technicians. It also acts like an overture, to introduce the themes in the film: the lettering is frantically scratched by hand, and jerks around on the screen. The design replicates the idolect – the private language – of the madman at the film's centre, with all sorts of meaningless lettering, scrapbook pages, biblical phrases, obliterations and scribbles.

Is this film intro-sequence the unified art form that so many have sought, since it combines literature, drama, music and graphic design?

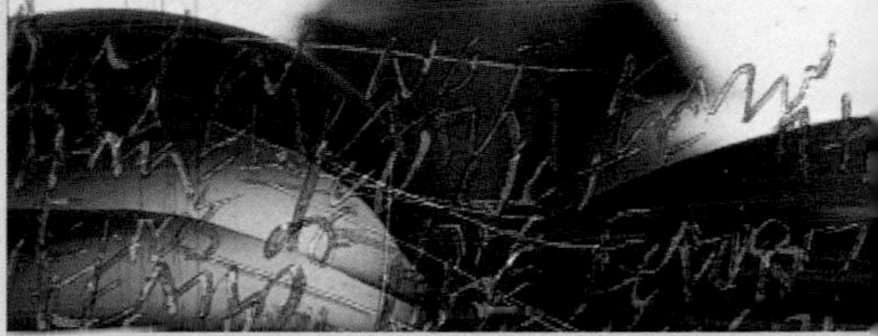

Changing the world

"First of all we think the world must be changed. We want the most liberating change of the society and life in which we find ourselves confined. We know that this change is possible through appropriate actions." This stirring call to action by French situationist, Guy Debord, might act as a rubric for all politically progressive art and design movements.

The desire for change is often very powerful, and this informs the language of the manifestos that simultaneously draw up the battle plan, and call others to the cause. This urge to remake society begs the question 'as what?' In the case of Marinetti and Wyndham Lewis, their vision ran perilously close to Fascism.

Early in the 20th century, design was seen to be an important part of the mechanism that would transform society and help to build a utopia. Industrialisation was seen as creating the context in which liberty for all could be realised. Futurism was just one aspect of this – Constructivism, Suprematism, the Bauhaus and its associated schools and teachers were others. Designers were to tap the energy of the machine, and use its qualities to create a new visual language. Machinery was so different to what was available in the past. It was rational, comprehensible, geometric, universal – it was classless and fantastically productive. Ellen Lupton points out aesthetic implications: "Modernism fetishised the very means of manufacture, using the systems of mechanical reproduction to build a mode of design that openly endorsed its technical origins".

Setting the tone
A detail from a fold-out page of 'Futurist Words of Liberty', written, typeset and published in 1909 by Filippo Tammaso Marinetti. "Except in struggle, there is no more beauty. No work without an aggressive character can be a masterpiece. Poetry must be conceived as a violent attack on unknown forces..." Marinetti's influence is still strongly felt. It epitomises the tone for any self-respecting manifesto: a verbal and intellectual assault on the established order, and the call for a new society. And although other manifestos had also done this (Marx's Communist Manifesto, for example) Marinetti heralds the new era with a fresh graphic language. He subverts the conventions of normal syntax: the words break apart, graphic devices, analphabetic characters, numbers and textures swirl about on the page surface, and all this can be seen simultaneously.

Marinetti wanted to herald the domination of the machine, and in part this meant the destruction of the romantic idea of the author, the individual attuned to nature, and all the traditions that seemed to support that. He flouted any previous form of comprehensibility, inventing a new championing of material form and implied complexity of temporality and meaning. Beware revolutions, as however alluring such forceful projects might be visually, we ought to remember that their very immediacy, virulence and tendency towards purity might disguise some half-baked, extremist political thinking.

5 mila
50 mila
50.000
5000
2000
1.033.750.00
150.000.00
60
34
er 100

'First Things First', written by Ken Garland in 1964, is a mild repost compared to manifestos from earlier in the century – it retains their urges without their ideals (shown right, it is available with a recent rewrite and all signatories at www.adbusters.org). Katherine McCoy on this gentle version of earlier utopian projects: "Too often our [design] graduates and their work emerge as charming mannequins, voiceless mouthpieces for the messages of ventriloquist clients. Let us instead give designers their voices so they may participate and contribute more fully in the world around them".

"The most significant choice of all, because it precedes everything else, is choosing what the design will be about" (Rick Poynor). Graphic design can be done with fairly minimal physical and financial means, but the means of putting it in people's hands require substantial capital. (The exception here is websites, which can be created for next to nothing, but publicising the URL is capital-intensive.) Because of this need for capital, designers will always remain locked in a commercial relationship with a client. Whilst the designer cannot simply take over and convert the material to her own purposes, she can work to infuse these commercial, or institutional, messages with political concerns and a greater social complexity. And this is surely where the future lies; change, but gradual change, raised expectations for designers and clients and readers alike.

"We, the undersigned, are graphic designers, photographers and students who have been brought up in a world in which the techniques and apparatus of advertising have persistently been presented to us as the most lucrative, effective and desirable means of using our talents. We have been bombarded with publications devoted to this belief, applauding the work of those who have flogged their skill and imagination to sell such things as:

cat food, stomach powders, detergent, hair restorer, striped toothpaste, aftershave lotion, before shave lotion, slimming diets, fattening diets, deodorants, fizzy water, cigarettes, roll-ons, pull-ons and slip-ons.

"By far the greatest time and effort of those working in the advertising industry are wasted on these trivial purposes, which contribute little or nothing to our national prosperity.

"In common with an increasing number of the general public, we have reached a saturation point at which the high-pitched scream of consumer selling is no more than sheer noise. We think that there are other things more worth using our skill and experience on. These are signs for streets and buildings, books and periodicals, catalogues, instructional manuals, industrial photography, educational aids, films, television features, scientific and industrial publications and all the other media through which we promote our trade, our education, our culture and our greater awareness of the world. We do not advocate the abolition of high pressure consumer advertising: this is not feasible. Nor do we want to take any of the fun out of life. We are proposing a reversal of priorities in that our society will tire of gimmick merchants, status salesmen and hidden persuaders, and that the prior call on our skills will be on worthwhile purposes. With this in mind, we propose to share our experience and opinions, and to make them available to colleagues, students and others who may be interested."

Speculation as revolution
The word 'experimental' has become highly charged in design writing and criticism. It always seems to attach to some sort of quasi-political claim, as though by playing with form, genuine social or economic movement can be opened up. Even if it were, it is not at all clear, as with the example of Marinetti, that experimental work always leads in positive and more democratic political directions. Type designer Jonathan Hoefler prefers the word 'speculative' rather than 'experimental'. It expresses the idea of chance, possibility, and chutzpah without the burden of social re-engineering.

Below: Nina Nägel applies Illustrator filters to the Arial typeface to explore the point at which the letterforms become pure pattern. The results are beautiful but accidental, unauthored and surprising.

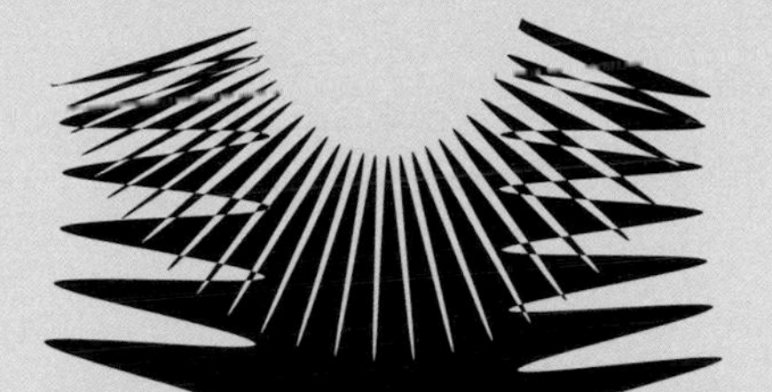

"Bless all English eyes"
'Blast' was the manifesto of the English Futurists, known as the Vorticists. Strongly influenced by Marinetti, Wyndham Lewis and a group of like-minded poets and painters wrote and produced two issues. Like the example below it was also a magazine for sale. The harsh typography lays out lists of the things the Vorticists hated (blast) and the things they admired (bless). There is a passion for machinery, and a wish to place this at the centre of a future society. "Technology has created a new Nature surrounding humanity... Now it is time for Art to keep up with this revolutionary step forward." Since the modern world was shaped by the industrial process, mechanisation was seen as the new source of beauty. Henri Gaudier-Brzeska, one of the group, said: "I shall derive my emotions solely from the arrangement of surfaces". The political dimension of their ideas was not overtly stated, but it errs towards the nasty, and is shot through with the extremism that pervaded all politics of the period. (Lewis was later an admirer of Hitler up to, during and after the Second World War.) But its very desire to achieve newness underwrote Lewis' development of a harsh, asymmetric typography that became, according to El Lissitzky, a founding example for the experimental typography that followed.

6

BLAST

years 1837 to 1900

Curse abysmal inexcusable middle-class (also Aristocracy and Proletariat).

BLAST

pasty shadow cast by gigantic Boehm (imagined at Introduction of BOURGEOIS VICTORIAN VISTAS).

WRING THE NECK OF all sick inventions born in that progressive white wake.

BLAST their weeping whiskers—hirsute
RHETORIC of EUNUCH and STYLIST—
SENTIMENTAL HYGIENICS
ROUSSEAUISMS (wild Nature cranks)
FRATERNIZING WITH MONKEYS
DIABOLICS—raptures and roses
of the erotic bookshelves
culminating in
PURGATORY OF
PUTNEY.

18

CHAOS OF ENOCH ARDENS
laughing Jennys
Ladies with Pains
good-for-nothing Guineveres.

SNOBBISH BORROVIAN running after
GIPSY KINGS and ESPADAS
bowing the knee to
wild Mother Nature,
her feminine contours,
Unimaginative insult to
MAN.

DAMN

all those to-day who have taken on that Rotten Menagerie, and still crack their whips and tumble in Piccadilly Circus, as though London were a provincial town.

WE WHISPER IN YOUR EAR A GREAT SECRET.

LONDON IS NOT A PROVINCIAL TOWN.

We will allow Wonder Zoos. But we do not want the
GLOOMY VICTORIAN CIRCUS in Piccadilly Circus.

IT IS PICCADILLY'S CIRCUS!

19

Buying dissent
Adbusters and Colors magazines, available on every high street, carry forward the language and cleansing impulses of manifestos. They treat commercial culture as intellectually corrosive, ideologically oppressive and propagandising, and call for a new, better world. It is a curious situation, as these magazines have cover prices, and compete for our commercial patronage. Dissent can be commodified like any other human need, "through the commercial mechanisms that control cultural activity, avant-garde tendencies are cut off from the segments of society that could support them" (Guy Debord). Who are these magazines really aimed at, and do the publishers really expect the readers to live out the extremist exhortations on their pages? Although Colors makes a much gentler comment on the world without Oliviero Toscani and Tibor Kalman at its helm, one is still left with the powerful, booby-trap-like incongruity of a magazine produced commercially, with pictures of the victims of landmines and machete attacks next to piles of brightly-coloured pullovers for teenagers. The complexity deepens when you realise several of Adbusters guest art directors are actively engaged in producing advertising. Has commercial culture split belief and action irrevocably?

Visual language

Design has flirted with French literary theory, often termed 'poststructuralism', over the past decade or so, plucking its most controversial and politically charged ideas and feeding them part-digested, with very mixed results, into education (especially Cranbrook in America), criticism (numerous articles in the magazines Eye and Emigre) and practice (usually marked by excessive use of the Photoshop program).

The dense and difficult work of French philosopher Jacques Derrida attempted to provide a basis for a whole new way of thinking about culture, and the use of the word 'deconstruction' – his name for his own theoretical ideas – has now become a commonplace word in any description of a certain kind of fragmented, deliberately clumsy typography. This happens whether or not the work has any actual relationship to Derrida's theory, usually neither designer nor critic care, it sounds so good. Yet critic Christopher Norris writes "to present 'deconstruction' as if it were a method, a system or a settled body of ideas would be to falsify its nature".

Whilst the raid on literary theory revived exciting ideas about 'open texts', and the mutability of interpretation was used to fuel an orgy of 'self-expression', the founding ideas of poststructuralism have yet to be fully understood, and their implications are huge.

Derrida, and all his fellow theorists, root their thinking in structuralism. In essence, structuralism states that all language (the definition of which encompasses all communication, including graphic design) is a system of relationships between signs. Each word or picture is a sign and each individual sign only has meaning because of its relationship to other signs. The word 'black' (also 'noir' or 'schwartz') only means what it does in reference to other colours. Meaning is created by a structure of relationships so vast that, as Roland Barthes said, "we cannot see its edges".

Derrida's importance in extending these ideas is paramount. Whilst he rejects any simple relationship between structure and meaning – indeed, his whole project has been to worry away at the link – he has shown "that there can be no spontaneous linguistic agency. He emphasises that whatever is said is pre-conditioned by the structural possibilities of what can be said" (Christa Knellwolf).

This would mean that design consists wholly of existing elements of meaning that are reused, recast, recombined. The scope for any movement, 'invention' or 'originality' in a conventional artistic sense, has to happen within strict limits. If every designer is recombining pre-existing material, drawing meaning from pre-established relationships, what role does 'originality' have?

Michel Foucault sees this in rather different terms. In a famous essay, 'What is an Author?', he describes the 'author-function' – an out-moded way of ascribing the creation of new meaning to a heroic artist. The hero-artist stems from the Romantic movement in art and literature; new ideas about creation that Isiah Berlin called "the greatest revolution ever in Western thought". Romanticism regarded every individual as genuinely and infinitely creative. Subjective feeling was all that mattered – it mattered so much that the 'common', existing patterns of expression were felt to be bankrupt, a threat to the only reality, that of the individual.

Structuralism and poststructuralism have been profound opponents of this idea; they doubt that self-expression even exists. Much

Monika Parrinder has captured a formula that underpins the idea of individual greatness in the hero-artist:

1 the creator
usually artist, writer or scientist – who rises above the ordinary mortal, acquiring a semi-divine status, in past times as a messenger for 'the original creator', God,

2 the individual
a pioneering, solitary non-conformist,

3 the madman
links between genius and madness are legion,

4 the intuitive person
whose work is 'natural' and unlearnt and hence cannot be analysed,

5 the pioneer
who is ahead of his or her (but rarely 'her') time and possibly a misunderstood or tortured soul (see 3 above).

We can see these ideas used in almost every article where the writer wants to lift up the designer or designers, and gild them. You will also notice many designers using the ideas to describe themselves. Parrinder's whole article 'The Myth of Genius', can be read in Eye magazine, issue 38.

design theory of recent years is an irreconcilable blend of two strains of thought: it proposes that structures of meaning create and transmit power, but then suggests that the heroic individual designer can use self-expression to usurp it. To propose that meaning is transpersonal, held in common, is to automatically call into question the Romantic individual, and whether she has any freedom of expression at all.

To use the analogy of a 'visual language' – an increasingly common term – brings with it structuralism, in some form or another. We are seemingly happy to regard spoken language as commonly created, commonly used. Derrida says "you are compelled in one way or another to make your text out of antecedent texts" – every text, every piece of design a kind of Frankenstein's monster made up of pre-existing parts. The full implications of these troublesome ideas have to be fully considered, not merely cherry-picked to give a contemporary zest to the hero-artist. We need to rethink the context in which design is made, how meaning is created, what its relationship is with antecedents, with tradition, what role does any individual actually play? With poststructuralism's grave questions about the 'self', exactly what is 'self-expression'?

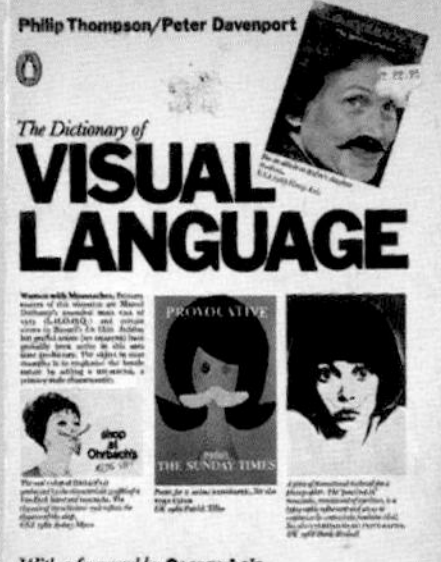

Right and overleaf: The Dictionary of Visual Language
The authors state: "Graphic design is a language. Like other languages it has a vocabulary, grammar, syntax, rhetoric". This book, published in 1974, explores what the authors call 'clichés'. The word 'cliché' has a derogatory sense, something tired and stale, an idea 'used' many times before. (How, they might have asked, can an idea be understood if it has not been used before?) It limits and diminishes the premise of the book to have used this word. The ideas of structuralism were stuck inside academia in the early 1970s, and perhaps Peter Davenport and Philip Thompson did not understand how significant a contribution they were making. Critic Terry Eagleton calls clichés "quotations without a source". In fact what the book shows is a sampling of the codes and metaphors intrinsic to a commonly created and understood visual language. Apart from Heller's 'Icons of Graphic Design' (see page 54), no other book has even attempted to catalogue the subtle shifts in use and meaning of the components of visual language.

Characteristic Style. The use of other styles of essentially characteristic typography, etc (seed packets, small ads, telephone directory, soap flake packs, etc), to achieve a particular result.

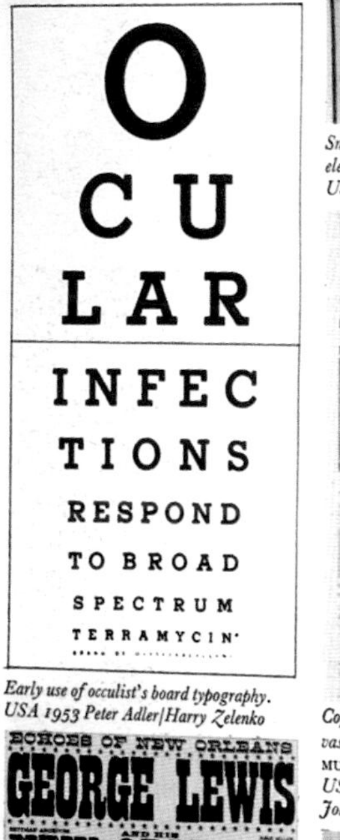

Early use of occulist's board typography.
USA 1953 Peter Adler/Harry Zelenko

Revival of playbill style.
USA 1956 Reid Miles

Small-ad style (missing person copy) made elegant.
USA 1957 Tom Courtos/Kurt Weihs

Copy reads, 'Wanted for holding captive a vast radio listening audience . . .' See also MUG SHOT.
USA 1959 Lou Dorfsman/Bert Newfeld/John Alcorn

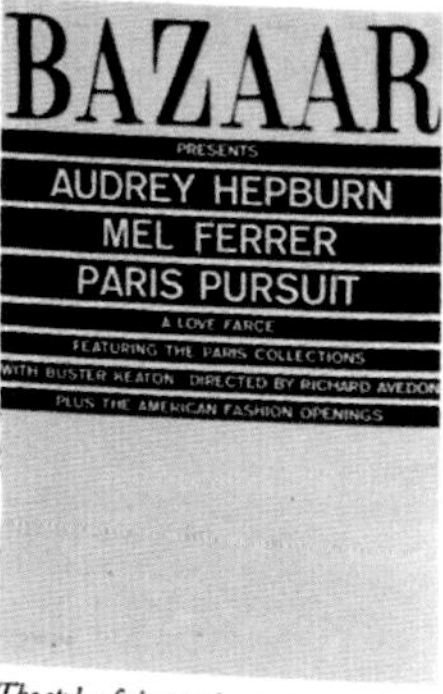

The style of cinema fascia typography.
USA 1959 Henry Wolf

Small-ad style is used to advertise weekly publication specialising in small-ads.
UK 1965 Philip Meyer

Seed packet style is used to symbolise the allergy.
UK 1967 John Dodson

50 **Characteristic Style**

The style of soap flake packs for a serious book on housewives (see HOUSEWIFE*).*
UK 1974 Paul McAlinden

Chess. As with many other board games (see GAMES), a well-established analogy for life, sometimes in its aggressive or even warlike form. The word pawn suggests manipulation but the image is not often visually realised.

Book jacket.
UK 1960 Larry Carter

Chess as an analogy for marital strife.
(Part of a three-frame strip.)
UK 1972 Mel Calman

Children's Bricks (Children's Blocks). Popular as a symbol for primary education. A 1950s cliché for simplicity (literally, it's child's play). Sometimes a symbol for the elementary facts. Naturally used by the building trade but also by investment and money lending firms (building for the future, etc).

For a building corporation. Children's building bricks as a substitute for the real thing.
USA 1962 George Tscherny

Children's Writing and Drawing. Sometimes infantilism is a solution especially when the subject matter is appropriate. The advantage of the child's drawing is its directness and lack of design niceties.

Poster for a cigar company.
USA 1958 Paul Rand

Bookjacket.
UK 1964 Derek Birdsall

Crystal Ball. Symbol for prediction.

UK 1970 Mel Calman

Cube. See GENERAL SIGNS.

Cup (Trophy). A natural prize symbol. It has strong association with the collector who makes gratuitous conquests.

Currency. The representation of coins or paper money is a symbol for private or public economics. A further condensing of information is achieved through the use of currency signs (see DOLLAR SIGN, POUND SIGN).

Small coin (dime or farthing) as letterform. See also SUBSTITUTION.
UK 1973 Derek Birdsall

Fusion of international paper currency with Buckminster Fuller map projection (see MAP*).*
UK 1973 Philip Thompson

Curtains. An old fashioned symbol for the theatre. Sometimes used to convey the idea of presentation to the public in a more general sense.

Copy says 'Eyes on Paris and America'. The EYE *peers through a curtain of gloves.*
USA 1959 Henry Wolf

Cut-out. A device derived from th language of children's annuals magazines (like COLOURING-IN). Th is the cutting out of the components a person or object waiting to be as sembled. Sometimes the inclusion a DOTTED LINE around the objec emphasises the device.

Personal Christmas card.
USA 1959 Brownjohn, Chermayeff & Geismar

USA 1969 Arnold Varga

Cut-up. A technique where th image is fragmented and sometim scattered around. As the technique analogous to dismemberment, in th case of human imagery, the effect ca be disturbing. Typographically sometimes creates a new dynami devoid of any symbolism.

Cover for Art Direction. *The missing letters are the important ones. See also* ALPHABET.
USA 1941 Paul Rand

70 **Crystal Ball**

opy asks, 'Like a piece of Skelton?' to ttract advertisers.
SA 1951 Lou Dorfsman

The fragmented logotype was a characteristic of the advertising on large poster hoardings and advertisements.
France 1954 Atelier Charles Loupot

Image reflects the technique of the film which analysed and dissected the story.
USA 1959 Saul Bass

Architectural Review *cover.*
UK 1962 Philip Thompson

Poster for Life *magazine.*
USA 1963 Dennis Wheeler

Poster.
Italy 1965 Bruno Munari

Dagger. Like the knife a symbol of sacrifice, vengeance, death. Because of its secret nature it has, unlike the SWORD, associations of treachery.

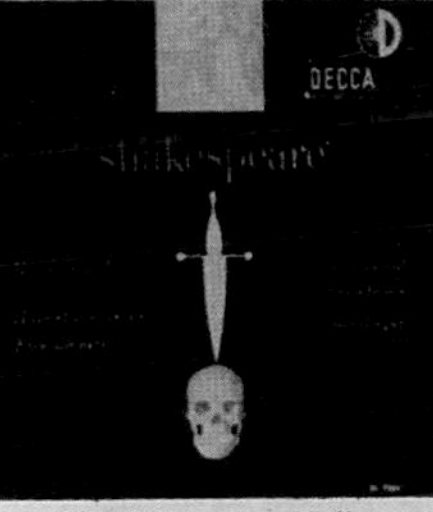

Record sleeve: Romeo and Juliet, Hamlet *soliloquies. See also* SKULL.
USA 1951 Erik Nitsche

Aggressive dagger determines the imagery. Book jacket for Edgar Allan Poe stories. See also SKULL.
Switzerland 1961 Heinz Stieger

Dagger 71

'Icons of Graphic Design'
This book, by Steven Heller and Mirko Ilic, gathers together work that utilises a common device or element – here, a pointing fist. Other subjects include shadows, squares, silhouettes, prisms and speeding trains. Heller retains the idea of the Romantic hero-artist, and suggests that there are two kinds of 'genius': a 'form genius' and a 'style genius' who take the common visual language and extend and expand it. He gives what he calls an 'icon' for every subject: a transformative and founding piece of design. He writes as if that one piece of design sprang fully formed from its creator's brow, untouched by anything the designer had previously seen or heard – almost as if they come from outside of culture or outside of history. Despite a lack of any deep examination of how exactly 'genius' breaks free of common recombination, this book presents a fabulously rich array of examples, and is one tiny step in acknowledging that all design is part of "a common vocabulary".

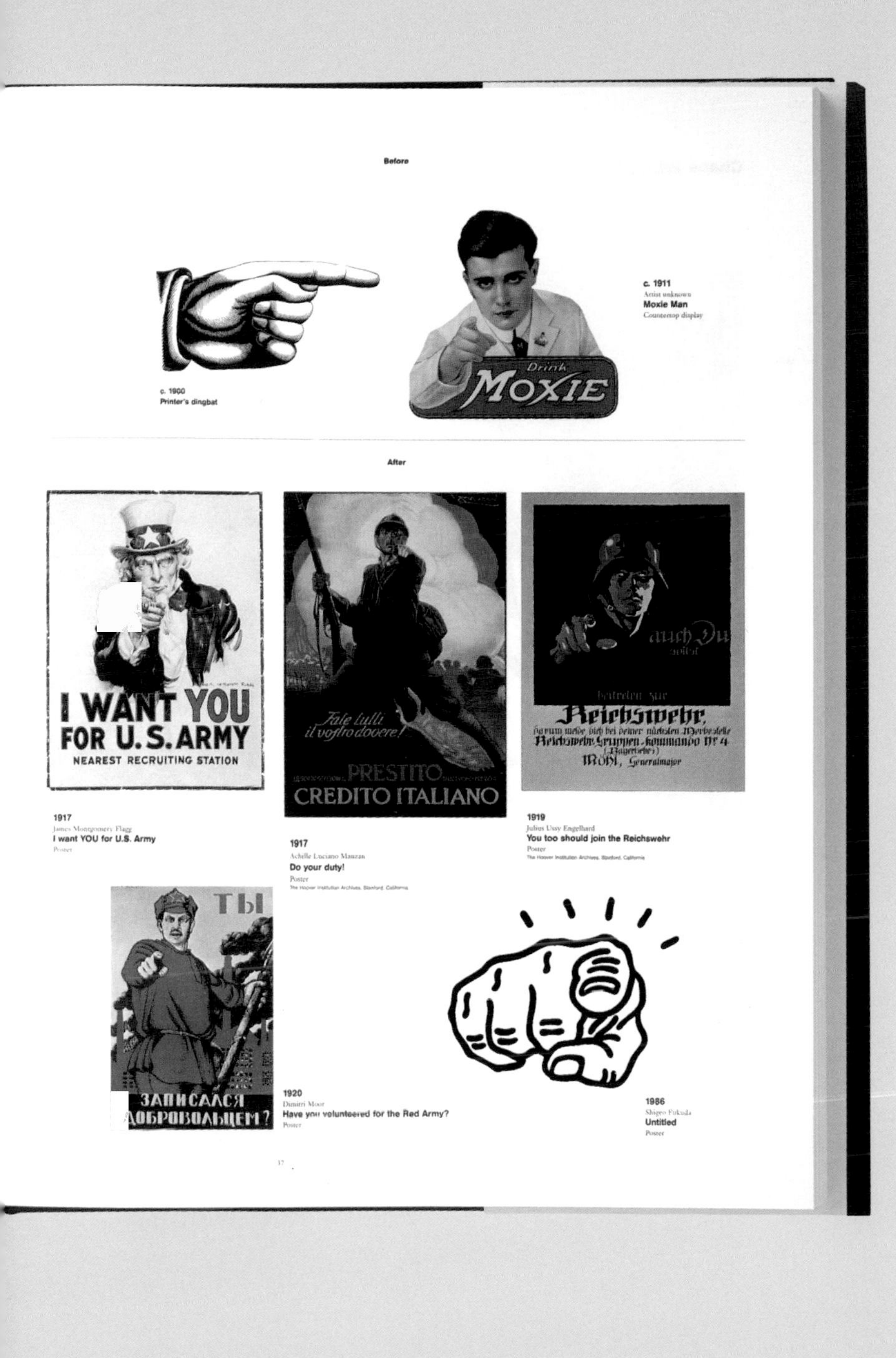

Before

c. 1900
Printer's dingbat

c. 1911
Artist unknown
Moxie Man
Counterop display

After

1917
James Montgomery Flagg
I want YOU for U.S. Army
Poster

1917
Achille Luciano Mauzan
Do your duty!
Poster
The Hoover Institution Archives, Stanford, California

1919
Julius Ussy Engelhard
You too should join the Reichswehr
Poster
The Hoover Institution Archives, Stanford, California

1920
Dimitri Moor
Have you volunteered for the Red Army?
Poster

1986
Shigeo Fukuda
Untitled
Poster

37

Attached to a framework
All these pieces use the same base: the moulded 'sprue' that holds the pieces of plastic models together before they are twisted off and constructed. Each design uses the sprue as a metaphor in the same basic way – this is a unified collection – but its tone and detailed meaning varies with each iteration. To compare two; the Dawkins book cover follows through the author's idea about genes. Every living creature is generated by their genetic codes, the sprue acts as a wry, tongue-in-cheek comment on this apparently mechanistic predetermination. (Note the little plastic Penguin logo.) In the essays in 'Anglo-English Attitudes', Geoff Dyer examines clichés in literature and the wider culture. The sprue here, with soldiers frozen in predictable and fixed postures, is a parallel for a set of clichéd intellectual ideas. With the overt militarism of the image and the type, critical of the essays' targets, there is purveyed a sense of ominous nastiness.

Clockwise: 'The Blind Watchmaker' published by Penguin Books, cover illustration by Liz Pyle; 'English Football Hooligan Set' by Mother; song titles for Feelings by David Byrne shown in 'Made You Look' by Stefan Sagmeister, published by Booth-Clibborn Editions; video of the band Space published by Gut Records Ltd.; 'Anglo-English Attitudes' published by Abacus; magazine advertising for the fashion magazine FHM.

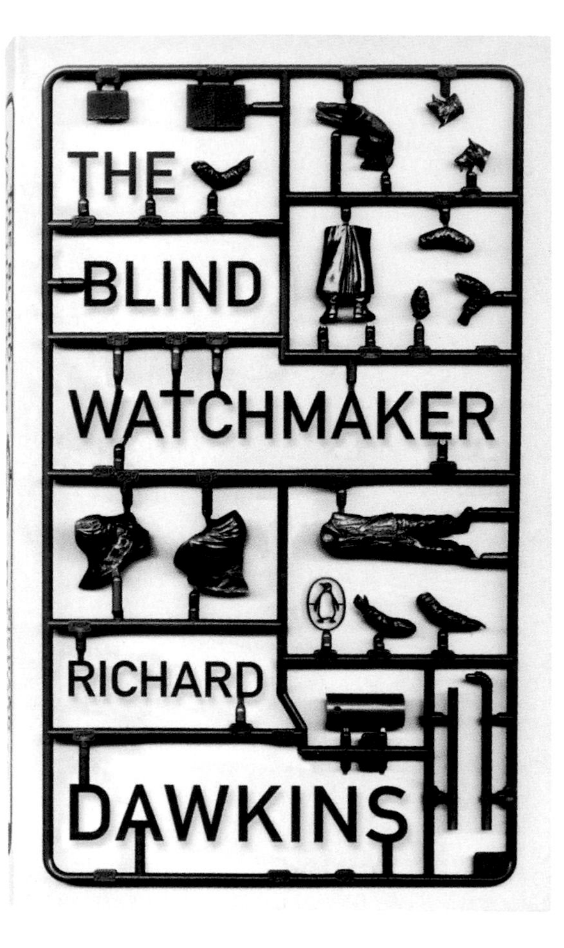

MOTHER MINIATURES
ENGLISH FOOTBALL HOOLIGAN SET
1/15 アメリカ現用陸軍歩兵セット
READY TO ASSEMBLE PLASTIC MODEL KIT
MODELLING SKILLS HELPFUL IF UNDER 10 YEARS OF AGE
MOTHER
GO ENGLAND!
mother
Feelings
DAVID BYRNE
FUZZY FREAKY
MISS AMERICA
A SOFT SEDUCTION
DANCE ON VASELINE
THE GATES OF PARADISE
AMNESIA
YOU DON'T KNOW ME
DADDY GO DOWN
FINITE=ALRIGHT
WICKED
BURNT BY THE SUN
LITTLE DOLL
THE CIVIL WARS
THEY ARE IN LOVE
Luaka Bop Inc
© 1997 Warner Bros. Records Inc
Made in U.S.A.

The Canon

The word 'kanon', Greek for 'measuring stick', was first applied to the religious writings that were gathered into the Bible. Many pieces had to be excluded, judged as not making the grade.

Literary critic Harold Bloom suggests that within a given era every artist struggles against the influence of "strong precursors", or great artists from the past, which can exert itself across many generations. The artist has two basic strategies to deal with this: "emulation", which can either be overt, or a rich synthesis of emulations of different precursors, and "avoidance". The danger with avoidance is that the work becomes an exact opposite of, but still informed by, what it set out to escape from. Bloom proposes that if the new artist is strong enough, she will completely digest, rewrite, and "conquer" the language of the stong precursor and become strong and canonical in her own right – a rare event.

Martha Scotford, a professor at North Carolina State University, has made a very detailed analysis of graphic design books, noting which designers have been featured, their gender, nationality, their works that have been referred to. The results are depressing, in that they slant in one particular direction, towards excessively male, almost wholly Western European and excessively avant-garde designers. Scotford concludes that "a canon creates heroes... in singling out individual designers and works, we may lose sight of the range of communication, expression, concepts, techniques, and formats that make up the wealth of design history... for students new to the study of graphic design, a canon creates the impression that they need go no further: the best is known, the rest is not worth knowing. This is unfair, dangerous and shortsighted."

There is a canon, but it is not made by the compilers of design books, or critics – the design canon is created by designers. Designers will seek out strong work in order to understand its strength, and be invigorated, influenced and changed by it. They enter a struggle, the majority never escaping the weight of their chosen precursors. The danger is that if designers do not have access to a very eclectic range of work from the past, then their choices will be limited. The best hope for design's future is to publish, exhibit, and mount on the web the greatest possible range of work from the past.

If the canon is by its very nature exclusive, the antidote then is an anti-canon. Michael Bierut has an anti-canon, a joyous celebration which is a long, liberal list of names, a kind of design rap. There is no aesthetic or ideological consistency, just the names of everyone who has made any kind of contribution to the field (the ones that Bierut knows of), one after the other. Bierut says, "I could list more graphic designers' names in any period of time than anyone else can... everyone else would have to quit, everyone else would be lying dead on the floor, and I would still be writing... Don Trusdell, Alexey Brodovitch, David Carson, Jilly Simons, Alex Isley, Laurie Haycock, Lester Beall, Woody Pirtle... what makes the field thrilling, and what always gives it a sense of possibility, is not just what I am going to do tomorrow, but what someone else is going to do tomorrow".

Young Caslon
An idea for a typeface by
Ian Chilvers of Atelier Works.

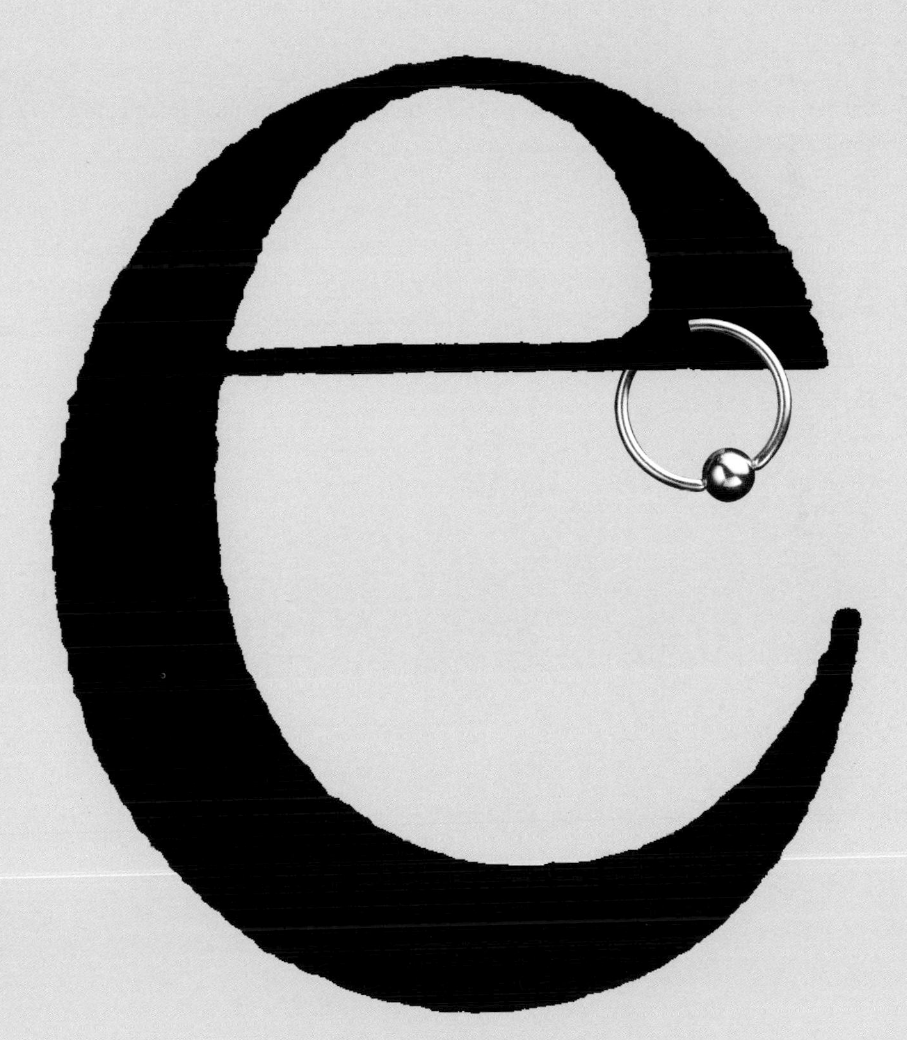

The last word

When we look at a book or a magazine about design, what are we actually looking at? All the work shown has been edited, resized, divested of its context. We are often shown one spread from a magazine, the cover of a book, one application of a logo. We have no idea of how it was received, the conditions of its commissioning, the circumstances of its reception, whether or not it worked.

Reviewing Steven Heller's book on Paul Rand, Lorraine Wild draws up a shopping list of what we need to know about design work in order to really understand it: "Explicit information about the communications [between designer and client], the chain of command, the schedules, the budgets, the strategies, the presence (or absence) of marketing, the documentation..."

Surely the starting point is to treat design like art. We need to see a piece of design as an artefact, a real physical thing with a specific place in history. Many pieces of design have become totemic, landmarks in design history, but how many of us have seen the actual pieces of design themselves: the actual poster, the actual pack? Most of us know them as reproductions, miniaturised printed copies, their texture, their fabric, and all their aura lost.

When we look at design work in this way, what exactly are we judging? It is shorn of all its context. Real, three-dimensional objects, painstakingly composed, are reduced to tiny, flat squares. You can't smell the ink, feel the paper surface, hear the page turn, or see the relationships between colour, type and image. Most commonly we see a stamp-sized image with a caption beneath it. This small image might be a logo (one version of it), a book cover (we do not see the book inside), one solitary spread from a thick magazine (in which we can't read the type), a poster (nothing near its original size, never on a wall). Often the image is squared-off, or not even a photograph of the thing itself, but an electronic file. In some cases, this may not even be what the client actually bought. (A designer I once worked alongside used to reprint disappointing jobs the way he thought they should have been done just for his portfolio, at another client's expense.)

If we compare design to other arts, literature, say, and film, then would we accept a book about a major poet, which consisted just of snippets from her poems? Or a book about a film-maker with just one scene from each film, with no sound? This would be regarded as a way of presenting their work that made it impossible to judge, a fragment that indicated certain values, but was incomplete. Why is design different? Almost all graphic design has a narrative, a sequence, pacing, it tells a story. It articulates different kinds of material, as dependent on all its parts for effect as any film or poem. Graphic design history and criticism needs to develop minimum standards, to treat design artefacts with integrity, photographing them complete, giving media, dimensions and provenance.

Design is at base a practical activity, the making of artefacts. Is there any need for theory at all? Can too much theory have an opposite effect – switching design from an intuitive, spontaneous, contingent activity to a way of working that is rigid? Johanna Drucker, designer and theorist, says "people who work from a theoretical perspective, whether it's in design or the visual arts, often do very stilted, self-conscious work that ultimately is only an illustration of the theoretical position".

We tend to think of theory as delivered fully formed in a book, but every piece of design has a theoretical basis, even if it has been made by a designer who has never read a book. A theory is a set of ideas: a particular reading of history, associated speculations and value judgements and ideas about the future. We all operate with a set of ideas underpinning what we do. Usually we do not call it theory, because it has built up slowly; an incremental growth of assumptions through hundreds of thousands of incidents, conversations, glancing at illustrated books and magazines, watching the television. Drucker says: "I don't think that design needs theory, but I think designers need theory". They need it as a counterweight, a litmus test for the second-hand ideas that bubble up through culture.

How are designers to get their theory? In my experience designers don't read much, they glance. The reasons for this are twofold: it is partly to do with design being perceived as non-intellectual – therefore designers are not encouraged to read theoretical texts – and partly to do with the genuinely non-literary way in which we develop visual skills. Reading has to be learned, especially the stamina to read difficult texts, and designers are often allowed to forgo this effort early on. Compare the amount a designer reads on a degree course with what an English student has to read. Why should it be different? Why should designers know less?

The reading of the late Paul Rand serves as an example of self-expansion. He published a partial bibliography for his last book 'From Lascaux to Brooklyn'. It covers some very diverse and difficult reading: mysticism, manifestos, sociology, history, the literary criticism of IA Richards and Harold Bloom, the philosophy of Hegel and John Dewey, the art history of Erwin Panofsky and Michel Foucault. There seems little doubt that his influence on several generations of other designers, and clients, is as much due to the thinking espoused in his books as to his design. Or put another way, his influence has been greatly intensified by his writing, which could not have been written without his reading.

If designers read more, the way they design would be more conscious of the work they produce being read. What designers consider important would change, they would be much more interested in finding ways of making the content into content worth reading.

"Design is not a neutral, value-free process. A design has no more integrity than its purpose or subject matter. Garbage in, garbage out" (Katherine McCoy). The best design has always worked backwards into its content to a greater or lesser extent, to create a satisfying unity. If the development of rich, sophisticated, supple design that deepens, redirects and even rewrites its content does not come from designers themselves – independent-minded, literate, politically sophisticated and historically aware – then where else will it come from?

Anatomy

Dividing up graphic design into categories is essentially a fruitless exercise. It ought to be clear, at this point in the book, that 'design' is a portmanteau term: it covers a number of interlaced activities that do not fall into distinct parts. But even an elementary analytical undertaking – the word 'analysis' itself means 'undoing' – leaves us no other choice.

This part of the book firstly examines typography and its components including the alphabet, typefaces and the grids that orchestrate type. The main forms of image-making follow, and then an extended look at the defining characteristic of graphic design: the juxtaposition of word and image.

Design is a process of creating – in the Tools section we consider the relationship between the eye and the technology that manifests visual thinking. The last section deals with Disciplines, those loose labels that segregate design activity. I have used terms that seemed to make most sense to me, but magazines might equally masquerade as 'editorial', and identity might have been 'branding'. So, we begin with forms of word and image, followed by the different ways these are used in combination.

Although, as in many professions, the computer is now the primary tool, any designer needs to be aware that what is constructed digitally on a flat surface is only one part of a process. A basic tenet of any craft is a thorough understanding of the materials being used, and these can extend to a bewilderingly extensive list. Some craft-like trends have recently crept into graphic design, perhaps due to an ever pressing need to 'innovate' and refresh the graphic vocabulary – or maybe because of the need to personalise the work and counter the globalising effects of mass production.

The graphic designer cannot avoid the fact that design is a preparatory activity for mass reproduction. This is manifest both in the processes and in the materials it makes use of. Not that mass production fully determines all the decisions a designer might take, but that mass production, or more strictly 'mass reproduction', implies a mass audience. And a mass audience includes various levels of literacy: poor or fading eye-sight; differences i n age, education, ethnicity, politics, and so on. Designing a typeface for 200 leaflets, with a readership of friends and associates, is a very different process from designing a national newspaper. This kind of commission makes decisions about the design inevitable, which brings us back to the ongoing debate between the model of the artist and the model of the artisan: the collision and choices between the values of the unique and the values of the repeatable, the experimental and the reliable.

This part concludes with a brief note on websites, and other film and digital work. Although these areas might appear to be free of the issues surrounding mass reproduction, they are as subject to them as any other area of design. A website, film or interactive CD aimed at the widest possible audience needs to be intellectually accessible, as well as taking into account its unpredictability and breadth of capability. The media in which the work will be delivered also exposes it to ready-made tests which it needs to pass: screen sizes, pixel values and the availability (or otherwise) of software plug-ins to view websites, for example. For film titles we could add screen ratios, projection or viewing methods and size of screen. Every time a film is screened, or a website visited, the work is being reproduced.

It is impossible to represent the huge range of graphic design in attempting to illustrate this section. Where possible, fresh, unpublished or unfamiliar examples are used to illustrate particular points.

Alphabets

Three thousand years ago, a revolution occurred when simple graphic marks were used to represent sound elements – phonemes – capable of endless recombination, as opposed to the complete pictographic systems of the Egyptians and Sumerians that run into many thousands of characters.

The development of letterforms, from their origin in the Phoenician Near East to today's alphabet is a long history. Every single piece of writing is, in some small way, a reinterpretation of letterforms. A good illustration of this is the copying of documents by hand. Throughout the late Classical and Mediaeval periods scribes economised on the Classical letterforms, using a style of writing called 'uncials' – the shapes were more comfortable and faster to form – in the process developing what we now call lowercase letters. (Lowercase and uppercase are so called because the two types were kept in two separate 'cases' see page 68.)

Linguist Ferdinand de Saussure made a very influential statement about spoken language and the concepts that language articulates. He said that the word for ox in English, and 'boeuf' in French showed that words had an arbitrary relationship to the world and that they are merely different sets of sounds used to describe the same thing. The sounds do not, in any way, correspond to objects in the physical world. The relationship between these sounds and the form of the letters used to represent them is also arbitrary – for example, how is the sound 'a' in any way related to the form of the letter 'a'?

Left: Rational alphabets
Five attempts at rationalisation, all fuelled by the modernist drive for universality. While interesting analytical exercises, they all suffer from more than a touch of arrogance. The overriding factor in the development of the alphabet is that it is not invented by any one person, but developed over thousands of years by thousands of people. Any substantial design development is only possible by democratic consent.
Top to bottom: Herbert Bayer's Universal, a version of his 'kleinschribung', based on lowercase letters; Jan Tschichold's Universal, a rationalisation aiming at one set of characters by making a marriage of upper- and lowercase; Wladyslav Strzeminski's alphabet modelled on pure geometric elements: circles, right angles and straight lines; Wim Crouwel's 'New Alphabet' based on a square – note the radical 'a' compared to the undramatic design of the other characters; Braille, an aesthetically beautiful matrix of two rows of three dots. Developed for the blind, it is usually embossed and meets all the criteria set by the most radical re-imagining: it uses only one 'case', has no accents, and allows for common words to be simplified as single characters.

Opposite: Legendary origins
A composite of the ideas of three linguists from the early 20th century. The Phoenician letters are real enough, but what they represent is largely guesswork.

PHOENICIAN			LATIN
𐤀	aleph	ox, then, head with horns	A
𐤁	beth	door, supports of roof	B
𐤂	gimel	neck of camel	C
𐤃	daleth	door, bottom stroke is ground	D
𐤄	he	man on knees, arms raised in joy	E
𐤅	vau	from nail to small flame	F
𐤆	zayin	sword in its sheath	I
𐤇	heth	flower, calix	
𐤈	teth	hand, fingers extended	
𐤉	yod	hand	J
𐤊	koph	folded hand, thumb extended	K
𐤋	lamedh	cross, cane, then shepherd's crook	L
𐤌	mem	water (but not Egyptian zig-zag)	M
𐤍	nun	serpent	N
𐤎	sameleh	fish in many forms	X
𐤏	ayin	eye	O
𐤐	pe	mouth, open mouth	P
𐤑	tsede	side of man in profile	Ts
𐤒	qoph	stomach with esophagus attached	Q
𐤓	res	head	
𐤔	sin	tooth	W
𐤕	tau	cross, a mark for a mark	T

Modules

"Acknowledge all constraints", says Anthony Froshaug, printer, typographer and teacher, by which he means: understand the nature of type and how it got that way. Almost every typeface in use today was first designed and cut for use in letterpress, which has strict physical constraints – everything has to lock together within a wooden frame called a 'forme'. Even many of the new, wholly electronic fonts are based on 16th- or 17th-century prototypes. Type is still designed on rectangular frameworks or bodies – bodies that hold the letterform in an invisible frame, separate from the letters next to, above and below it. Many of these conventions have been carried into the typography of our computers, the skeleton and structure of ethereal 21st century digital type is still firmly physical. The language of type betrays this: even the word typeface refers to the 'face' that is presented to be inked. The conventions developed during the centuries of the letterpress era are so embedded in how type has evolved that it is impossible to separate type from the process that brought it about.

Mechanisation necessitates measurement and repeatability. It requires modular relationships within each typeface, and between different typefaces, but, as examples on this page show, modularity is part of a process that had long been part of the harmonious construction of letterforms even when they were still hand-drawn.

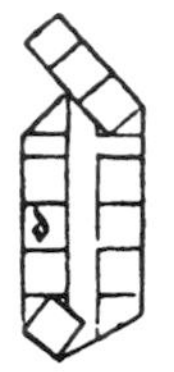

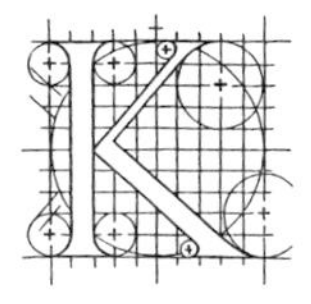

Opposite: Modularity
In this poster by English designer Phil Baines, printed using letterpress type, the relationships and patterns that typography creates are laid bare. It is easy to see how the grid – central to most graphic design – is a natural outcome of modular typography.

Left: Modular letters
Examples of modularity in letter design – the main purpose of which is to create unity across all the letters of the alphabet.
Top to bottom: Albrecht Dürer, 1525; Geoffrey Tory, 1529; a modern bitmap font; even Arabic script (bottom) has a modular basis.

going again

going against the grain

W ng as

art In the thick of it In the sticks A dry old stick Come down from the trees In a cleft stick All bark no bite Being at loggerheads Turning over a new leaf Shaking like a leaf Something rotten in the woods hed Coming out of the woodwork Barking up the wrong tree Your neck

Eaves dropping Up a gum tree Reduced to pulp Don't upset the apple c

your tree old blut Round and round the mulberry bush Taking a leaf out of

oak the tr

a knotty problem

s ok S log he ro k i t & hic rt plan esn't g Heardi e grape ff one's twig T wiglets Backw

meone's boo leeping like a Cutting out dead wood C w's nest Hac branch As t k as two sho ks Money do row on trees through the vine Fallin

oods Don't beat about the bush Have you twigged it yet There are other avenues Something in the forest is stirring Taking the stick There's sap in it Trunk road Seeds of doubt Trunk call Local branch A hatchet job Splinter group Local branch Branch meeting Something to be axed Stripping the willow A thorny problem He was hedging his bets Bearing fruit Out of joint Up sticks At one's beam ends Off-shoot Up-ro

oted Root-less Logarithm Whittled down Rooting for you Branchlines Leaf through Shady goings on Backlog Logjam Lumbering along Log book Out on a limb Hedged in Hedged around Budding talent Rising sap Walking the plank Shiver me timbers Rooting about Family tree Special branch Deeply rooted Tracing yo ur roots G etting spru ced u p In a nutshell An old c hestnu t Off be am Roo ting it o ut Win dfalls W illowy Speed of knots Chock-a- bloc k R ooting fo r Resting on yo ur laurels Yardstick E V E RGREEN I've been l um bered wit h Touch wo od N igger in the woodpile Sh e's nut s Papering o ver the crack s Off th e peg Eavesdr opping Up a g um tree I n the thick of i t Reduced to p ulp Don't u pset the apple c art In the sticks A dry old sti ck Come down f rom the trees N ot out of the w ood yet Being at loggerheads Turn ing over a new l eaf Shaking like a leaf Something rotten in the woodshed Coming out of the woodwork In a cleft stick Barking up the wrong tree Your neck of the woods Respect your elders Scraping the barrel A bird in the hand is worth two in the bush Sapping your energy You look as though you've been through a hedge backwards Out of your t

ound & re af out of a log Cut st Hackir as two sh n trees H ff one's tw he bush

if you go down to the woods today

orest is n a nutshell glets Se oubt Ta stick Tr d Trunk nter gro e's sap i atchet j ter group Leaf through Branch meeting Something to be axed

stirring I hell Twi eds of d king the unk roa call Spli up Ther n it A h ob Splin

Strippi ng the willow A thor ny pro blem H e was h edging his bets

Bearing fruit Out of joint Up sticks At ones beam ends Ro t-less Of shoot Up rooted Lo garithum Whittling down Rooting for you Branchlines (Dr. Beeching) Leaf through Shady goings on Backlog Logjam Lumbering along Log book Out on a limb Hedged in Hedged around Budding talent Rising sap Walking the plank Shiver me timbers Rooting about Family tree Special branch Deeply rooted Tracing your roots Getting spruced up Hear in a nutshell An old chestn

beam Ro -a-block A chip of Shaking l Round a Sapping y Trunk ca Family tr Walking

Typefaces

Recent discussion surrounding typefaces has tended to harden into two opposed readings of the history of typeface design. The first view – brutally summarised – is that there has been a clear line of improvement in typeface design since Gutenberg. The form of letters has become increasingly more rational. This reached its zenith with the universalising designs of the Bauhaus, and the typefaces within that tradition, such as Helvetica and the appropriately named Univers. Tiny adjustments and deferent revisions are all that is required.

The second reading is roughly similar with different conclusions: it has more time for the typefaces that got left behind, and holds that what it calls 'the certainties of Modernism' are oppressive, and not relevant in the present day. It calls for typefaces that are more 'expressive' and appropriate to contemporary society.

Both outlooks are 'diachronic' readings of typeface design in that they look at the development of typefaces over time and make judgements about the relationship between those developments – being either steps forward or steps backward.

However, these are not the only contexts within which to consider type. A more inclusive approach is to think of all typeface designs as being more or less successful, in their own right. The history of typefaces can be viewed as an unending experiment with the forms of letters – the effect of history on the alphabet.

Opposite: Interchangeable
Taken from the play, 'Measure for Measure', the verse has been set in two different fonts. How does each typeface effect us? As you read these passages, do you 'hear' the language, or do you understand the words in some other way? Do we understand the meaning of Shakespeare's words differently in each typeface? Do we 'hear' a different tone, or voice? Can Shakespeare's work be set, with equal effect, in any typeface?

Above: Mutable
Nine versions taken from typefaces designed between 1900 and 1940 that illustrate the wide parameters of form for each letter. There is no ideal typeface and there is no single model. Rather, the form of each letter – in Walt Whitman's words – "contains multitudes". All typefaces are simply interpretations of this non-existent original.

Below: Cases
The phrase 'upper- and lower-case' stems from physically splitting a typeface into capitals and small letters, kept in a case.

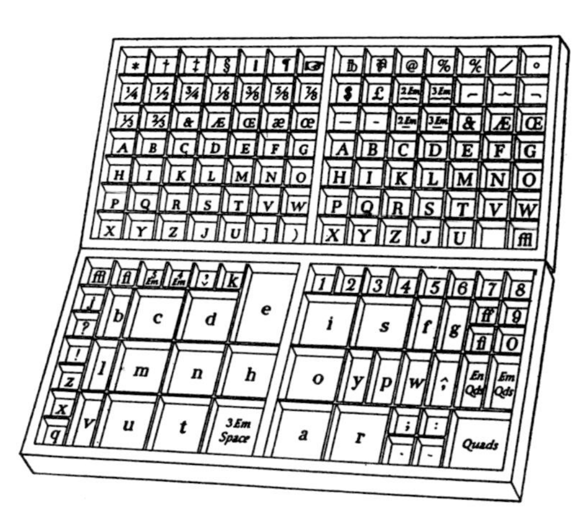

O place! O form!
How often dost thou with thy case, thy habit,
wrench awe from fools, and tie the wiser souls
to thy false seeming.

**O place! O form!
How often dost thou with thy case, thy habit,
wrench awe from fools, and tie the wiser souls
to thy false seeming.**

Digital type

Type designer Matthew Carter describes the transition from type designed for specific, physical form, to type now: "In a world of multiple, co-existing technologies we can no longer design type for a particular technology, even if we wanted to. Now, today, the life-expectancy of a decent typeface is longer than that of the technology that reproduces it. A type design dedicated to a particular technology is a self-obsoleting typeface.

"I cannot predict how you will use it – on a laser printer at 300, 400 or 600 dots per inch (dpi), a typesetter at 1200 or 2000 dpi, on a screen display, film recorder, broadcast video system, or architectural sign-making system. But I have to assume that sooner or later it will be used on all of those things, and probably more, as yet uninvented."

Continuing developments in software will enable a significant movement forwards in typeface design and use. Existing fonts consist of a maximum of 256 characters, whereas software such as Microsoft's OpenType will allow 65,000, enough for a single typeface to set all the world's languages.

The combination of precision and encylopedic comprehensiveness, alongside randomisation and the ability to modify or create fonts for specific projects or single applications, makes for a new era in typeface design. As Carter himself says, "We have had 550 years of moveable type, now we have mutable type".

BBB

Above: Beowolf
Beowolf was designed in 1989 by Eric van Blokland and Just van Rossum, two Dutch type designers who go by the name of LettError. It heralds new possibilities for digital type that were impossible for physical or photographic type. It has a 'randomisation routine' which means every time a key is struck it alters the font, so every character is slightly different. They say, "The only reason we have grown accustomed to non-varying type is because of the way people have been making type: take one form and copy it over and over... but for reading this sameness is not necessary: we can read handwritten text, type superimposed on flickering TV images." More than any other design development in the past few years, the wilful randomness of this font offers a genuine alternative to uniformity and universalisation.

Opposite: Enigma
The design of Jeremy Tankard's Enigma typeface in progress. The basic ideas behind this font are a marriage between the strong pen strokes of mediaeval black letter and the supple curves of Roman type. Although he uses historical inspiration, the resolution and technical perfection of this font is wholly contemporary.

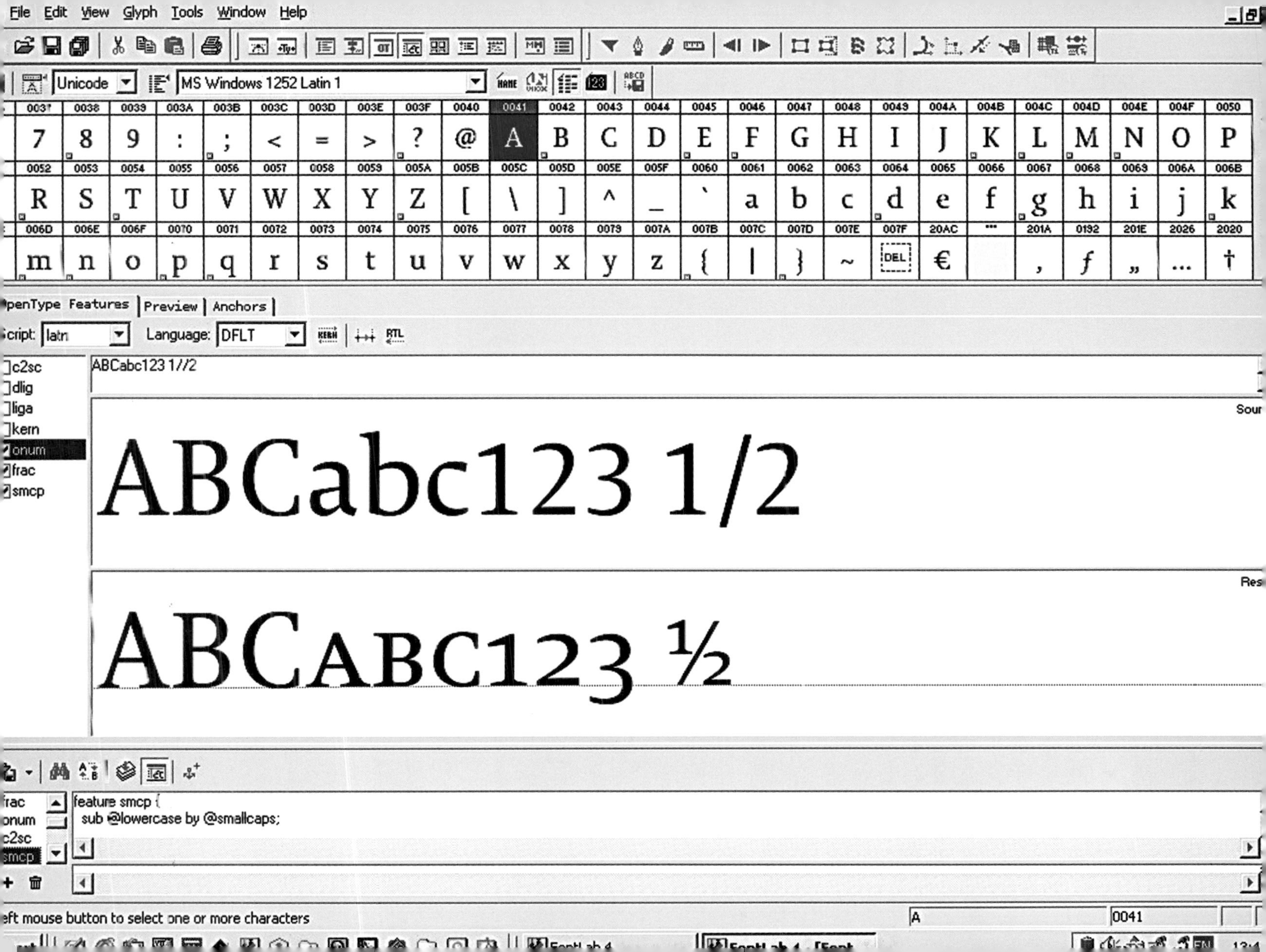

File Edit View Glyph Tools Window Help

Unicode | MS Windows 1252 Latin 1

0037	0038	0039	003A	003B	003C	003D	003E	003F	0040	0041	0042	0043	0044	0045	0046	0047	0048	0049	004A	004B	004C	004D	004E	004F	0050
7	8	9	:	;	<	=	>	?	@	A	B	C	D	E	F	G	H	I	J	K	L	M	N	O	P
0052	0053	0054	0055	0056	0057	0058	0059	005A	005B	005C	005D	005E	005F	0060	0061	0062	0063	0064	0065	0066	0067	0068	0069	006A	006B
R	S	T	U	V	W	X	Y	Z	[	\	]	^	_	`	a	b	c	d	e	f	g	h	i	j	k
006D	006E	006F	0070	0071	0072	0073	0074	0075	0076	0077	0078	0079	007A	007B	007C	007D	007E	007F	20AC	***	201A	0192	201E	2026	2020
m	n	o	p	q	r	s	t	u	v	w	x	y	z	{	|	}	~	DEL	€		,	ƒ	„	…	†

OpenType Features | Preview | Anchors

Script: latn Language: DFLT

c2sc
dlig
liga
kern
onum
frac
smcp

ABCabc123 1//2

Source

ABCabc123 1/2

Result

ABCABC123 ½

frac
onum
c2sc
smcp

```
feature smcp {
  sub @lowercase by @smallcaps;
```

Left mouse button to select one or more characters

A 0041

Full character set

The typeface also contains many elements that we can not translate into spoken language. These elements are 'analphabetic' symbols.

The full character set that most modern typefaces have is decreed by the ISO (International Standards Organisation) – it provides for most languages that use the Latin alphabet, except some – such as Danish, Lapp and Maltese – that need specially expanded fonts and keyboards.

Some analphabetic characters are directly related to sound. The comma, full stop, parentheses and question mark are used to signal inflections of or pauses in speech. Others are stylised letters – like the $ and % signs – typographic abbreviations of a phrase or word. Some are silent, and serve a purely typographic function, such as *. A few analphabetic characters have found their way back into speech – the use of the word 'period' at the end of a sentence to emphasise that something has ended, for example.

With the reassignment of the old fashioned and near-redundant accounting symbol @, and the advent of the Euro sign, €, the character set will continue to grow.

Opposite: Even fuller
There is no limit to the potential number of typographic characters. Martin Spector designed the 'interrobang' (top) in the 1960s for rhetorical questions that might normally carry both question and exclamation mark. Fred Flanagan and Stan Merritt followed his lead and invented the 'flabbergastrix', (middle) and the 'stupendapoint', (bottom), to give more power to jaded typography.

Below: Full window
The 'full character set' window on the Mac, showing the basic extras available in most fonts.

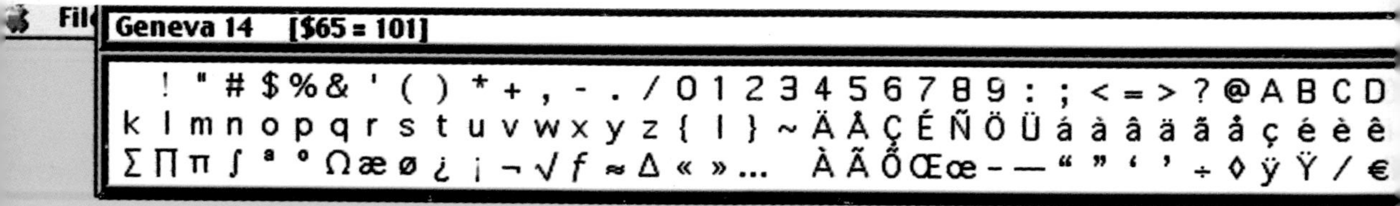

Geneva 14 [$65 = 101]

! " # $ % & ' ( ) * + , - . / 0 1 2 3 4 5 6 7 8 9 : ; < = > ? @ A B C D
k l m n o p q r s t u v w x y z { | } ~ Ä Å Ç É Ñ Ö Ü á à â ä ã å ç é è ê
Σ Π π ∫ ª º Ω æ ø ¿ ¡ ¬ √ ƒ ≈ Δ « » … À Ã Õ Œ œ – — " " ' ' ÷ ◊ ÿ Ÿ / €

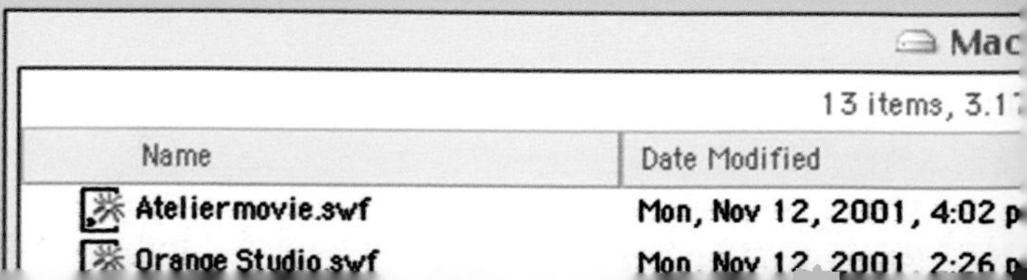

Mac
13 items, 3.1
Name | Date Modified
Ateliermovie.swf | Mon, Nov 12, 2001, 4:02 p
Orange Studio.swf | Mon, Nov 12, 2001, 2:26 p

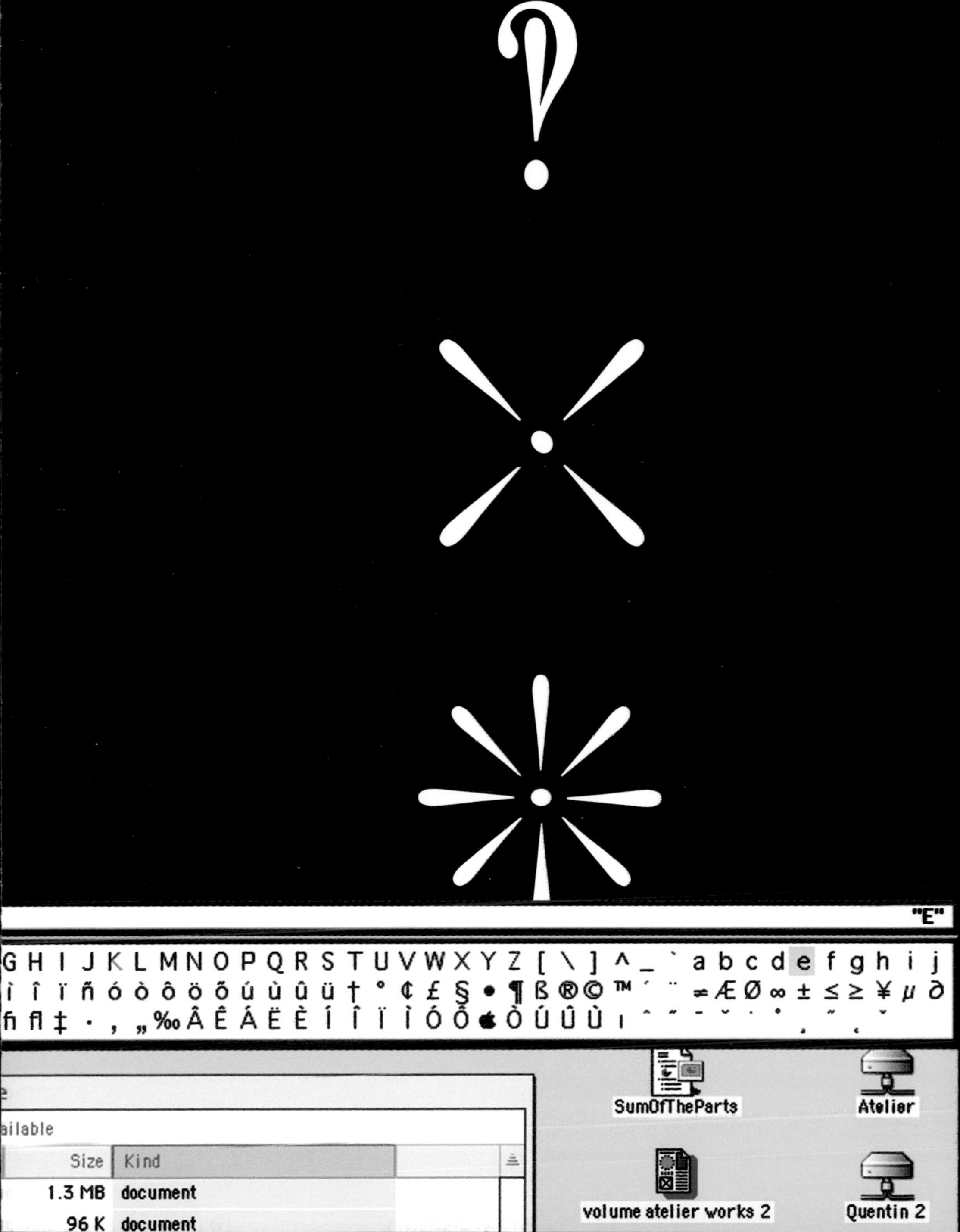

"E"
G H I J K L M N O P Q R S T U V W X Y Z [\ ] ^ _ ` a b c d e f g h i j
ì î ï ñ ó ò ô ö õ ú ù û ü † ° ¢ £ § • ¶ ß ® © ™ ´ ¨ ≠ Æ Ø ∞ ± ≤ ≥ ¥ µ ∂
ﬁ ﬂ ‡ · ‚ „ ‰ Â Ê Á Ë È Í Î Ï Ì Ó Ô Ò Ú Û Ù ı
SumOfTheParts
Atelier
Size
Kind
1.3 MB
document
96 K
document
volume atelier works 2
Quentin 2

Languages

English is the only version of the Latin alphabet that does not use accents, apart from assimilated foreign words. All other users of the Latin alphabet have to create accented letters to represent specific sounds additional to the 26 basic letters used in English. This is achieved with the addition of 'diacritics', little extra marks on certain letters that distinguish a specific sound: ç, ó, ø for example.

The project shown opposite – a modification of the alphabet – has produced new letters to represent certain sounds in the German language more efficiently. Why is this not done more often? The original Latin alphabet had several new letters added to it for European language use: j, u, w, y and z. New graphic forms are made to stand for scientific and mathematical processes and values, so why not expand the range of letterforms with new characters that sit apart from the others, rather than simply add curlicues to existing ones?

Some type designers try to add politics or a dash of controversy, often in very questionable taste, naming their typefaces after murderers or swear words. For those with genuine altruistic political feelings, and a belief in the power of language, it is possible to bring about change with design that can benefit millions of people. There are many marginalised communities in the world who need the type designer's skills and cannot join the modern world until their alphabet, therefore their language, is digitised.

Above: Tuareg
Pierre di Sciullo has designed 'Akatab', a font in five variants of 'Tifinagh' – the language of the Tuareg. It is the first version of Tifinagh that can be used with electronic media, giving the Tuareg people – disseminated across five countries – the ability to benefit from the advantages of information technology. Leaders of the Tuareg put it this way: "We are poor. Our families find it difficult to make a living... we want to take an active part in our future, as far as our own resources will take us, with the support of competent individuals and with the resources provided in solidarity, along with access to good technical training. It is a vital challenge for us."

Opposite: German
Using the precedent of the letter ß, Philipp Stamm took a whole issue of the magazine, Typografische Monatsblätter, and explored a redesign of the German alphabet, creating characters for sounds unaccounted for by the Latin alphabet. He draws a new character rather than using one letter to modify a second letter.

Laut und zeiden in der reatsrebun | *Sound and signs in conventional spelling*

fast fast
vieh fiː

mais mais
reis rais
laus laus
läuse lɔyzə
keule kɔylə
apfel apfl
kerze kertsə
rutsch rutʃ

herzwärts
hertsverts

muskulöse
muskuløːzə

tal taːl
staat ʃtaːt
mahl maːl
maße maːsə

stil ʃtiːl
stiel ʃtiːl
stiehl ʃtiːl

bank baŋk
masse masə
sack zak
stadt ʃtat
katze katsə

2

More adequate phonetic scripts

beinhalten bəˈʔinhaltn

feststätte fɛstʃtɛtə
festshtätte

schön ʃøːn
sachte zaxtə
dicht diçt
lange laŋə

orientieren orjenˈtiːrən
orienteren

dornröschen ˈdɔrnrøːsçən
dornröschen

schmal ʃmaːl šmal shmal
spröde ʃprøːdə špröde shpröde

3

Typography

You cannot use a typeface without typography. Anthony Froshaug puts this very clearly: "The word typography means to write/print using standard elements; to use standard elements implies some modular relationship between such elements; since such a relationship is two-dimensional, it implies the determination of dimensions which are both horizontal and vertical". In fact this holds true whether a typeface is handwritten or a mechanical font – there is still the same issue of relationships. They are all inseparable: language must be written with a typeface, and using a typeface necessitates typography.

While French literary theory has undoubtedly had an electrifying effect on the practice of, and thinking about, typography (see pages 48 and 60), it has perhaps rehearsed some old experiments, rather than led to any genuine change or invention.

This is a typical assertion from Katherine McCoy, once leader of the design course at Cranbrook: "Many pieces have explored the possibilities of de-stabilized 'open' meaning, which provokes the audience to actively consider multiple interpretations of meaning". Of course the paradox here is that even the most 'open' typography – whatever that means – has to finally be fixed into a single form, however elaborate. This fixed form becomes as stabilised, and as 'closed', as any other kind of typography ever was.

Opposite: Two in one
An inventive and economic application of typography: the menu of a French restaurant on its plate.

RESTAURANT
A TOUTE HEURE
2 œufs sur le plat
Salade
Fromages divers
Confitures
PAIN COMPRIS
Carte des Vins
Vins Rouges
Bordeaux
St Emilion
Médoc
St Estèphe
Beaune
Château Laffitte
Vins Blancs
Chablis
Graves
Barsac
Champagne
CONSOMMATIONS
DE
PREMIER CHOIX
BIÈRE le Quart 15c
Malaga, Porto, Muscat 20c
Sirops et Liqueurs
Grog, Cognac, Rhum, Kirsch 25c
Grog Américain 50c
GRANDE BRASSERIE NATIONALE
33 Rue de la République 33
La Maison n'a pas de Succursale
Serviette 0.10c
Soupe à l'oignon 40c
Choucroute saucisse ou jambon 50c
Saucisse nature 50c
Jambon do 50c
Bifteck cresson 60c
Côtelette do 60c

The grid

As we have seen, the placing of a letter on a surface with boundaries means that that letter has certain relationships between the edges, and the space it creates around itself. As more letters, images or anything else are placed, the more complicated relationships become. This process can be managed in an apparently random way, by 'eye', or alternatively decisions can be predicted and determined by the use of a grid – the invisible framework that organises graphic material on a surface.

The graphic designer Otl Aicher, famous for the rigidity and austerity of his typography and layouts, described a grid as "a tool not of coercion but of liberation". The purpose of the grid is twofold: firstly, it helps the designer choose how to arrange the elements on each page, by limiting the choices. The grid can be as complex and nuanced as it needs to be, but in designing the grid, the designer is creating the character of her design, choosing a set of physical values and rejecting others. Secondly, the grid brings a unity to a design. As Aicher says, the use of a grid makes for a design that will "look coherent even while containing pages that are different from one another".

Arch proponent of the grid, Josef Müller-Brockmann said, "To function successfully, the grid system, like all workable systems, must be interpreted as freely as necessary. It is this very freedom which adds richness and a note of surprise to what might... be potentially lifeless."

Below and opposite: Grid for Design magazine
The example below shows the grid for a magazine in red. The pages that it underlies are shown below it. Any grid is only ever a starting point, it rarely defines every decision about position, size of text or size of pictures, as this content varies from page to page. The countless possibilities it offers still need to be worked through. The greater the variety of content – magazines being a good example – the greater the potential flexibility the grid needs to offer. This contrasts strongly with the grid for a paperback novel: one simple grid is used throughout as a basis for identical pages with continuous, unbroken text in one typesize, apart from chapter openings, if there are any (see page 80). Design by Atelier Works.

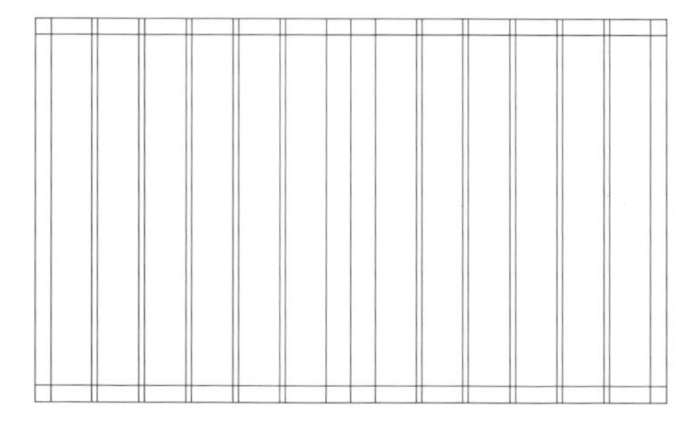

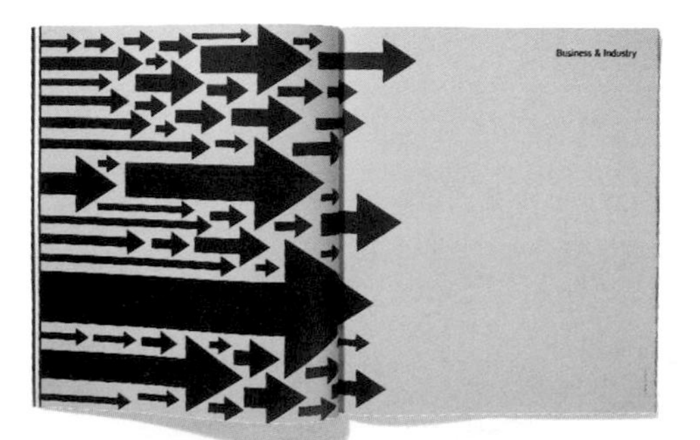

The gizmo man
I HAVE WORKED HARD
TO IMPROVE ENGLISH FOOTBALL.
NOW IT MUST BE DESTROYED.
Shoes with attitude
United in design?
How to win the Indy
500
Home-made men
in sight
in sight
Hearts of glass
The conversion
of St Michael
The ties have it
1955 to 1959

Hierarchy

Within the grid's framework, there are subsequent decisions to be made about the detailed organisation of any text. Hierarchy lies at the very heart of typography. The word is derived from the Greek words for 'sacred' and 'ruler', in other words, the one who came first. It is almost unimaginable that a text might be written without hierarchy. Hierarchy is the most important feature in absorbing meaning from a text – be it a newpaper or a book.

There have been many experiments that have attempted to break away from a single pre-determined text, and many have proposed that different meanings and experiences of texts might be preferable – for example, books in sections that can be shuffled by the reader, books and brochures with multiple simultaneous texts, and 'cut-ups', most famously used by David Bowie and William Burroughs as a way of destroying conventional sequence and creating unexpected new meanings.

Despite these forays, conventional text predominates. And this leads to a conventional design response: a limited vocabulary of typographic labels and treatments; headings and titles to be read first; naming the author of a text; introductions and prefaces before the main text; contents pages; the introductory 'stand-first' that explains the article in magazines; pull-quotes; sub-heads; captions; chart titles; setting titles and foreign words in italic etc.

Opposite:
The Pakistan Post Typeset in Urdu, this paper shows the most simple device in creating hierarchy: altering the size of the title or most prominent element. This can also be done by other means: space, colour, different typeface, emboldening and so on.

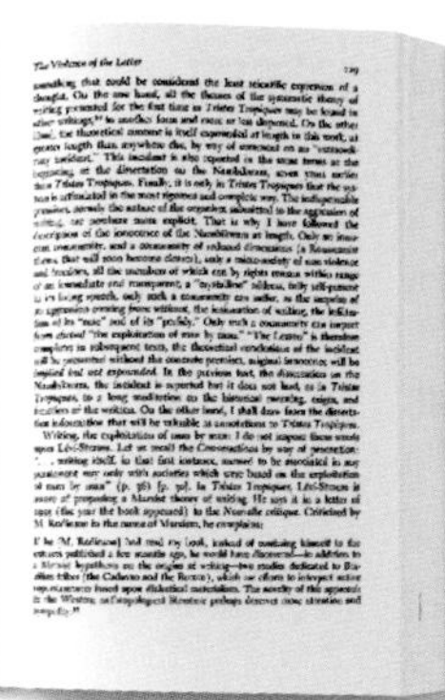

Above: Of Grammatology
A book by the widely admired textual theorist and philosopher, Jacques Derrida. He has spent his whole life in microscopic examination of the shifting and contestable meanings of words; the impossibility of a single truth; the partisan and rhetorical nature of science. However, all his books (with one exception) have been produced using the most conventional design. This book is based on a perfectly ordinary grid, using a legible book typeface, long, but recognisable sentences in novel-style justified columns, and folios. He might assault received ideas in society, but is happy to utilise them in the design of his books. It is the actual content that is radical, not its means of transmission.

ہفت روزہ
دی پاکستان پوسٹ
The Pakistan Post

جلد نمبر 1 | جمعہ 30 نومبر 2001ء، ۱۴ رمضان المبارک 1422ھ قیمت 70 P | شمارہ نمبر 34

KASHIMR POST
کشمیر پوسٹ
صفحہ نمبر 5-6

نمبر 1 کے کھیل میں الجھنا نہیں چاہتا
سنجے دت
صفحہ نمبر 13

شمالی اتحاد کے قبضے کے بعد افغانستان پر کیا گزری
صفحہ نمبر 11

اے آر وائی ڈیجیٹل ٹی وی چینل کے مینجنگ ڈائریکٹر سلمان اقبال سے انٹرویو
صفحہ نمبر 7

امریکہ مجاہدین سے نمٹنے میں بھارت کی مدد کرے گا

پاکستان کے تعاون کا صلہ

پہلی کھیپ کے طور پر کشمیر میں مجاہدین کو داخل ہونے سے روکنے کیلئے انفرا ریڈ کی فضائی گاڑیاں، ٹرانسپونڈر اور دیگر فنی سامان فراہم کرنے کی پیشکش

اسرائیل کے تعاون سے بھارت مجاہدین کے خلاف خصوصی فورس استعمال کرے گا، طیارہ بردار جنگی جہاز اور متوسط تربیتی طیارے تیار کرنے کا بھی منصوبہ

صدر پرویز نے خوشحال کشمیر پروگرام کی منظوری دیدی

کراچی: طالبان اور القاعدہ کیخلاف آپریشن، مرکزی دفتر سیل

وزیر اعظم آزاد کشمیر ٹریفک حادثہ میں زخمی

امریکہ کشمیر کا رخ کر گئے تو وہ ہمارا موقف نہیں بدل سکتا: واجپائی

بھارت اور امریکہ کی دوستی ڈھکی چھپی نہیں، وہ سرحد پار سے ہونے والی مداخلت کیخلاف پہلے بھی مدد کرتا رہا

کنٹرول لائن پر جھڑپیں، 16 پاکستانی فوجی شہید کرنے کا دعویٰ مسترد

پاکستان کشمیر پر بھارت سے مذاکرات کرے، بے نظیر بھٹو

بھارت سمندری حدود میں مزید 10 فوجی چوکیاں قائم کرے گا

جیکب آباد ایئر بیس، جنگل اور قبرستان صاف کر دیا گیا

600 امریکہ اور شمالی اتحاد نے جنیوا کنونشن کی دھجیاں اڑا دیں

قیدیوں کی لاشیں جب ریڈ کراس کے حوالے کی گئیں تو بیشتر قیدیوں کے ہاتھ بندھے ہوئے تھے

بنگلہ دیش میں محصور پاکستانیوں کی نئی نسل وطن نہیں آنا چاہتی

ISSN 1473-9984

Rules and other devices

Rules, bars, pi characters, dingbats and numerous other devices are used to aid the organisation and clarification of divisions and associations within a text.

A novel is a single continuous text, traditionally self-contained. By contrast, a newspaper or magazine is a mass of discontinuous texts of varying lengths, subject matter, types of irony, humour, and so on, unified by an editorial attitude. These need careful physical organisation: subject headings, small extra text explaining the main text, and all manner of pictures, icons and emblems to break up and signal asides. This is also true of lists, tables, charts and catalogues.

Opposite: The Guardian
Detail of a design by David Hillman of Pentagram, extended and developed by Simon Esterson and the current art director, Mark Porter. It remains the most distinctive daily newspaper, largely because it shows a typographic sensitivity far greater than any other. It does its hard informational work with a contrast of heavy sans serif titles against a softer tone of serif text, and an extensive use of rules to delineate articles and different forms of data within an article.

Below: Landmark Trust
Bars of tone and graphic emblems are used to convey complex variations in pricing for holiday homes owned by the Landmark Trust. Design by Atelier Works.

Property	Sleeps	Beds	Facilities	Winter			Early Spring			Easter		Late Spring		
Prices quoted are per property for the period stated and not per person				4 Jan to 12 Feb			12 Feb to 1 Apr			1 Apr to 6 Apr	6 Apr to 9 Apr	9 Apr to 30 Apr		
				Short Stays		Weeks	Short Stays		Weeks			Short Stays		Weeks
				Fri to Sun	Mon to Thurs	Start Fri to Mon	Fri to Sun	Mon to Thurs	Start Fri to Mon	Thurs to Tues	Tues to Thurs	Fri to Sun	Mon to Thurs	Start Fri or Mon
Danescombe Mine	4	TD	%	241	174	321	252	185	336	707	261	397	296	534
East Banqueting House	6	TDTs	x2	578	424	739	606	450	774	1155	627	678	512	874
Edale Mill	4	TD		224	153	309	235	162	325	526	243	284	200	397
The Egyptian House														
First Floor	3	ST	%	222	152	261	234	161	274	401	242	256	180	303
Second Floor	4	TD	%	226	154	268	237	163	281	438	245	276	194	331
Third Floor	4	TD	%	226	154	268	237	163	281	438	245	276	194	331
Elton House	10	2S 3T D	x4	543	389	703	570	413	736	1295	645	634	468	827
Endsleigh														
Swiss Cottage	4	DB	%	288	213	413	304	225	433	750	314	394	299	567
Pond Cottage	5	STD	%	329	242	454	346	257	475	905	356	499	380	696
Field House	7	S 2T D	x2	526	360	657	552	381	689	1066	570	587	414	740
Fort Clonque	11	4T III	x3 H %	£124 per night*		703	£127 per night*		737	1412	731	£161 per night*		1065
Fox Hall	4	T(D)		399	239	469	418	253	492	716	432	445	274	528
Frenchman's Creek	4	TD		284	211	393	298	222	412	888	308	484	367	673
Gargunnock House	16	5T 3D	x5	874	565	1097	945	617	1184	2495	1397	1347	867	1650
Goddards	12	4S 3T D	x3	1033	853	1535	1083	905	1609	2995	1547	1488	1089	1984
Gothic Temple	4	2D	H	441	322	557	463	341	584	896	479	534	401	681
The Grammar School	4	2T	%	196	174	344	226	203	379	587	277	256	221	406
Gurney Manor	9	S 2T 2D	x3	720	406	876	755	430	919	1385	797	799	465	985
Hampton Court Palace*														
Fish Court	6	2S T D	x2	619	527	927	643	546	963	1226	691	673	560	987

...ans, aged 76, union leader 21

...evision's loss 9

Reviews

Lord of the dance Joaquin Cortes and his ego almost pull it off 16

...port

Same old story Manchester United go top for the first time this season after Arsenal draw with Liverpool 1

Australian Open Seven Russians who are better than Anna Kournikova 16

Return of the blob What's that mystery blob on the bottom of every euro note? 2

Green berets Why we joined the commandos 8

The Monday Interview

...rpal Virdi I'm more of a fighter ...4

...en

...ll, ladies Woman's Journal is ...fter 75 years. It was lovely ...ted, says Liz Hoggard 6

...re

...tion It is so... but...

New graffiti threatening Catholics appeared overnight...

Two arrested as U...

Rosie Cowan
Ireland correspondent

Nationalists in Northern Ireland fear an intensified campaign of loyalist terrorism after the Ulster Defence Association yesterday admit... murder of a ... Catholic post... Two m... conn... D...

Royal Mail, the Co... tions Workers U... constable, ... gan, ... sid...

Images

Many designers are happy to be known as typographers, but not much design is just text alone. Eventually, even the most iconoclastic typographer will have to handle an image.

How these images are arrived at can vary enormously: they can be 'found' (produced or reproduced by some previous method); commissioned; self-created or accidental. And, as illustrated opposite, every medium can be utilised and yields subtly different effects.

How images are used is yet another variable: in sequence (randomly, chronologically, following the text, using various types of category); singly; multiple; captioned; embedded in text, and so on.

The use of images in combination with text is at the heart of the definition of graphic design. This combination increases graphic possibilities by many times of magnitude.

Miniatures
A selection from the 48 Millennium stamps issued by the UK's Royal Mail in 1999. Art directed by Mike Dempsey the stamps feature a variety of image-makers including Bridget Riley, David Hockney, Howard Hodgkin and Don McCullen. The method of image-making was unique to each stamp: photography; oil pastels; watercolour; montage; found photography; collage; letterpress; oil paint; screenprinting and so on. Although each stamp was different the simple typographic structure gives a generic quality that ties the series together.

Millennium 1999/48
Timekeeping/D Gentleman
20
26
43
Millennium 1999/45
Computers/E Paolozzi
63
20
26
43
63
DEEDS
NOT
WORDS
VOTES FOR WOMEN
19
26
Millennium 1999/22
Right to learn/A Drummond
44
Millennium 1999/15
Mechanical farming/C Wormell
19
26
44
64
19
26
44
64
Millennium 1999/4
World of the stage/A Jones
19
26
Millennium 1999/2
World of literature/L Milroy
44
64

Illustration

Illustration returns us to the presence of a person, a distinctive and idiosyncratic point of view.

Certain ideas can only be communicated through illustration, which is the part of graphic design most directly linked with art. A few designers make their illustration a signal part of their work, through an integration of type and illustration – for example Milton Glaser, Sheigo Fukuda, Alan Fletcher, André François, AM Cassandre, and in this book, Koichi Sato. More often it is used in contrast to photography, or for those jobs that it does more successfully.

Illustration is a form of meticulous and painstaking editing. Each tiny part of a drawing has been consciously produced. This can be seen most clearly in a quick sketch that sets out to capture the most essential features of a face or an animal for example. Any illustration is an extended sketch, gradually layering in and adding more telling detail to the essence.

An illustration is the exact opposite of a photograph. A photograph uses mechanical processes to de-personalise the picture. This perceived objective, machine-like quality has been eagerly sought by many designers over the years. But, if any designer is looking for the greater perceived values of 'authorship', she will find it most intensely in a hand-drawn image.

Above:
Portrait of the author
An horrific vision by English illustrator Ben Kirchner. Certain details have been selected, grotesquely emphasised and thrust forward. Designer transmutes into gangster.

Opposite: The New Yorker
Pages from 'Covering the New Yorker' by Françoise Mouly. The covers of this magazine, an American institution, present probably the best and most consistent use of illustration in the world. It is nearly impossible to find a poor drawing or uninventive idea in nearly 76 years of covers. At their best the drawings summarise or comment on themes or events in American society – fear and violence in schools or the nature of the typical family. One of the simplest was a picture of a half-empty glass of orange juice by Bob Zoell. It appeared on the eve of the controversial trial of OJ Simpson (orange juice is known as OJ in America). Is the glass half-empty or half-full?

Price $3.00
Sept. 14, 1998
THE NEW YORKER
BACK TO SCHOOL by William Joyce
September 14, 1998
160
Sept. 13, 1993
Price $1.95
THE NEW YORKER
THE GUNS OF SEPTEMBER by Art Spiegelman
September 13, 1993
Since 1993, several groups lobbying for gun control have asked for permission to use this image.
161

Nov. 23, 1968
Price 50 cents
THE NEW YORKER
NOVEMBER 23, 1968
by Saul Steinberg
230
April 22, 1996
Price $2.95
THE NEW YORKER
FAMILY VALUES by Art Spiegelman
April 22, 1996
231

Graphic authorship

The term 'graphic authorship' has been doing the rounds over the last few years as something designers ought to do more of. It might sound like 'writing about graphic design', but the term seems infinitely re-interpretable without one clear, agreed definition. Many 'graphic authors' use text they have not written and pictures they have not taken in layouts that seem quite similar to layouts produced by plain old graphic designers.
The term carries with it an air of stridency and rebellion – a wish that graphic design play its part in putting the world to rights and for designers to break away from their restrictive commercial clients. But graphic design is already a broad church, with thousands of examples of 'overtly-authored' publications, books, exhibitions and magazines. It takes more than attitude, wish and a loose term to create something genuinely fresh and exciting.

If someone was looking for any unequivocal recent examples of graphic authorship to help set a central point for a definition, they might look to the masterly books by David Gentleman. He has covered Italy, India and the UK so far. He plans his trips in detail and then travels each country for six months, making hundreds of drawings, taking photographs and keeping an extraordinarily detailed diary. He then plans the book, writes it, makes each illustration, and designs and produces the final artwork. Every inch of Gentleman's books is by his own hand. (He has not yet designed his own typeface.) This picture shows the page plan in miniature of 'David Gentleman's Italy' in progress.

RAISINS

Photography

It is commonplace to say that the invention of photography revolutionised art. Ernst Gombrich saw photography as one of the progenitors of the whole development of modern art: "There was no need for painting to perform a task which a mechanical device could perform better and more cheaply". If painting affected art, photography catapulted design into another realm altogether, vastly extending its vocabulary, and proving itself perfectly suited to mechanical reproduction.

It also fitted a new ideological and theoretical need. It seemed to be de-personalised, and to offer objectivity. Josef Müller-Brockmann stated that it "provides an objective picture of reality and thus conveys an impression of authenticity".

Photography has been so successful at depicting 'reality' that it has pushed illustration into second place – to the point that many designers never use handmade images. It is not quite true to say that illustration has been ghettoised, but it is rare for it to be used for the depiction of anything 'real' (except exploded technical diagrams). It appears more frequently on seductive packaging, magazines, bookcovers, and children's books.

Historian Richard Bolton says, "The photograph continues to be a primary source of information about both the world and ourselves". But photography's objectivity, and "authenticity" is much overstated, as we have discovered that it can be as subjective and emotional as any drawing.

Above: Pictures of reality
A charming and clever use of photography by Dieter Graf. His book, 'Point It', can be used anywhere in the world to order food, communicate with doctors or barter in markets, just by pointing at photos. The style of photography might seem kitsch, and therefore fake; it is instantly understood as representation of the physical world.

Opposite: Neue Grafik
Pages taken from two copies of Neue Grafik magazine, published between 1958 and 1965. It defined and promoted 'Swiss style', which was marked by high contrast black-and-white photography integrated with sans serif typography. Joseph Müller-Brockmann made the grand claim that photography provided "the unretouched, unadulterated illustration of things... a vision which leaves intact the essential nature of the subject".

Graphic Design
and Jazz Records
Hans Neuburg, Zurich
AFTER HOURS JAZZ
fontana
STAR BRIGHT DIZZY REECE
The Essential Count Basie
best
COOTIE
GARNER IN PARIS
ART TATUM

Schweizer Plakate der letzten fünf Jahre
Swiss Posters of the Past Five Years
Affiches suisses des cinq années écoulées
chum mach mit
achte den andern
weniger Lärm
Winterhilfe 59

Using photography

Photography is still burdened, or blessed, with the myth of objectivity, and, by extension, universality – if it is an objective depiction of the world, then anyone and everyone can accept it.

As it matures – it is only 150 years old – photography is growing increasingly supple, and as capable of the expression and subtle gradation of emotion as other forms of image-making ever were. The endless choices of film stock, filters, lighting, depth of field and processing, allow photographers – and designers working with photographers – to imprint immediate atmosphere and character before the subject matter is even considered.

There are two basic ways to use photography: respectfully (uncropped, squared up, type placed very discreetly), or as another graphic element. The great leap forward in the designer's use of photography was montage, intervening with the picture – cutting, cropping and overlaying it with colour and type. The modern version of this is the cut-out, which removes the photograph from its background, making it a free-floating element to be combined with other equivalent graphic elements like type, rules, shapes, charging it with graphic power.

New computer programs, like Photoshop, have enabled extensive reworking of photographs and have introduced painting techniques which had hitherto seemed to be completely divorced from photography.

The following seven pages show different approaches to using photography, proving it is no mere automatic replication of 'real life'.

Opposite: Surreality
Stationery for a headhunting company designed by Michael Johnson of Johnson Banks, with photography by Mike Parsons. Johnson uses instantly recognisable pairs – pairs that belong together – as a metaphor for their effectiveness. The photographs are intensely coloured, like a cartoon. The comic effect is enhanced by straightforward presentation. Nothing about the picture pairs links them – they are brutally cut together and, like surrealism, the association happens in your head.

CANNA KENDALL & CO.
Telephone
Facsimile

Right:
Impressionistic verité
For a series of brochures for the Royal College of Art, London. Rebecca Foster used crude and energetic blurring of video stills as a version of 'cinema verité', tying the college into its west London geography.

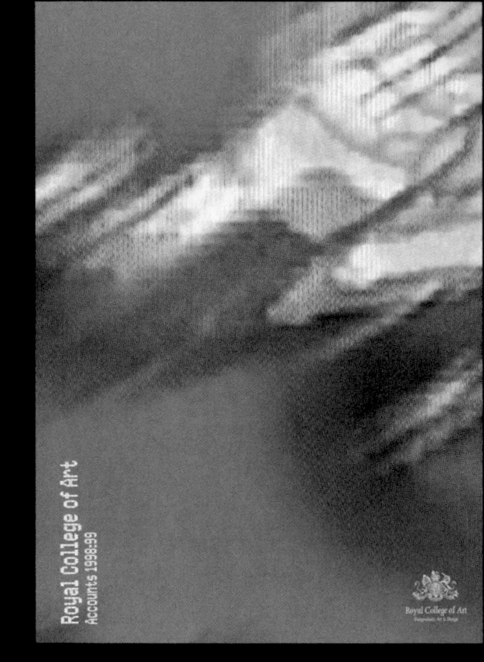

Left: Testament

Designer Simon Esterson quietly organises portraits of Cambodians in Reportage magazine. Only on careful inspection do you realise that these pictures were all taken by Khmer Rouge cadres minutes before each person was executed. The horror is intensified by the neutral layout. There is a school of photography, known as 'reportage', and usually black-and-white, that we have grown to accept without question as 'real'. Its subject matter is often morbid, or depressing, it utilises only 'available' natural light, and seeks to capture moments of uninhibited emotion.

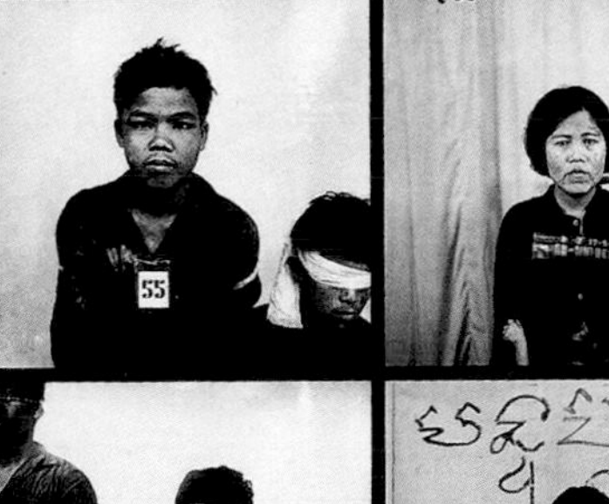

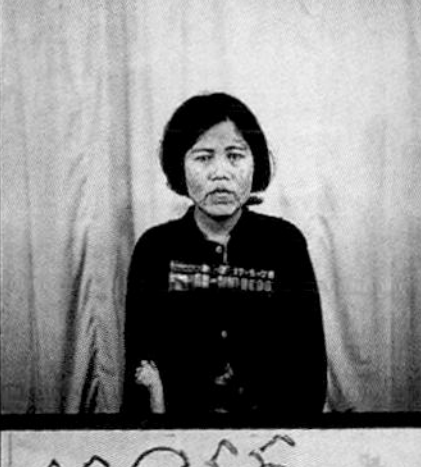

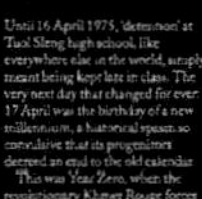

Until 16 April 1975, 'detention' at Tuol Sleng high school, like everywhere else in the world, simply meant being kept late in class. The very next day that changed for ever. 17 April was the birthday of a new millennium, a historical spasm so convulsive that its progenitors decreed an end to the old calendar.

This was Year Zero, when the revolutionary Khmer Rouge forces commanded by Pol Pot and his Paris-educated cadres overthrew 'bourgeois rule' and forced the citizens of Cambodia out of the cities to work in the fields. Under this crash-course scheme of Maoist re-education, detention at the high school at Tuol Sleng acquired an altogether more sinister and brutal aspect. The Khmer Rouge turned it into a prison, where those suspected of harbouring counter-revolutionary sentiments were interrogated, harassed, humiliated, forced into writing confessions and then, in any case, executed.

The Khmer Rouge's blunt renaming of the building 'S-21' was unintentionally eloquent, prefiguring the way in which the 14,000 Cambodians who passed through the school gates and died inside were themselves deprived of names, becoming numbers. The grim irony of their fate was that their killers – the self-styled enemies of bureaucracy – were themselves expert and meticulous bureaucrats, who kept not only a written record of each prisoner, including copies of confessions, but also a photograph of every one.

By the time the Vietnamese intervention of 1979 forced the former schoolteacher Pol Pot into exile, one million Cambodians – approximately one in seven of the population – had died of disease or starvation. Another 200,000 were killed as enemies of the state, many of them crudely dispatched by blows to the skull with agricultural implements. After Year Zero, ploughshares were turned into swords.

The Khmer Rouge followed the precedent of Stalin's and Mao's repressions, yet there was something still more dementedly paranoid about Pol Pot's depredations. For all that it was a grotesque charade, the Maoist ritual of rectification and self-criticism did at least allow for eventual rehabilitation; likewise, Stalin's show trials were grim parodies of judicial process but they were conducted in public and a death sentence was not automatic.

The confessions extracted in Tuol Sleng were for the Party's private satisfaction only, they provided no grounds for clemency. Only seven people are known to have survived the prison. When the Vietnamese finally overran Phnom Penh, they found the bodies of prisoners executed only hours earlier, their spilt blood not yet dried.

Following the chaotic retreat of Pol Pot's forces, a large part of the archive was looted and destroyed, and what remained was scattered, filthy and mildewed. Still, with the efforts of the US-based Photo Archive Group, some 6,000 negatives survived to be housed in archives when the former school was turned into a museum to commemorate the holocaust that Cambodia, now Kampuchea, had endured.

Recently, the photographer responsible for these haunting images was discovered in Kampuchea. Nhem Ein, now 37, joined the Khmer Rouge as a 10-year-old. He was sent to China for training and returned in May 1976 aged 16 to be chief photographer at Tuol Sleng. Interviewed in Phnom Penh by Robin McDowell of the Associated Press, Nhem Ein estimated that he took about 10,000 photographs at S-21 and recalled seeing face after face filled with fear and a deep sadness. "I knew that I was taking the pictures of innocent people, but I knew that if I said anything, I would be killed."

Nostalgic
Photographer Peter Wood emulates the American great, O Winston Link, with this study of a steam train at night. It was taken as a test shot for a Royal Mail stamp series, but not used. It presented substantial technical problems, especially the lighting of such a large, complex form. Its style is created by different elements: objective recording with a hefty dollop of emotional sculpting. It is difficult not to be impressed by the train in this picture.

Overleaf

Left: Dreamscape
An image by Me Company for a Kenzo advertising campaign, Autumn/Winter 2001.
David Hockney has said that the computer is "putting the hand back in the camera". This image departs from photography and begins to become something else, so extensively are the images worked over by hand. Direct personal judgement overrides the mediation of automatic processes. The 'boy' standing in a cataclysmic jungle, has been digitally created by changing the facial structure of a female model using a morphing process. The whole confection is designed to oscillate between categories: female/male; lovely/horrific; photo/painting.

Right: Sensual
A close-up of a Dachshund by Mette Heinz for a book cover. There is no attempt to place the subject within a context, instead we are invited to concentrate on physical details, like the texture and colour of the fur and the dog's moist eye.

5029

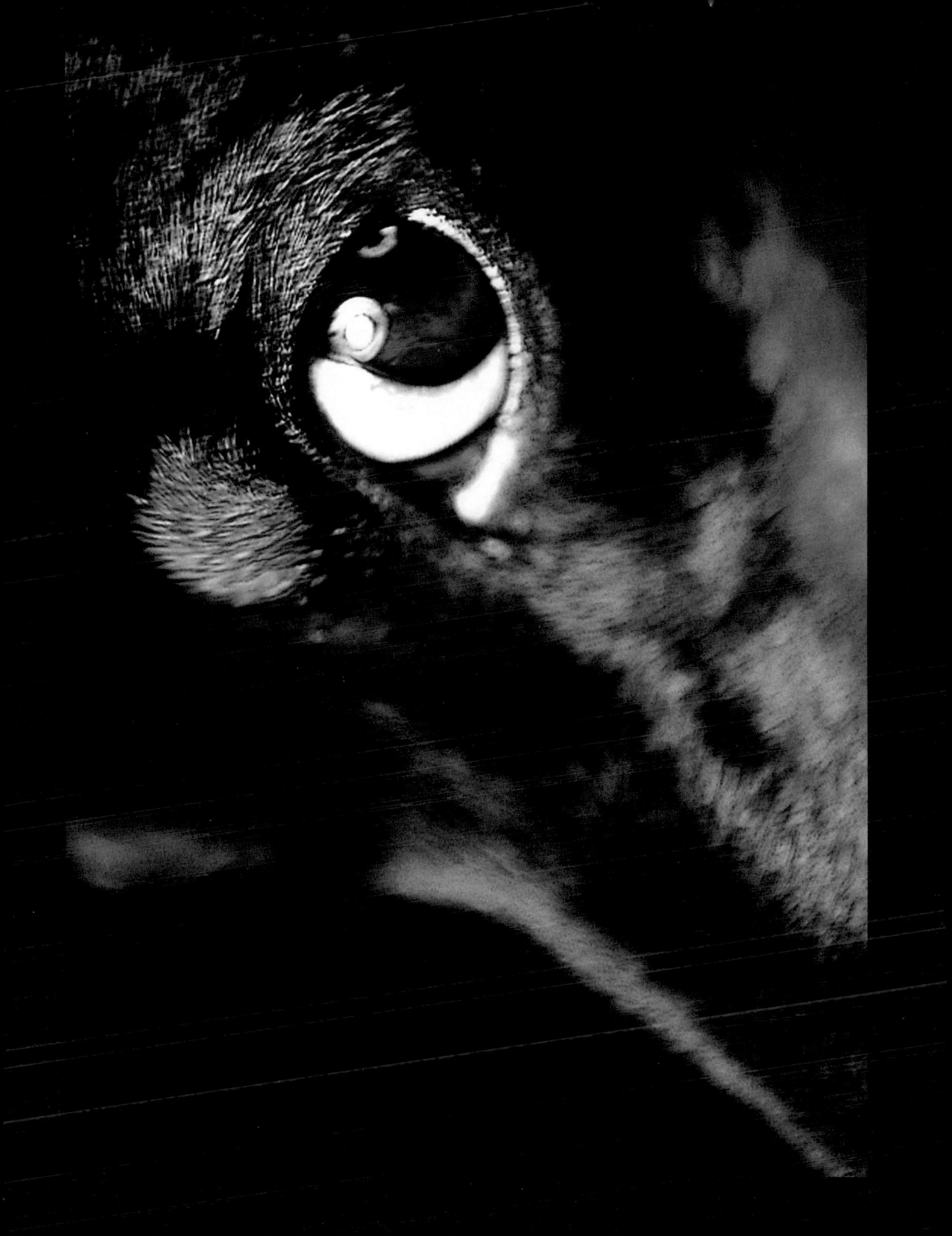

Word and image

It is not entirely clear who first used the term 'typophoto', but in 1925 László Moholy-Nagy announced that the combination of typography and photography was "the new visual literature". The next seven pages show some examples of the defining activity of graphic design – integration of type and photo.

Moholy-Nagy went on to describe how typophoto worked: "Typography bears much resemblance to cinema, just as the reading of print puts the reader in the role of the movie projector. The reader moves the series of imprinted letters before him at a speed consistent with apprehending the motions of the author's mind". Here we might take "author" to mean whoever has made the sequence: a combination of writer or writers, editor, photographer, and above all, designer.

The examples shown here are almost all snatched from a longer sequence, but it is fundamentally as a linear sequence that word and image work together, in an infinite variety of combinations. Rudolf Arnheim sees word and image like this: "Language is used linearly because each word or cluster of words stands for an intellectual concept, and such concepts can be combined only in succession".

The difference between word and image, and words on their own, especially en masse, is that images are comprehended more immediately – word and image "is not a delayed system; information is conveyed directly. The greatest power of visual language lies in its immediacy, its spontaneous evidence. Visually, you see content and form simultaneously", says psychologist A Dondis. The organisation of material – the design– is in and of itself investing the words and images with meaning and comprehensibility. The design helps us understand what we are looking at. Marshall McLuhan, always one for a neat turn of phrase, called the process of understanding word and image "an extreme specialism of sense".

Each element in the design – page size, space, folio, caption, passage of text, image – becomes charged with meaning as it is organised, piece by piece. Ludwig Wittgenstein's famous definition of the meaning of words, "The meaning of a word is its use in the language", could also be written as, 'The meaning of a graphic element is its use in the design'.

I would suggest that the marriage of pictures and text is often unsuccessful, in fact, almost always unsuccessful. Many designers (not those shown here!) rely on a small number of conventions, such as placing a caption under a picture, or embedding a picture into text. They slavishly follow these limited means without specific adaptation to the material in hand.

What follows is a sample of the myriad ways word and image can be successfully combined. These show that in the hands of a highly skilled designer, the categorical distinctions between words and images melt away into a new combination: graphic design.

Words with no pictures

Images of the Century
A stunning piece of invention by designer Peter Davenport, whose first idea was to collect 100 of the most significant images from the 20th century. When he saw the high fees for use of the pictures, he had to rethink. The result is remarkable, as Davenport presents us with the captions and no pictures, and yet it works just as well as if the pictures were there. So deeply are these images imprinted in our visual memories, they can be summoned instantly. László Moholy-Nagy's prediction has come to fruition – "From now on 'imagination' will tend more and more to refer to the powers of visualisation". The design is disingenuously unassuming, extremely polite for such a radical concept. Words as pictures.

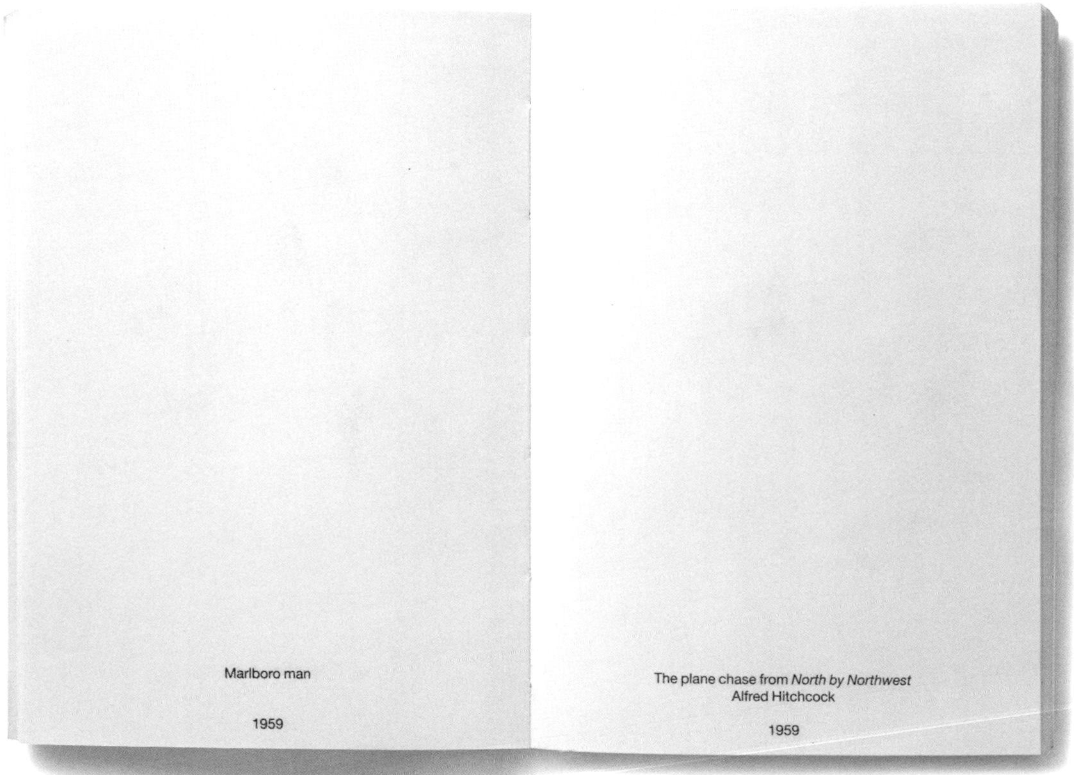

Marlboro man

1959

The plane chase from *North by Northwest*
Alfred Hitchcock

1959

Pictures with no words

Right: Nazis
This is simply a collection of pictures of Nazis, as depicted in 'popular culture'. It has no introduction and no captions, except a bare list at the end. The images are fitted into the pages with very little manipulation. The sequence is random (ignoring Wurman's five criteria, see p128). The design invites you to write your own commentary, provoked by the juxtapositions. The snarling face of Malcolm McDowell (top left) who has played sociopaths throughout his career as an actor, is placed opposite Roger Moore, who never fills the role of a villain... except here. My favourite combination is Derren Nesbitt (bottom left) who has played Nazis in many films – this image shows him in Where Eagles Dare, a film in which my father played a shouting Obergruppenführer who tries to shoot an abseiling Clint Eastwood off a rope. Nesbitt sits opposite Marlon Brando, my father's hero. Design by Piotr Ulanski and Hanna Koller.

Opposite: Full Moon
Described as a "photographic journey to the moon and back", this book uses scans from NASA's original negatives. It is a mixture of epic journey, popular science, landscape, and highly aestheticised photography. The images stop short of the page, giving every picture a black border – black is used as a metaphor for space throughout. The pictures are given narrative thrust by the sequence of the journey – the book has the same inevitability as any road movie, any odyssey. Design by Michael Light.

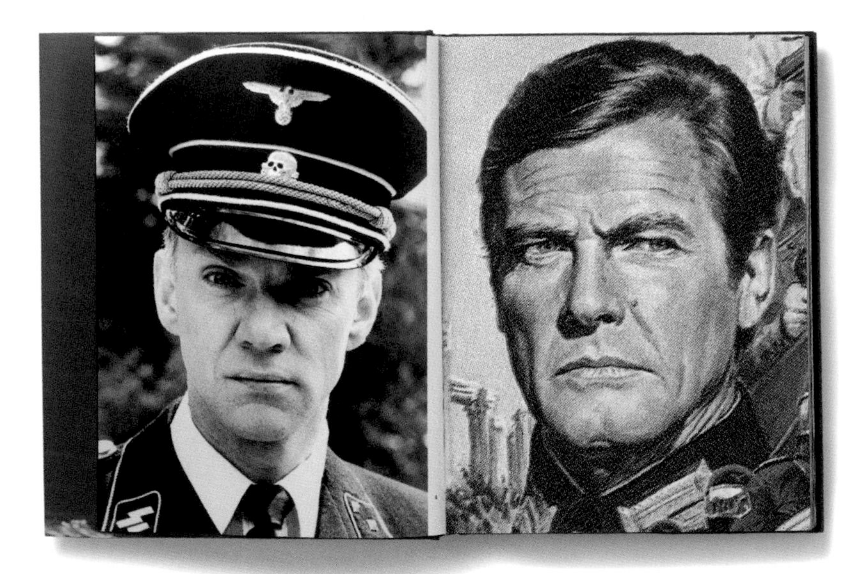

Pictures with a few words

Right: Chairman
This stumpy palm-sized book tells the story of the chairman of Vitra, Rolf Feldbaum. Vitra make chairs, hence the title. It has the drive of a film with images flickering past like a movie: the blue pages act like caption cards in a silent film, introducing turns in the 'through line' of the story. The book is good at humour and sleights-of-eye, but poor at anything more detailed, and at dealing with confusions that the pictures present: are those Vitra's wheelchairs? It is memorable, charming and makes you love Herr Feldbaum. Design by Tibor Kalman.

Opposite above: Artificial Nature
A catalogue for an exhibition in Greece. This piece of work is one of the most regularly copied designs of recent years and is now almost an archetype. Its influence – cynical tone, juxtapositions of kitsch images, harsh, contradictory captions – is to be felt in almost every design monograph that attempts to comment on the destructive power of popular culture. The energy that comes from its discordant images and statements is impressive and irrefutable, but what it all amounts to (apart from a condemnation) is more questionable. Design by Dan Friedman.

Opposite below: The Commissar Vanishes
Important, path-finding historical work by designer, archivist, historian and author David King on Stalin's tampering with images as a way of re-making history. The design is fairly straightforward – a combination of annotation and images – some enlarged for graphic impact, and all meticulously sequenced.

spiritualizing it
42
infusing it with
43
TEN YEARS OF UZBEKISTAN/3
Faizulla Khodzhaev. Soviet chairman of commissars in Uzbekistan. Cofounder of the nationalist Young Bokhara movement. Did not join the Bolsheviks until 1922. Arrested on Stalin's orders, accused of bourgeois nationalism and conspiring to deliver Central Asia into the hands of the British. Tried and shot with Bukharin and others in 1938.
, OzSSR MIQ RAIS OKUNBASARI
D. Abidova, member of the Council of People's Commissars in Uzbekistan. Her exact fate is unknown.

Pictures with words

Right: Ways of Seeing
This book caused a considerable stir when it appeared in the 1970s, due to its Marxist view of art, and its stark, didactic design. Rather than treat the pictures with curatorial reverence – large, in colour – designer Richard Hollis sets them into the prose, where they are mentioned as black-and-white typographic elements. They are not pictures, but referents. The effect is that words and images form one smooth strand. There are two picture essays in the book (bottom spread) and Hollis treats these in a way that mimics how we encounter them – unexpectedly, abutting the images as if in a scrapbook. A model design, emulated almost as frequently as 'Artificial Nature'.

Words as pictures

Opposite: Frozen Sky
This playful, witty book consists of the alphabetic codes used to represent airports (BOM is Bombay, RIO is Rio). The design uses the geometric rigor of the Futura typeface at a large size to make two-dimensional sculptures of the codes – word as image. The sequence of material is without a clear narrative purpose – the reader is no wiser at the end than at the start. The whole concept is rather an interplay of the ideas of randomness and pattern. (An extravagant intellectual luxury that marks it out as 'art'.) The spread below is a joke, splitting the book's title as if it were two airports: FRO/ZEN. Design by Langlands & Bell, with Peter Willberg and Clementine Deliss.

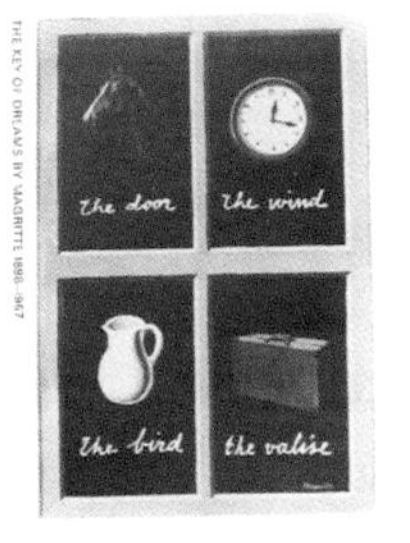

The way we see things is affected by what we know or what we believe. In the Middle Ages when men believed in the physical existence of Hell the sight of fire must have meant something different from what it means today. Nevertheless their idea of Hell owed a lot to the sight of fire consuming and the ashes remaining – as well as to their experience of the pain of burns.

When in love, the sight of the beloved has a completeness which no words and no embrace can match : a completeness which only the act of making love can temporarily accommodate.

Yet this seeing which comes before words, and can never be quite covered by them, is not a question of mechanically reacting to stimuli. (It can only be thought of in this way if one isolates the small part of the process which concerns the eye's retina.) We only see what we look at. To look is an act of choice. As a result of this act, what we see is brought within our reach – though not necessarily within arm's reach. To touch something is to situate oneself in relation to it. (Close your eyes, move round the room and

8

notice how the faculty of touch is like a static, limited form of sight.) We never look at just one thing; we are always looking at the relation between things and ourselves. Our vision is continually active, continually moving, continually holding things in a circle around itself, constituting what is present to us as we are.

Soon after we can see, we are aware that we can also be seen. The eye of the other combines with our own eye to make it fully credible that we are part of the visible world.

If we accept that we can see that hill over there, we propose that from that hill we can be seen. The reciprocal nature of vision is more fundamental than that of spoken dialogue. And often dialogue is an attempt to verbalize this – an attempt to explain how, either metaphorically or literally, 'you see things', and an attempt to discover how 'he sees things'.

In the sense in which we use the word in this book, all images are man-made.

An image is a sight which has been recreated or reproduced. It is an appearance, or a set of appearances, which has been detached from the place and time

9

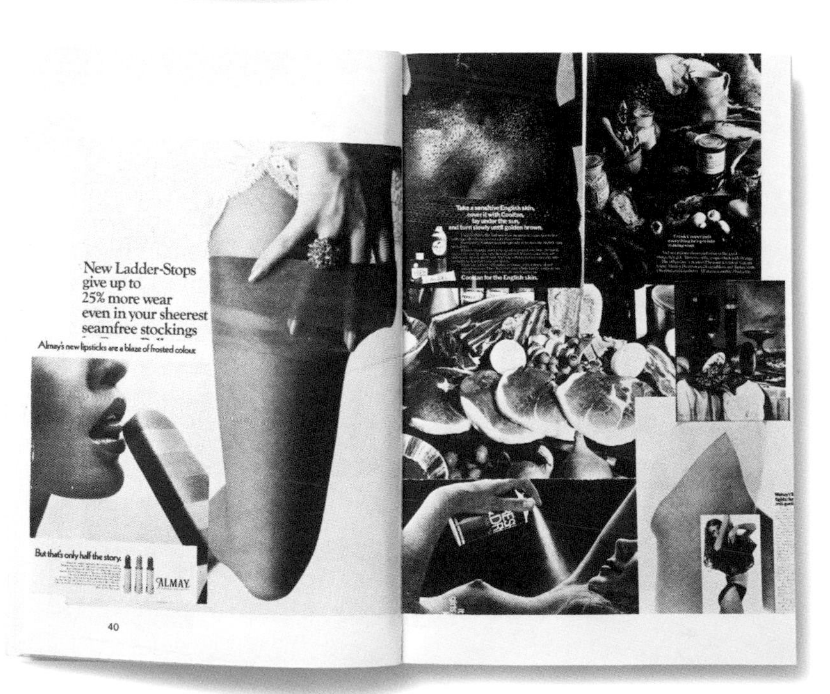

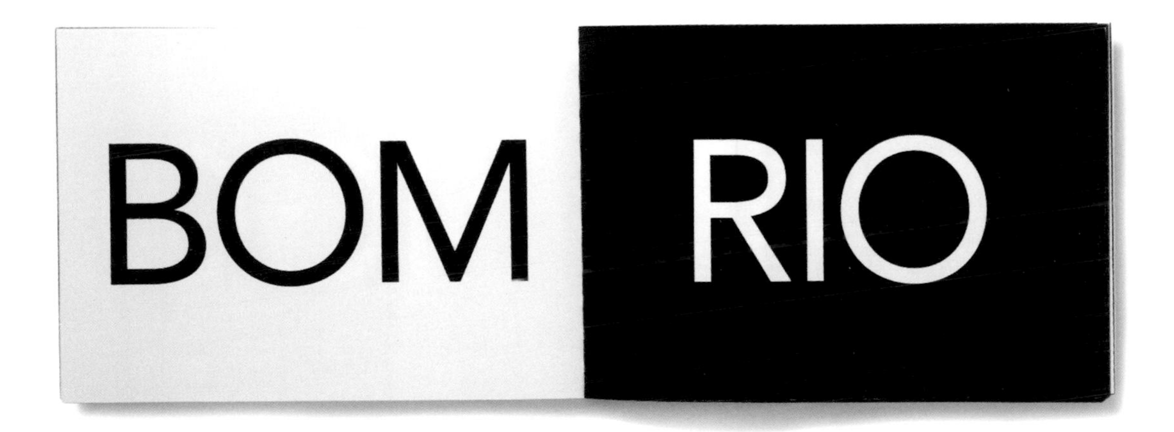
BOM
RIO

FRO
ZEN

Tools

Design is a process of making, it is the transfer of ideas to a surface by means of tools. Eric Gill used the image of a hand and eye as an emblem in his design. Graphic design exploits the visual and sensual in equal measure.

If the computer deprives us of anything in exchange for its bounteous gifts, it is the physical pleasures of making. When using the (near redundant) letterpress process, every action has an effect: if the ink is carefully thinned, it prints thinly; if the colours are bled, they print that way, but differently each time; you can see the dust from the paper swirling in the sunlight; you can hear the treacley crackle as you ink the roller; you reel at the bitter smell of the turpentine. Each little piece of type bites itself into the paper. The surface of work printed by letterpress undulates minutely – the type sinks back, the ink has a sheen. Each print differs, even if only by a fraction, from its fellows.

This loss of sensuality is felt by even the fiercest devotees of digital design: "What I really want on the Macintosh is a virtual reality interface – armholes in either size of the box so you can reach in and move logos around; a real paintbrush so you can feel the texture of the surface underneath", says Neville Brody.

Perhaps the most important tool of any designer is the voice: calming, cajoling, questioning and asserting. Design is above all else a social activity: even the simplest letterhead might involve lengthy meetings and discussion with a long cast-list: client, assistant, photographer, plate-maker, printer and paper supplier. The needs of every cast member vary.

Above: Plus ça change
However many tools are made available, the designer's problems remain the same: the difficulty of creating good work, failures of courage, obtuse clients, the pressures of budgets and time.

Opposite: Tools are only as good as the workman
Image by Charles Barsotti

SHARP PENCILS, CLEAN PAPER, GOOD LIGHT, COMFORTABLE CHAIR, HOT COFFEE, WARM ROOM... READY TO WORK... PERHAPS THE ROOM IS TOO WARM...
CBarsotti

Pencil

The traditional instrument of rapid transfer of thought to a surface – the pencil – is so easy to use. It does not need booting up, does not dry up, and it can draw on almost any surface. It has become a cliché: that of quickly scribbling and capturing an idea – an emblem of inspiration.

There is a school of design that the approximation of the pencil suits perfectly. Informed by American advertising of the 1950s, it is a form of design sometimes referred to as the 'big idea' (see page 26), and is based on one key idea activating and acting as the central element of a design, whether it be a logo or a book. One of its early proponents was Bob Gill, who famously said that your idea was poor unless you could describe it over the phone.

This echoes László Moholy-Nagy's assertion that the essence of art and design lay in a concept, not in the final execution. He used to have an assistant, Gyorgy Kepes (who went on to have a prestigious career of his own) who carried out artwork based on his instructions.

While the pencil excels at organising and trying relationships in an approximate way, it is not so useful for design that relies on detail, or the exact relationships of interlocking elements. For many designers, it has been replaced by the mouse, particularly as programs are beginning to appear that match the ease and immediacy of graphite on paper.

My only gizmo
and its mouse.

Above: Access to ideas
A typically light-hearted tease by Jon Gorham.

Opposite: Pencil as idea
British Design & Art Direction (D&AD) use the pencil as their highly prized award: fetishising the successful manifesting of an idea.

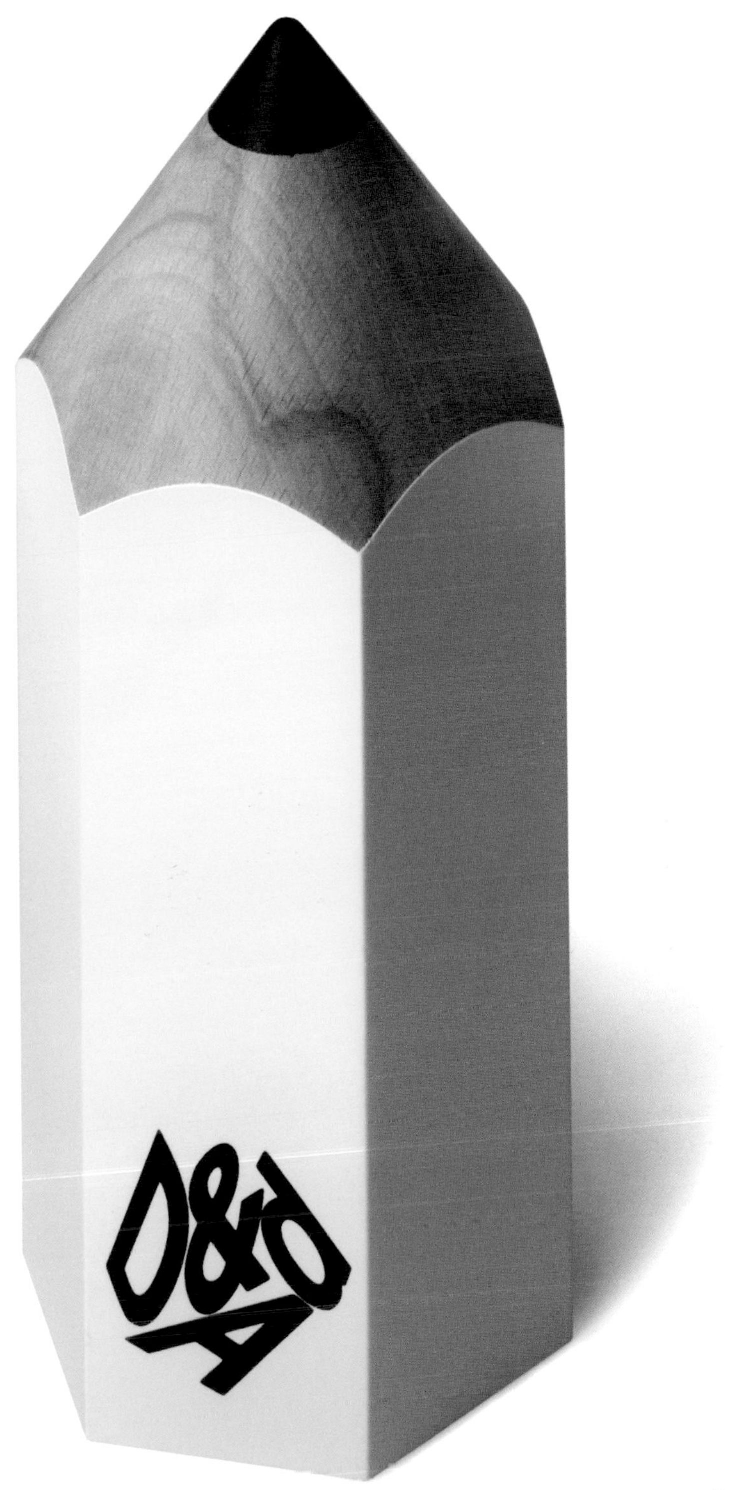

Materials

The primary material of graphic design may still be paper, but any designer will encounter huge variation beyond that. As well as book-cloth, and every variety of card, board, and plastic laminate, it is not so unusual to work with neon tubing, steel, slate, fire-resistant plasterboard, concrete, gilded wood, sandblasted glass or boiled leather.

Designers that need to go into the territory of new materials possess, or develop, a cautious, methodological approach of experimentation and constant questioning to ascertain how these materials behave, and establish how best to transfer and apply designs to them using partially or fully mechanised processes.

Below: Permutations
An array of materials frequently encountered by graphic designers, each of which needs particular allowances made in the design and the artwork given to the manufacturer. For example, the paper bag is printed using rubber sheets which spread the ink, so all the type needs extra letter spacing. From left to right: toughened glass, greaseproof paper and single-side coated card, waterproof cloth, recycled paper, and polypropylene, all designed by Atelier Works.

Opposite: Sweet
Even more rare materials sometimes present themselves. Johnson Banks – who more usually design identities, posters, literature and sign schemes – make a rare foray into confectionery, and cast themselves in chocolate. (One of them is a real dog.)

An Assortment of
Johnson Banks
Michael
Georgia
Luke
Harriet
Chris
Sarah
Jo

Paper

A book by the acerbic, revolutionary political theorist Guy Debord used sandpaper as its cover, so it would rub away at and damage other books on the shelf – a wonderful example of paper as expression of content.

Despite the significance of paper to graphic design, its invention and supply is confined to quite a narrowly-defined band that suits commercial printing. Most designers find themselves having to use industrially produced papers with slim tolerances of variation, designed specifically for offset lithographic printing, or vast rolls for web printing.

The eccentric designer and printer, Hendrik Werkman, was famous for exploiting the expressive qualities of paper in his work: "Some paper is so beautiful that you would like just to caress it and leave it chaste".

Opposite: Vespa catalogue
For a charitable sale of Vespa scooters, customised by a selection of celebrities, including fashion designer Paul Smith. The catalogue is wrapped in a blueprint, which does several things at once: it is an emblem of an idea; it shows a generic, unadorned Vespa (all the scooters for sale had been radically altered); and it brings the reader into unusual contact with the ammonia smell and chalky texture of this very distinctive form of printing. Design by Rebecca Foster.

Below: The Mennonites
A book by Larry Towell about the Mennonite religious sect who live in Canada and Mexico. It uses a contrast of paper types: the photographs are richly printed on thick-coated paper and the text on translucent, fragile Bible paper, emphasising the different experiences of looking (at pictures) and reading (text). The design also makes reference to the only book the Mennonites allow themselves: the Bible. Design by Atelier Works.

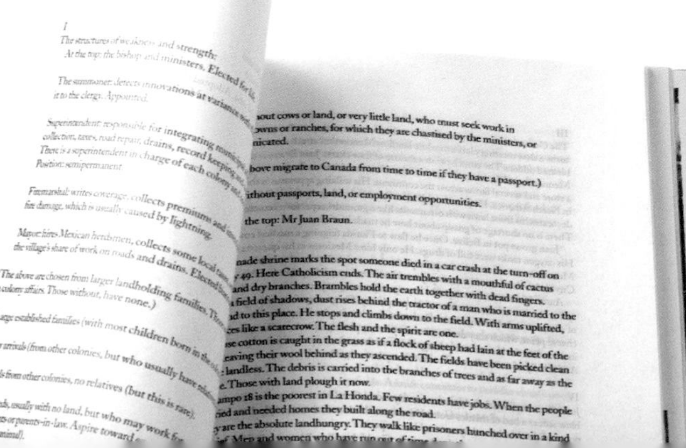

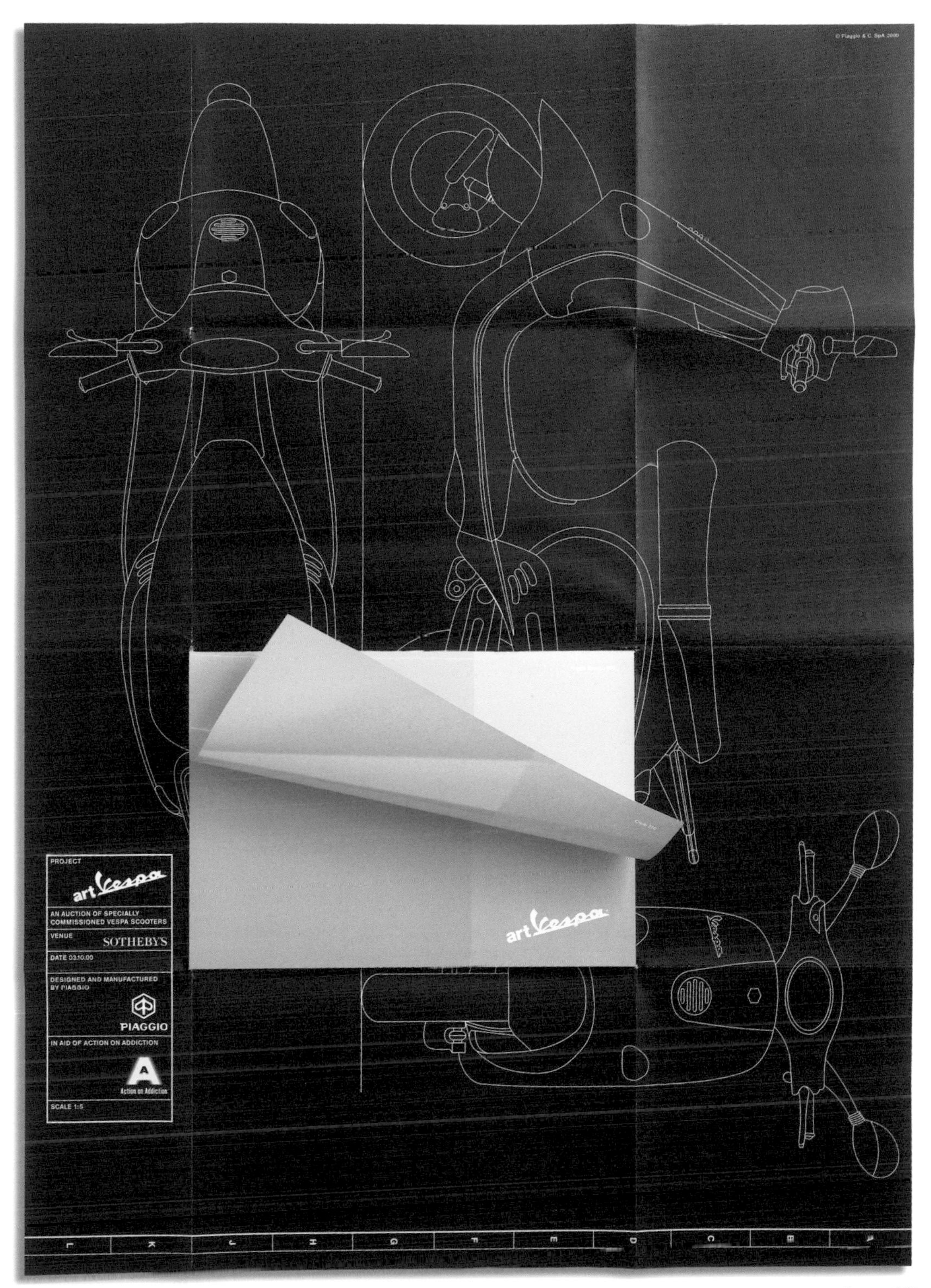
© Piaggio & C. SpA 2000
PROJECT
art Vespa
AN AUCTION OF SPECIALLY COMMISSIONED VESPA SCOOTERS
VENUE
SOTHEBYS
DATE 03.10.00
DESIGNED AND MANUFACTURED BY PIAGGIO
PIAGGIO
IN AID OF ACTION ON ADDICTION
A
Action on Addiction
SCALE 1:5
art Vespa
L
K
J
H
G
F
E
D
C
B

Computer

The computer is now the primary tool for almost all designers. Any vestige of concern about the dominance of the computer lies in the educative profession, with its emphasis on using the steps in the development of each area of design to expose the underlying principles.

What the computer does is to unify processes, vastly increasing the designer's power. The industrial revolution created machines that aimed to replicate and then simplify craft processes, making them thousands of times more efficient by taking them out of individual homes, and centralising them in factories. The computer is having a similar but exactly opposite effect – the process of manufacture has become vastly more efficient, but has allowed individuals to opt out of centralised places of work.

The computer has now combined almost every design activity (including using the internet and email): information gathering; writing; editing; image acquisition; manipulation and creation; typeface creation and minute management of its spacing and arrangement; preparation and delivery of artwork; combining text and image in motion; website design etc. Almost never before have designers had such control of every aspect of what they produce.

A typically sober and salty note is struck by Luddite, Bob Gill: "One of the things I do that a computer can't do is think. Layout is not the imperative anymore. We have to think and do what the computer can't do."

The multi-tool
A series of screen-grabs showing some of the processes that take place on every designer's computer: web browsing; integrated layout; emailing; illustration and font creation; word processing and reprographic preparation.

Atelier Works
Back
Forward
Stop
Refresh
Address
http://www.atelierworks.co.uk/
invite
Please send us your email address and we will invite you to the imminent
Click here to send email invite@atelierworks.co.uk
Search
Contacts
Check
QuickMail Pro
Who
Date Received
8/100
london.cpre 6/12/01
bloodbank 5/12/01
Latenightlondon.co.uk 3/12/01
Giovanni 3/12/01
images 3/12/01
QuickTime News
Cheapestflights.co.uk
Apple eNews
Quentin
Martin Lee
Glenn
10/100
No A
RE: RIBA
Glenn,
esign. The firs
eading, brutall
ummerized, is
ere has been
Style Sheets
No Style
01 Body Text (Scala)
02 Big Headings
03 Captions Body
05 Body Text (Akzidenz)
Normal
04 Caption Titles Bold
pattern obsessive <300%>
Character
Paragraph
Font: Helvetica
Regular
Swatches
Brushes
Color
Attributes
Stroke
Weight:
Miter Limit:
Dashed Line
Preview
Marquee
Adjust
Reset
0.0
EPSON TWAIN Pro
Document Source: Flatbed
Image Type 24-bit Color (Std)
Destination Prepress 150 lpi
Resolution: 300
Source: W 2550.00 H 3510.00
Target: W 2550.00 H 3510.00
9 4266
Scale:
Preview
Scan
Close
Settings...
Ready

Disciplines

Like all the categories in this book, disciplines are porous. There can be no corporate identity without understanding of logos or no packaging design without addressing the principles of publicity and information design. All these disciplines are joined by their articulation of word and image.

As an example of how leaky these disciplines are, where would the clock below fit? Designed for British Council language classrooms by Michael Johnson, it carries images that typify Britain or rather draw attention to clichés used to describe it. Part two-dimensional, part three-dimensional, it has no pages, no typography, only a sequence of images, fitting perfectly into the British Council identity scheme.

No designer experiences disciplinary boundaries when they work.

Opposite: Ambiguity
An essay by Rick Poynor in a recent book, 'Lost & Found: Critical Voices in New British Design' suggested a new term, 'visual communication', "which is being used more and more to describe overtly-authored projects by practitioners whose output goes well beyond the classic boundaries of graphic design". As an alternative for graphic design, the term is not new – the design course Max Bill established at Ulm in 1951, successor to the Bauhaus, was called 'visual communication'. The question is not a quibble over terminology, only over what the classic boundaries of graphic design might be, and who set them. (Rick Poynor does not say.) The examples opposite stand as a challenge to the idea that a few young designers are doing something either new, or particularly expanded.

Herbert Bayer had a remarkable career spanning 60 years: he taught at the Bauhaus, produced banknotes, posters, magazines, logotypes and typefaces – all of the highest quality. He taught and wrote influentially, took photographs and was a significant developer of the new form of montage. He acted as commissioning client on behalf of the Container Corporation of America, art directing a benchmark series of ads using philosophical and political statements. He undertook a redesign of the Latin alphabet ('klein-schribung', based on lowercase, and another version using phonetics) and was involved in the founding of the Institute of Humanistic Studies for which he designed the 'World Geo-Graphic Atlas' with a pioneering use of informational diagrams. Also an architect, he designed all the Institute's buildings in Aspen, Colorado. He was also a noted painter and sculptor.

The black-and-white picture shows Herbert Bayer's exhibition of the Deutscher Werkbund, German architecture and furniture, using his '360° field-of-vision' principles. The colour image shows a design for a pavilion at a 1924 industrial fair – note the type made out of smoke.

Any attempt to set up a new description of an 'expanded' definition of design has a long way to go before it covers even a fraction of Bayer's astonishing 'overtly-authored' oeuvre well within the "classic borders" of the disciplines he worked in.

REGINA
R
Regina

Logos

Paul Rand, designer of the logo for IBM said, “A trademark is created by a designer, but made by a corporation”. (Or unmade.)

The full name is ‘logotype’ from the Greek words ‘logos’ for word, and ‘tupos’, meaning impression. It can also be called a trademark, service mark, mark, or marque, but logo is the word that has entered common parlance. It can be a piece of type, a symbol, a picture, or a combination of any or all of these.

It is always a specific formulation – a repeatable and legally protectable signature. Devising logos, or brandmarks as they are becoming known, is at the core of modern graphic design. Almost all designers create logos. It sums up the joint and connected tasks of conceiving a distinctive graphic form that can create commercial value.

Superlative logo designers (for Mobil and Chase Manhattan Bank among dozens of others) Ivan Chermayeff, Tom Geismar and Steff Geisbuhler give this thorough formula: “A mark is both form and substance, image and idea. To be effective, its forms must be familiar enough to be recognisable, and unusual enough to be memorable. The design must be simple enough to be read in an instant, and rich enough in detail or meaning to be interesting. It must be contemporary enough to reflect its epoch, yet not so much of its time as to appear dated before the decade is out. Finally, it must be memorable, and appropriate to the ideas and activities it represents.”

Opposite: Per Mollerup
Perhaps the most experienced and prolific logo and identity designer in Scandinavia, Mollerup invests all his work with humour and warmth. Although he is reductive, and stringently ‘modernist’ in his choice of typefaces and layout, his logos avoid the banal austerity of pure geometry, and always include some clever and playful idea. This approach perfectly meets psychologist Douwe Draaisma’s ‘mnemonic requirements’ – unusual or unexpected features that the mind needs in order to remember.

Below: Evolution
Many of the best known (and therefore most successful?) logos evolve over decades rather than get re-invented. Working from scratch sometimes happens for sound strategic reasons, but there are many circumstances where a designer could tidy and redraw a logo rather than toss it aside completely. Several logos have their genealogy traced in Per Mollerup’s book ‘Marks of Excellence’.

Clockwise: Home
Logo for a real estate agents who specialise in flats and family houses. The fat, friendly type and hearth colour are pierced by a keyhole: a symbol of domestic security.

Oslo airport
One visual experience shared by all visitors to an airport is that things get smaller. If you leave the airport by air, you see houses getter smaller and smaller. If you remain on the ground, you see planes getting smaller and smaller.

Rødby
The name of this town translates as ‘red town’. The green ‘ø’ is a diagram of the town – which has one main road passing through it – as well as announcing the green countryside surrounding it, and the ‘green’ ambitions of the town council.

Schiang
Logo for a furniture manufacturer, a slightly uncomfortable rebus, where the picture of a chair stands for the letter ‘h’.

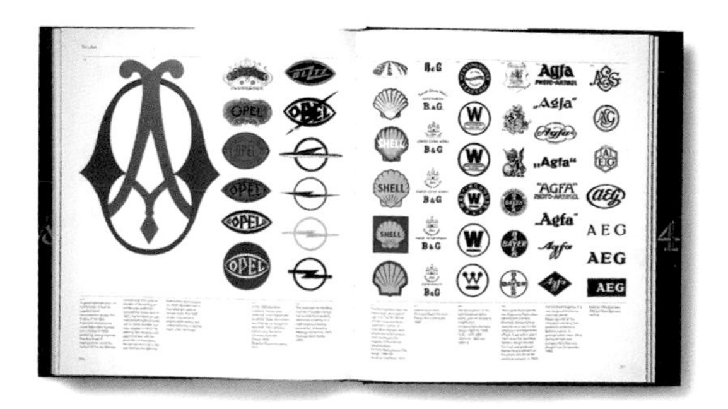

home

Schiang

RØDBY

Stock Trademarks
In 1975, American designer Jerry Herring produced these crisp parodies of logo design. He mailed them out in the form of a leaflet, introduced as follows: "Are you in need of a dynamic new image... but you are hesitant to act because of the expense and uncertainty of selecting an image... that is precisely why the Herring Design Studio of Houston, Texas has produced this collection of Stock Trademarks. Long a leader in the design of trademarks and logotypes, HDS now draws on this vast experience to offer trademarks that are not only inexpensive, but can be used for almost any company... All the designs are available in black, green and blue. A few are available in red. Allow 2–3 weeks for delivery".

Tree Trademark
A must for a real estate project. Goes real well with woodsy names like Oakmont or Pinesap Apartments.

Star Trademark
Perfect for those doing movie, government or occult work. Special clearance needed to use in red.

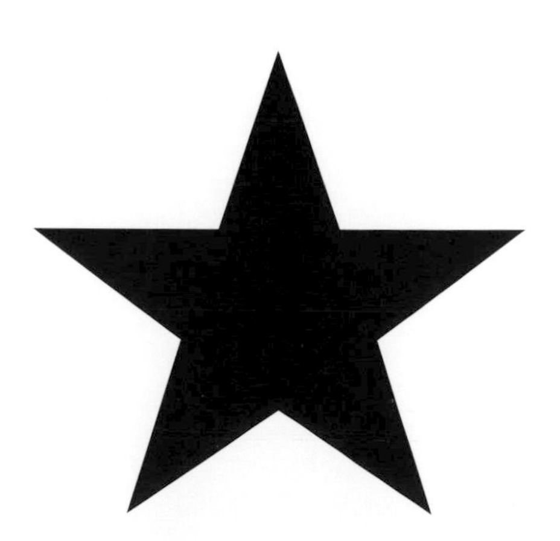

Modern Trademark
Can be interpreted in many ways. An ideal choice when dealing with a committee.

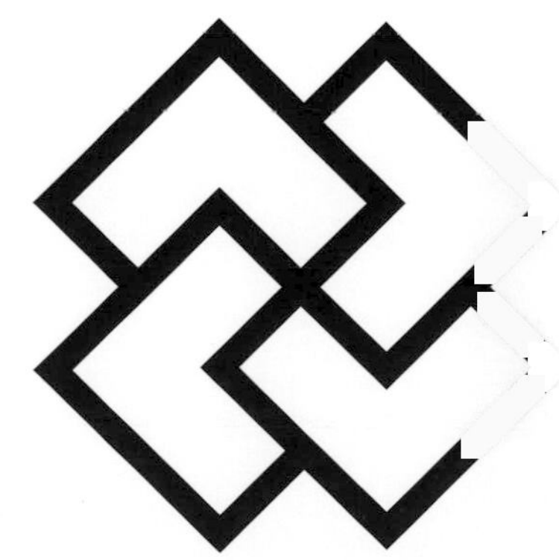

Crest Trademark
Has a quiet dignity. Especially good for new restaurants in need of a long history.

Rainbow Trademark
Good for companies with a bright outlook, or one dealing in gold futures.

Arrow Trademark
For companies on the move, on the way up or on the go. Specify whether going straight up or to the right.

Eagle Trademark
An excellent choice for patriotic firms. A big favourite among banks for some reason. Specify brown or black.

Identity

The logo is only part of an organisation's identity. It is no more than the moniker, a label, or an emblem, like a name is only a part of an individual's personality.

What has come to be known as the 'corporate identity' covers how the logo is used, as well as all the other elements: tone of language, typefaces, colours, paperstocks, pictures, publication formats, signs, and so on. Other names are 'house style', and in recent years, 'branding'.

For large organisations, creating a corporate identity can be a huge undertaking, sometimes lasting years, and needing constant attention ever after. Organisations that do not coordinate graphic work are, by default, creating a diffuse and disjointed identity. The choice seems straightforward, but Paul Rand, doyen of big American corporate identity schemes, warns that "a certain sameness seems to pervade all fields of design... The emphasis on simple shapes, the absence of ornamentation, and the universal acceptance of certain art forms, tends to encourage anonymity." This is taken further by Ken Garland: "A ubiquitous and successful corporate identity is, in the last resort, a calamity just because it is ubiquitous". He sees identity as "infused with over-weaning, elitist notions of power and the imposition of order".

Perhaps the problem lies not with the principle of a singular, unified design, but with whether or not we agree with the direction in which many of the corporations displaying them are moving.

Royal Institute of British Architects (RIBA)
Forty years in the life of an identity.
Top: An identity scheme by Herbert Spencer designed in 1961. Its primary element is a heraldic crest, used by RIBA since its inception in 1836.
Bottom: The first page of a design 'audit' – a collection of all the materials produced by RIBA in the year 2000. Spencer's scheme, by this time 40 years old, needed updating to cover new items, new media and new sensibilities.
Opposite: The new scheme, launched in 2001. Its principle element the letters RIBA, drawn by John Rushworth of Pentagram, with a redrawn, more geometric crest used in a subsidiary role. The new crest is used generously in one or two applications, such as the 'site board', used on every building site in Britain. Design by Atelier Works.

Royal Institute
of British Architects
'This is how all architecture can be: relevant, surprising and human'
Marco Goldschmied, President
Annual Review 2000/2001

RIBA

Membership 2002

RIBA

President's midsummer party

RIBA

Royal Institute of British Architects

Code of Professional Conduct

and Standard of Professional Performance

RIBA Architect

Peterson Williams Johnson & Smith

Telephone 012 3456 1890 Other data may be included providing it doesn't extend beyond a single line

Print – publicity

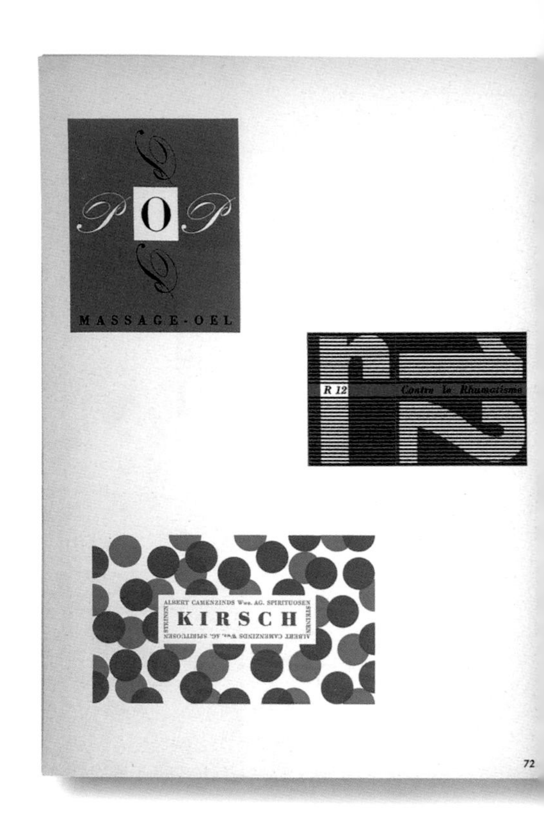

Printed matter can be very broadly sliced into two types: material that publicises, and material that conveys information. Obviously, literature that has the primary function of publicising, promoting, or selling products or services, may have some informational aspect – prices, dates or application forms – but it is structured around making a positive impression.

The requirements of publicity are best observed in its most abbreviated form, with only a single surface on which to pack an attention-grabbing blast of seduction: the flyer or poster. This category contains some of design's most taxing work which is routinely sent to unsuspecting, or hostile recipients: direct mail.

The way most publicity material works can be compared to the formula for a good piece of newspaper journalism: 'hey, what? how? so'. 'Hey' is the attention grabber, usually an intriguing image or powerful piece of typography, 'what?' is the brief introduction to the product or service, 'how?' is the fuller story, and 'so' is what you do as a consequence.

Although flyers, leaflets and brochures are the bread and butter of many, if not most, graphic design studios the world over – much of the design can be impossible to elevate. To design something enchanting for direct (junk) mail is one of the hardest tasks imaginable. Even the aesthetically beautiful examples of avant-garde adverts and leaflets, when lifted from history books and put back into magazines, or dumped on your doormat, become candyfloss.

Left: Walter Marti
An unsung Swiss designer of the early 20th century. Unsung, perhaps because Marti's work is all small scale, and consists largely of beautifully composed promotional cards, leaflets, signs and ads.

Below left: Unknown
A promotional card that works in the most direct way, combining promotion with information, and showing the product itself – a device that used to be common. This is a modern piece however. Somehow a designer in Kirknewton has retained, or developed, skills of drawing and composition more common a hundred years ago, almost as if Modernism never happened. Although outmoded, this design is delicately resolved.

Right: Morag Myerscough
In her book that describes apartments in a newly converted building, Myerscough avoids unadulterated property clichés by turning all the imagery – photography of the interiors and surrounding area, floor plans – into intensely coloured paintings. She also adds a few non-sequitur, surrealistic pictures, like penguins, indicating that she is not taking the work too seriously. It is more like an art book, and comes supplied with a bookmark cut into the shape of the site.

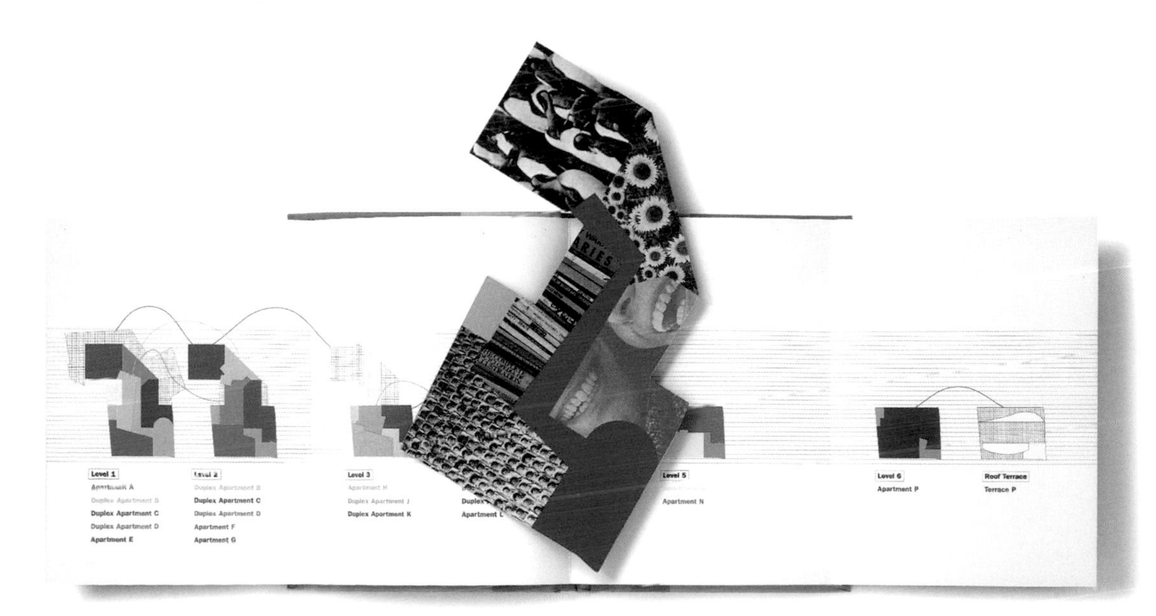

Print – information

Informational graphics is 'cognitive art'. Like all graphic design 'categories', this is a huge and diverse area – from run-of-the-mill leaflets to complex charts, tables, diagrams, graphs, maps, plans, and so on.

Richard Saul Wurman, originally an architect who has become a multi-millionaire through a series of brilliantly designed guides to drugs, investing and travel, says "the only means we have of comprehending information is through words, numbers and pictures... Despite the critical role that graphic designers play in the delivery of information, most of the curriculum in design schools is concerned with how to make things look good. This is later reinforced by the profession, which bestows awards primarily for appearance, rather than for understanding or even accuracy."

Wurman, who has invented a special term for himself and others like him – 'information architect' – asserts that there are only five basic ways to organise any information: location (maps); alphabet; time (timelines, timetables); category (this includes organising by colour and material) and hierarchy (from largest to smallest, darkest to lightest). I have discovered three more: randomly (many catalogues); intuitively (magazines, often organised by the editor's instinct) and traditionally (the Bible).

Work in this area stresses the functional aspects of design: the legible as opposed to expressive aspects of typography; cross-referencing paraphernalia; numbering systems and so on.

Above: Knoll catalogue
Herbert Matter's lifelong interest in biomorphic form led to this simple juxtaposition of photographs with drawings showing the dimensions of the products. The photographs were cut out in order to emphasise the striking shapes of the chairs. Their inherent beauty was clear to Matter: although this catalogue dates from 1950, almost all the furniture is still in production. The spiral binding allows the catalogue to be laid flat and the products pored over.

Opposite:
Book of Common Worship
Derek Birdsall of Omnific, with assistants John Morgan, and Shirley and Elsa Birdsall, recently redesigned this book for the Church of England. Very mindful of the congregation being unable to read easily in poor light, or with old eyes, Birdsall set the type size first, then the grid and page size, which followed the longest line length. After attending services, he broke the text to ensure that noisy page turns did not occur in the middle of a prayer. The re-design retains the most logical aspects of hundreds of years of ecclesiastical typography: rubric (the priest's passages are set in red) and thin paper (specially made in a soft 'ivory' colour to reduce bulk).

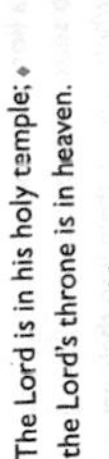

4 The Lord is in his holy temple; ♦
the Lord's throne is in heaven.

5 His eyes behold, ♦
his eyelids try every mortal being.

6 The Lord tries the righteous as well as the wicked, ♦
but those who delight in violence his soul abhors.

7 Upon the wicked he shall rain coals of fire
  and burning sulphur; ♦
scorching wind shall be their portion to drink.

8 For the Lord is righteous;
  he loves righteous deeds, ♦
and those who are upright shall behold his face.

Psalm 12

1 Help me, Lord, for no one godly is left; ♦
the faithful have vanished from the whole human race.

2 They all speak falsely with their neighbour; ♦
they flatter with their lips, but speak from a double heart.

3 O that the Lord would cut off all flattering lips ♦
and the tongue that speaks proud boasts!

4 Those who say, 'With our tongue will we prevail; ♦
our lips we will use; who is lord over us?'

5 'Because of the oppression of the needy,
  and the groaning of the poor, ♦
I will rise up now,' says the Lord,
  'and set them in the safety that they long for.'

6 The words of the Lord are pure words, ♦
like silver refined in the furnace
  and purified seven times in the fire.

7 You, O Lord, will watch over us ♦
and guard us from this generation for ever.

8 The wicked strut on every side, ♦
when what is vile is exalted by the whole human race.

604 *Psalm 12*

Psalm 13

1 How long will you forget me, O Lord; for ever? ♦
How long will you hide your face from me?

2 How long shall I have anguish in my soul
  and grief in my heart, day after day? ♦
How long shall my enemy triumph over me?

3 Look upon me and answer, O Lord my God; ♦
lighten my eyes, lest I sleep in death;

4 Lest my enemy say, 'I have prevailed against him,' ♦
and my foes rejoice that I have fallen.

5 But I put my trust in your steadfast love; ♦
my heart will rejoice in your salvation.

6 I will sing to the Lord, ♦
for he has dealt so bountifully with me.

Psalm 14

1 The fool has said in his heart, 'There is no God.' ♦
Corrupt are they, and abominable in their wickedness;
  there is no one that does good.

2 The Lord has looked down from heaven
  upon the children of earth, ♦
to see if there is anyone who is wise
  and seeks after God.

3 But every one has turned back;
  all alike have become corrupt: ♦
there is none that does good; no, not one.

4 Have they no knowledge, those evildoers, ♦
who eat up my people as if they ate bread
  and do not call upon the Lord?

5 There shall they be in great fear; ♦
for God is in the company of the righteous.

Psalm 14 605

Packaging

Packaging is storytelling in a compressed area – like posters in miniature. Packs must mark out and differentiate the product from competitors, which they attempt in the most demanding of circumstances, often sitting next to direct competitors, on shelves brimming with distractions.

One might think that this was a field best suited for graphic experimentation, given the compelling need to stand out, however packaging tends to be one of the most conservative areas of design, dominated by the 'marketing department' of the manufacturers. Writer Thomas Hine asserts that "packaging, with its severe limits on individual expression, is one of the few design disciplines that values continuity over bold new [design] statements." Most packaging borrows heavily from broad trends, or perceived traditions, to make it acceptable, especially where mass production, involving high capital investment, is concerned.

One notable aspect of packaging is its role as a source for a design phenomenon best called 'cross-dressing', where the conventions of a niche area of packaging are borrowed for a refreshing and ironic shock effect in some other area – for example, the sensuous photography and use of space in fashion packaging applied to that of food. One area regularly raided is medical packaging, with its rigid sans serif and acidic colours. Dance music, always hungry for new treatments, is promiscuous territory: CDs are often dressed up as pills, jam, machine parts, magazines and art.

Right: Storytelling
A set of chocolates created to mark the Voyages of Discovery exhibition at the Science Musem. Together the six wrappers tell the story of how chocolate was encountered by Sir Hans Sloane on a voyage to South America, brought back and served at his dinner parties – one of which was attended by a certain John Cadbury. Design by John Powner of Atelier Works.

Opposite: Cross-dressing
Tradition is still favoured for much food packaging – selling the idea that the product has been produced by family firms for decades and therefore not been industrially farmed, and has qualities deeper than exigent commercial ones. Real tradition does feel different to created tradition – there is subtle conviction in the way that packaging is assembled, and in the details of how the image is drawn – the colours ignore fashion and there are idiosyncracies that have escaped customer focus groups. This pan forte (dense Italian cake) communicates its deliciousness with sumptuous illustration and charming lettering.

PAOLO
Atti
E FIGLI
BOLOGNA
VIA CAPRARIE, 7 - TEL. 220425
VIA DRAPPERIE, 6 - TEL. 233349
P.ZZA XX SETTEMBRE, 4 - TEL. 224480

Books

The book is the birthplace of graphic design. Historian Lucien Febvre said that it "assembled permanently the works of the most sublime creative spirits in all fields... [and] created new habits of thought not only within the small circle of the learned, but far beyond, in the intellectual life of all who used their minds."

Hans Peter Willberg, a highly experienced book designer, has roughly categorised types of book based on conventions of subject matter. This determines how they are designed. Roughly, Willberg's categories are: typography for linear reading (novels; plays, books of poetry and illustrated storybooks usually follow a linear sequence, but need more sophisticated treatments); typography for information (scientific and instructional books); typography for consultation and selective reading (reference books, encyclopedias, the Bible); and typography for units of meaning (teaching books of individual lessons with accompanying commentary and exercises).

Dutch book designer Jost Hochuli draws a distinction between macro- and micro-typography – macro being the book as a whole, its navigational elements, and each page, and micro being the spaces around and between the lines, words and letters. The majority of books are designed according to systems, pre-conceived grids and typographic schemes – a precious few are designed page by page. Books are written and designed to last – one of the few products that graphic designers work on that do.

Below: Harboard covers
A series of covers for an English publisher, producing only Russian novelists translated into English. The covers are designed as rich slabs, like a Russian 'iconostasis': the illustrated walls in Orthodox churches. The back covers feature a close-up portrait of the author. Design by Atelier Works.

Opposite: The People's Art
This book was made to accompany an exhibition. It is half book, half catalogue – or catalogue in the form of a book. The pictures are pushed onto the outside, and carried on a series of double-sided covers. You can choose which artist you like best, and personalise the book. The text inside is treated in contrast to the rich images outside: stark and unrelenting. Design by Experimental Jetset.

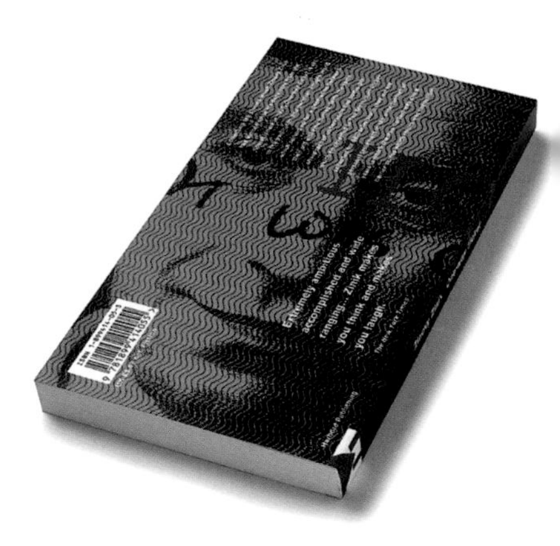

The People's Art
A Arte do Povo

Porto 2001

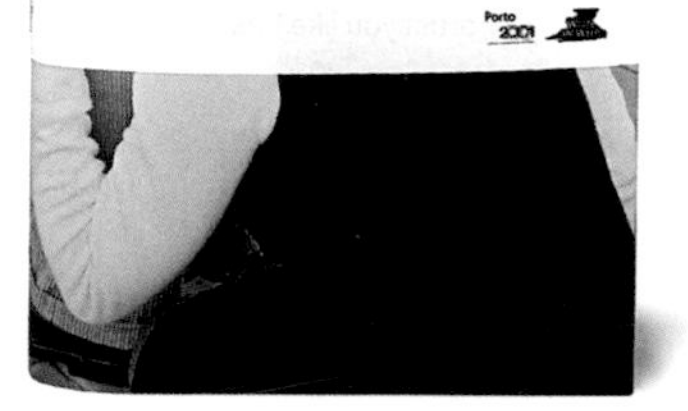

The People's Art
A Arte do Povo

Porto 2001

A Arte do Povo
Bartomeu Marí

Página 06
A Arte do Povo

Desde as últimas décadas do século passado que as grandes exposições que apresentam a arte de um país em concreto – a arte nacional – têm vindo a modificar substancialmente o seu carácter. A questão nacional ou regional apenas sobrevive no intercâmbio de artistas entre instituições cujo carácter é mais representativo e político do que científico. E isto aconteceu a favor de uma maior internacionalização das grandes manifestações expositivas, esporádicas ou com uma certa continuidade. O novo internacionalismo expandiu as fronteiras geográficas da arte contemporânea, oscilando também até regiões até há pouco tempo ausentes dos circuitos de grandes exposições. Artistas da antiga Europa de Leste, América Latina, Ásia ou África começam a fazer parte das listas de participantes de grandes exposições, publicações internacionais, mesas redondas... A exposição que origina estas linhas e que fica registada nesta publicação é atípica em relação ao que acabo de descrever.
A organização do Porto 2001, Capital Europeia da Cultura encarregou-me de organizar uma exposição que proporcione uma visão da arte contemporânea holandesa. Esta mostra vai ser apresentada na Central Eléctrica do Freixo. Trata-se de um enorme edifício industrial, inserido na colina que rodeia o início da desembocadura do rio, mas em plena cidade. Uma ponte colossal voa por sobre o edifício como um toucado, um monumento à velocidade, de quem desde a Central só se apercebe da serenidade plana e rígida da engenharia moderna, onde o betão veio substituir o agora romântico aço das pontes de Eiffel.
O interior do edifício tem um aspecto surpreendente. É como se os últimos iões positivos e negativos tivessem acabado de deixar o lugar, como se a maquinaria tivesse estado a funcionar até ao dia anterior à nossa primeira visita. Este é um lugar que respira electricidade por todos os poros; transmite de imediato um ambiente de esforço, de dínamos encadeados,

A Arte do Povo
Bartomeu Marí

Página 07
A Arte do Povo

de turbinas em contínua actividade.
O que posso dizer sobre a arte contemporânea holandesa? Elaborei a exposição seguindo uma velha intuição que se mantém válida hoje em dia. A resposta a esta interrogação quanto à forma da exposição que agora apresentamos, não seria nem objectiva nem exaustiva, mas sim representativa de um determinado fenómeno que é objecto de representação. Há quase seis anos que dirijo um centro de arte contemporânea na Holanda e estou rodeado por todos os lados de arte holandesa, em directa e contínua confrontação com a arte do resto do mundo.
Muitos colegas da minha geração partilham comigo o facto de detestarem as noções de nacionalidade ligadas à arte. De uma forma mais ou menos ingénua, cremos que a arte é uma linguagem universal, que o artista cria a sua obra potencialmente para todo o ser humano consciente e curioso e que a arte é património de todos, independentemente da atribuição do seu autor a uma ou outra nação. Mas a realidade contradiz-nos. Não só manifestações internacionais de grande prestígio como a Bienal de Veneza seriam impossíveis sem a noção de 'arte nacional' que explica a sobrevivência dos pavilhões nacionais, como também uma grande parte do sistema ocidental da arte funciona sustentado pelos institutos nacionais de promoção.
Ainda que o mundo da arte seja muito mais poroso, e se esteja a tornar cada dia mais diáfano e flexível, a rejeição inicial à relação arte/nação converteu-se num paradoxo fascinante. A questão sobre até que ponto se encontra a obra de tal ou tal artista ligada a um lugar preciso, à sua gente, às suas tradições e valores recorda-nos períodos escuros da História do Velho Continente. Desde o início do século que uma série de opiniões e teorias estéticas e pseudo-científicas se esforçaram por demonstrar a pertinência da arte de tal ou tal nação, ao definir critérios de pureza, pertinência ou

The People's Art
A Arte do Povo

Porto 2001

Identity/Reality
Carel Blotkamp

Page 34
The People's Art

landscape made by a camera tied to a kite. They lack the sharpness and purposiveness of those aerial survey photographs made from a plane on which Holland invariably appears as a neatly-tilled cultivated landscape, organized with mathematical precision; on De Ruijter's photographs we see the untidy loose edges, picturesque details rendered visible with the aid of controlled chance.
Holland in fact does not have any nature; everything here is made by human hands, everything is designed. That is a cliché, but one based on reality. An artificial urban layer has been imposed on the formerly empty, artificial countryside, now stretching inland from the coast like a Los Angeles of the polder. This twofold artificiality is reflected in the work of artists such as Jeroen Offerman and Edwin Zwakman. Offerman's video *The Rise and Fall of Nunhead Cemetary* is projected on a large screen and gives a convincing illusionistic image of a half-rural, half-urban environment, until the viewer discovers that the video camera is installed in front of a comparatively primitive maquette with separate photographic elements against a background of yet another video recording of a sky with clouds. What looked so true to life disintegrates into fragments. Viewed superficially, Zwakman's photographs look like ordinary shots in the tradition of landscape and architectural photography, with a mixture of documentary and artistic pretensions. They show a view of a dockland area for instance or the nondescript front of an apartment block from the 1960s on a sunny day. But on closer inspection, you can see from small details that this is a world of wood and cardboard, constructed in small scale in his studio with the sole purpose of being photographed.
These artificial realities remind one a little of a film set that has been abandoned by crew and actors. The association with film also occurs in the work of artists like Anneke A. de Boer and Philippine Hoegen. Admittedly their photographs

Identity/Reality
Carel Blotkamp

Page 35
The People's Art

were taken on real locations, but the people and things one sees there are clearly 'directed' by them. The characters in De Boer's sequences of photographs give one the impression of belonging in a story; this feeling however is subverted by the camera being moved around, so that one's attention is distracted by details whose relevance is unclear. In Hoegen's photographs furniture and locations take on a disturbing, living presence due to the suggestive lighting and the way the camera is installed. In her recent book *The Crack in the Wall*, tension is generated through the sequence of photographs being interspersed with fragments from literary texts in a manner that makes one think of Polanski's film *Repulsion*. It comes as no surprise then that the book ends with the sentence, 'It was murder'.
Soaps and sitcoms, pseudo-documentaries and thrillers – the world of TV and film apparently supplies the majority of the artists represented in this exhibition with a wealth of inspiration; in their work they are above all concerned with the staged position of characters in their environment, the staged relation of people with each other and with objects. People's behavior and actions are removed from their everyday context and to a degree enlarged, isolated, distorted or dramatized. Psychological factors play a certain role in the work of some of these artists but only at a collective level. In this art human beings do not appear as individuals but rather as socially conditioned types – just as city and landscape appear not as concrete places, but as types.

Is this art typically Dutch and made in the tradition of Dutch art? On occasions like this authors tend to hark back to historical genres such as landscape painting, portraiture and the still life to suggest a continuity in the artistic production of their country, but personally I don't think this is particularly meaningful. The notion of an uninterrupted tradition is a fiction.

Magazines

Alexey Brodovitch is the grandfather of modern magazine design. His cry of "astonish me", is what every reader is thinking when thumbing through a magazine. However, the primary tasks of magazine design are complex and effortful: a lot of organising, chasing material, endless revisions of the page plan, careful management of lots of text. The art director (the graphic designer gets a title when working on a magazine) must develop an intimate understanding with the editor. Tibor Kalman – art director of Andy Warhol's Interview, and Colors magazine – said that it takes a designer/editor team ten issues to understand what a magazine is really about, and then they have ten or 20 really great issues in them. (After that, perhaps one of them needs to move on.)

It is easy to see why many magazine designers seek refuge in the simplicity of using an eccentric typeface, or one or two semi-pornographic photographs, or some other flouting of expectation and convention, such as making text illegible by setting it in dingbats. Some of these 'innovations' do serve to refresh and energise the content of a magazine, and act as a banner for its editorial attitude, but many are hollow efforts, making one or two pages interesting, and leaving the rest of the magazine unspiced and dreary. Magazine design is about establishing a design system, a palette, that can adopt various tones and yet remain coherent.

Opposite: Domus
Simon Esterson is fast becoming the UK's most prolific editorial and newspaper designer. His favourite word for a successfully designed magazine is 'rich'. His approach to the Italian architecture and interiors magazine, Domus, is to build layouts out of big, hefty slabs of type, colour, space and pictures which slide against one another, jostle and interlock. He sets up a rhythm that ties together the diverse material throughout the magazine with a small number of elements – squares, one typeface, a limited suite of colours – repeating in varying scales in different locations on the grid. Although parts of Domus deal with a number of smaller items grouped together, many spreads are dedicated to a single feature and are quite simple and spare. For this magazine, the richness comes from lavish, beautifully printed colour photography used as large and as frequently as budgets and text will allow.

In order to demonstrate how a magazine needs to work, almost all of a single issue of Domus is shown over the next five pages. This way of looking at a magazine takes our attention away from the elegant typography of one particular spread, and shows us how it does its real job: coordinating and giving refreshing vitality to potentially disconnected material.

domus
Dicembre/December 2001
Curvare
la strada
Bending
the street
Il paesaggio
domestico
The domestic
landscape

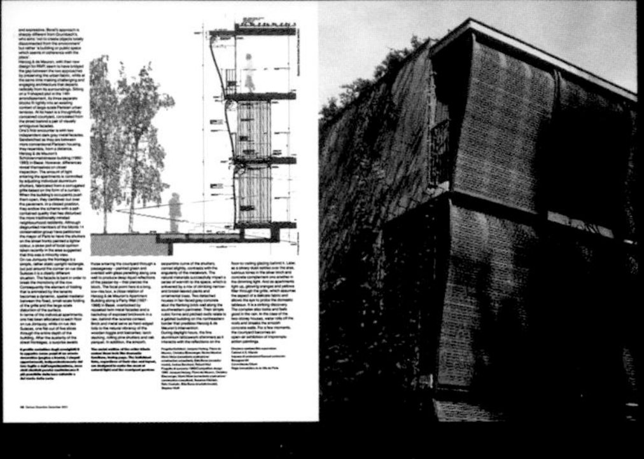

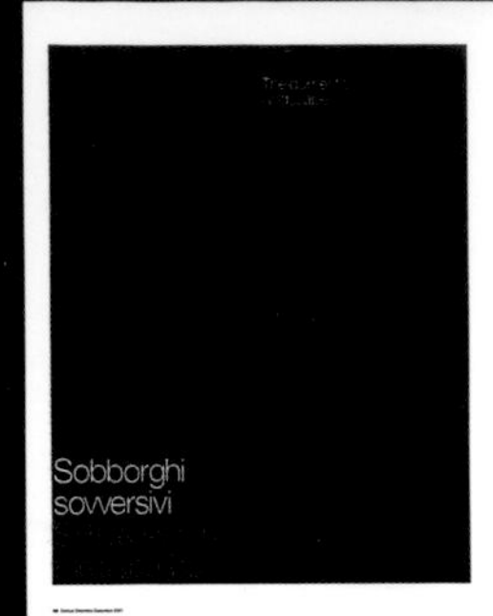
Sobborghi
sovversivi

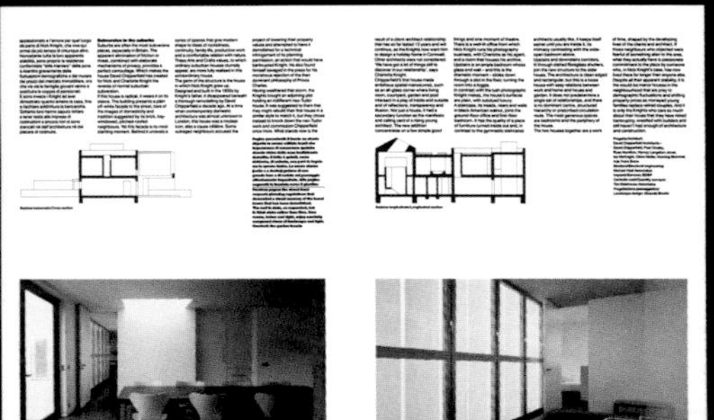

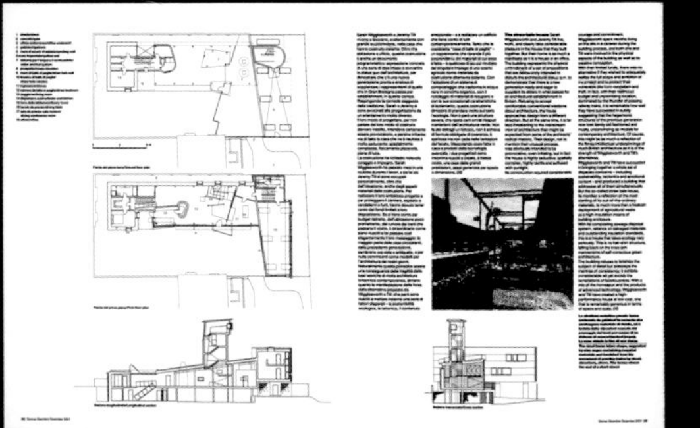

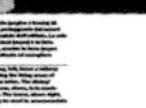

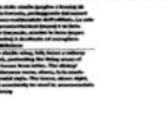

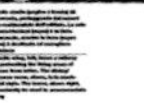

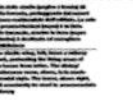

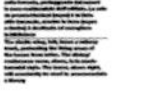

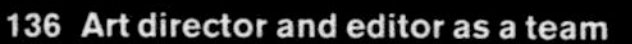

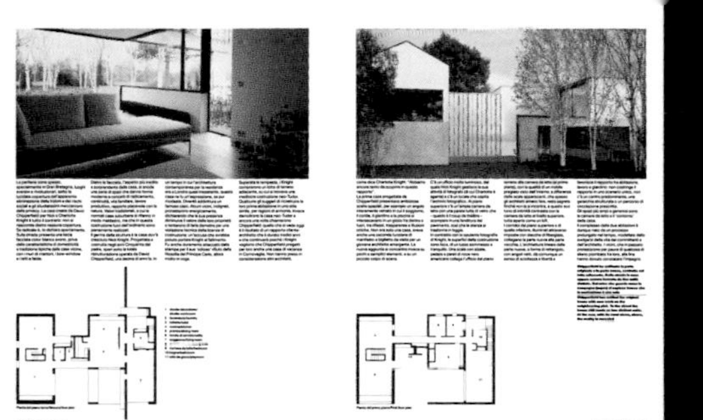

La casa di Bucky
The house that Bucky built

Casa di paglia
The straw bale house

Il paesaggio

The domestic landscape

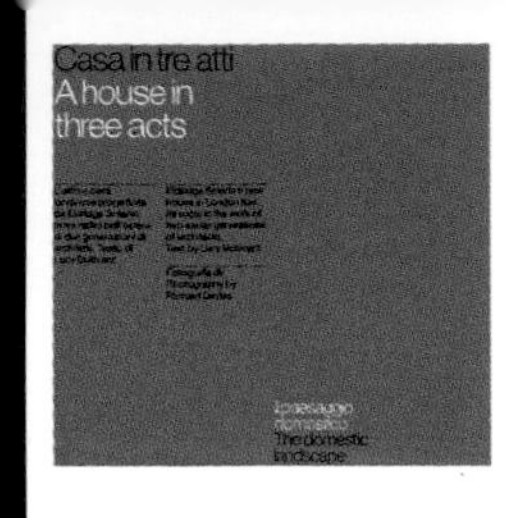

Casa in tre atti
A house in three acts

Il paesaggio domestico
The domestic landscape

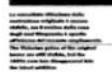

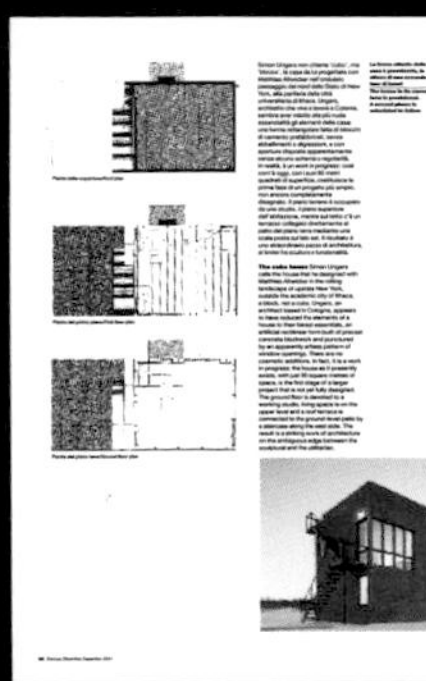

L'incontro di alcuni maestri portoghesi contemporanei con la tradizione dell'artigianato, visti da Francesca Picchi

Francesca Picchi looks at a collaboration between traditional craftsmen and contemporary Portuguese designers

Fotografie di/
Photos by Lee Funnell

Le ceramiche degli architetti
Architectural ceramics

Il paesaggio domestico
The domestic landscape

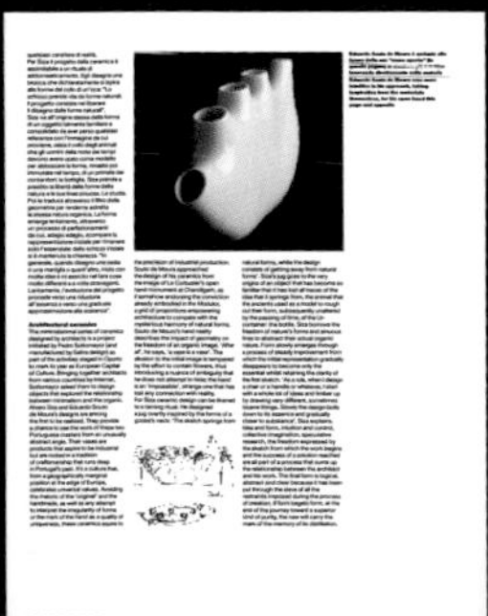

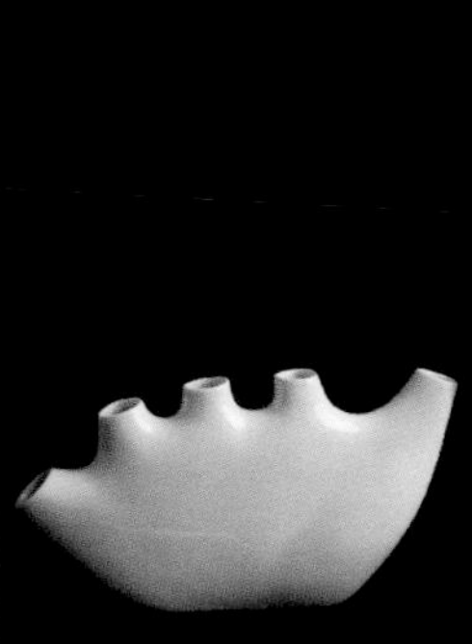

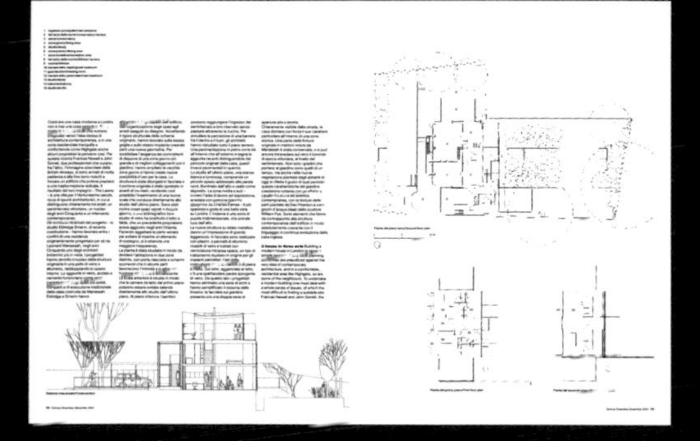

Casa cubo
The cube house

Nel nord dello Stato di New York, la casa progettata da Simon Ungers riduce l'ambiente domestico al minimo essenziale

Simon Ungers' house in upstate New York reduces domesticity to the bare minimum

Fotografia di/Photography by Eduard Hueber/Arch Photo

Il paesaggio domestico
The domestic landscape

Dal Bauhaus a casa mia
From Bauhaus to My House

Il paesaggio domestico

Il Guggenheim di Rem Koolhaas non è ciò che Venturi aveva in mente quando invitava a "imparare da Las Vegas", sostiene Mark Irving

Rem Koolhaas's Guggenheim isn't what Robert Venturi had in mind when he learnt from Las Vegas, says Mark Irving

Fotografia di/Photography by Michael Moran

Un'altra lezione da Las Vegas

Another lesson from Las Vegas

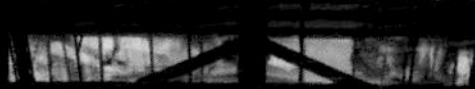

Exhibitions

An area of design rarely mass reproduced, exhibitions are almost always one-offs. They can be permanent or temporary, fitted to a particular space or designed to tour. Included under this heading are those aspects of graphic design that fit into existing architecture, that might not be exhibiting but are a more gentle display of graphic elements. This includes shops, corporate headquarters, lobbies and restaurants.

This form of design is about an architectural experience: the exploitation of space, use of light, creation of large structures, and relationships of materials.

Much is related to everyday graphic design, just on a much larger scale. It is more to do with the feet than the hand. The organisation of the content of exhibitions has already been covered in previous sections (see pages 100 and 128).

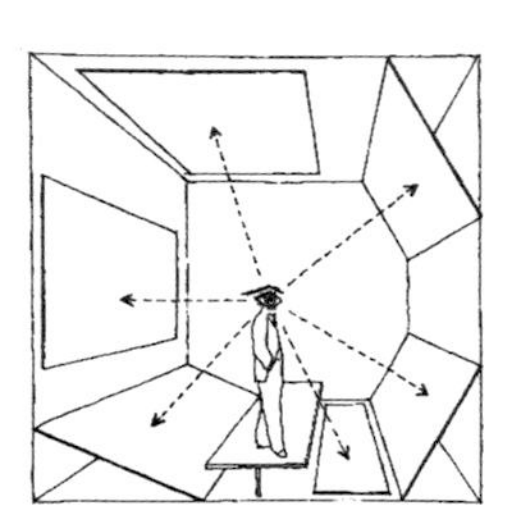

Above: Field-of-vision
Herbert Bayer was called "one of the most influential exhibition designers of the modern period". Above is his 360° field-of-vision diagram showing his exhibition principles; the visitor is surrounded by a rich, multi-faceted, out-of-the-ordinary array of pictures and information. (See this idea in use, page 119.)

Above: Super-cinematic
The visitor is immersed in pulsing light, shimmering colour, scrolling text and sound. An intuitive use of Bayer's field-of-vision principle by Morag Myerscough.

Opposite: Parade of years
Simple in its mechanism, but striving for a monumental effect – an exhibition for the 25th year anniversary of a furniture company. Myerscough celebrates the passing years with numbers on the lights.

83
85
89
88
91
92
93
94
95
96
97
+
99
98
2000
2000
2000

Signs

There are two types of sign: those you want to see (toilet, pub), and those you are compelled to see (fire collection points, speed restrictions). Signs that announce or decorate perform an advertising, promotional function. Almost all the others represent some kind of failure: you would rather have a choice of what to view than an arrow pointing to something specific.

Sign-making is an ancient activity: an arrow and letters scratched onto a piece of wood nailed to a tree; the horseshoe nailed outside a smithy; a wooden coffee pot outside a coffee shop. Pub signs have rightfully been claimed as the first surrealism – the relationship between activity and symbolism is often highly arbitrary.

Sign design is driven more by what is perceived as function than almost any other area of graphic design. Typeface, size, colour and iconography are dictated by legislation, as well as on-site testing, and extensive consultations with 'user groups'.

There are basic physical difficulties with sign-making that no graphic designer has ever resolved completely, such as an arrow that clearly points forward rather than up into the air. Many signs fail, or can be made to fail with the addition of another sign. Many public sign schemes (hospitals, schools, etc) are applied (with varied success) without the use of any graphic designers at all.

Above and below:
David Chipperfield's River & Rowing Museum in Henley-on-Thames has floor-to-ceiling glazing throughout the ground floor. By law such glazing must be adorned with 'manifestations'; dots and lines to prevent people walking into it. Rather than hundreds of dreary dots, silhouettes of the wildlife of the Thames, such as birds, fish and insects, were used. Design by Atelier Works.

Opposite:
This sign in New York is by Rigo, who describes himself as a 'visual rapper'. It is a piece of 'culture jamming', an intervention that uses the language of graphic design, but has a different purpose. Instead of what might be seen as a banal intention, directing you to a car park, this sign has a poetic, cerebral intention. Is it graphic design? (See Is graphic design the same as art?, page 28). Photo by Iain Crockart.

SKY

Web and film

If there were still any doubts about the future direction of graphic design, this one fact should dispel them: in 1993 there were 50 websites, in 2001 there were 350 million.

Any discussion of new media means we must turn to the great media prophet, Marshall McLuhan. He said that any new medium goes through a period of mimicry before exploiting its own specific forms properly. Currently, computer software and the web use physical analogues: the desktop, icons and tools, even type. All these have been used to give meaning, what John Maeda calls "semantic camouflage", to clusters of pure data.

Once this mimicry melts away, designers will be able to explore word and image with an unprecedented flexibility that has never existed before: mobility through any and every angle and speed, types of transition and morphing of forms and sound. This is in complete contrast to fixing type and images in one place.

I have placed web and film together because both forms seem to be drawing closer, but there are also games, moving advertising and sports screens, television, even new interfaces on mobile phones. We are now seeing websites and interactive displays that ask questions, learn your name, respond to your voice, show films, and reconfigure the equivalent of tens of thousands of pages of data at a single touch.

But, however sophisticated web and film become, ultimately, they are still graphic design: combinations of word and image.

www.etc.co.uk
Playful use of movement on a website for ETC, a furniture and space planning consultancy. The site features an office, which as you watch, is populated by staff who sit at their desks, go to the toilet, go for lunch. It is play with a serious point, illustrating the need for efficient and well-planned spaces. After they all go home, a cleaner appears. Design by Tonic Design.

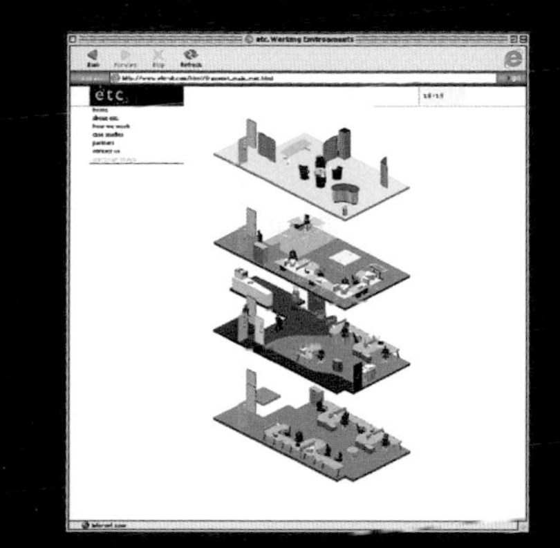

The Island of Dr Moreau
This is a stunning film sequence: the type fragments, mutates and grows ugly over a background of dilating human and animal eyes. This acts as a metaphor of the story by HG Wells, in which Moreau merges the genes of animals and men in terrible and unsuccessful experiments. Design by Kyle Cooper at Imaginary Forces.

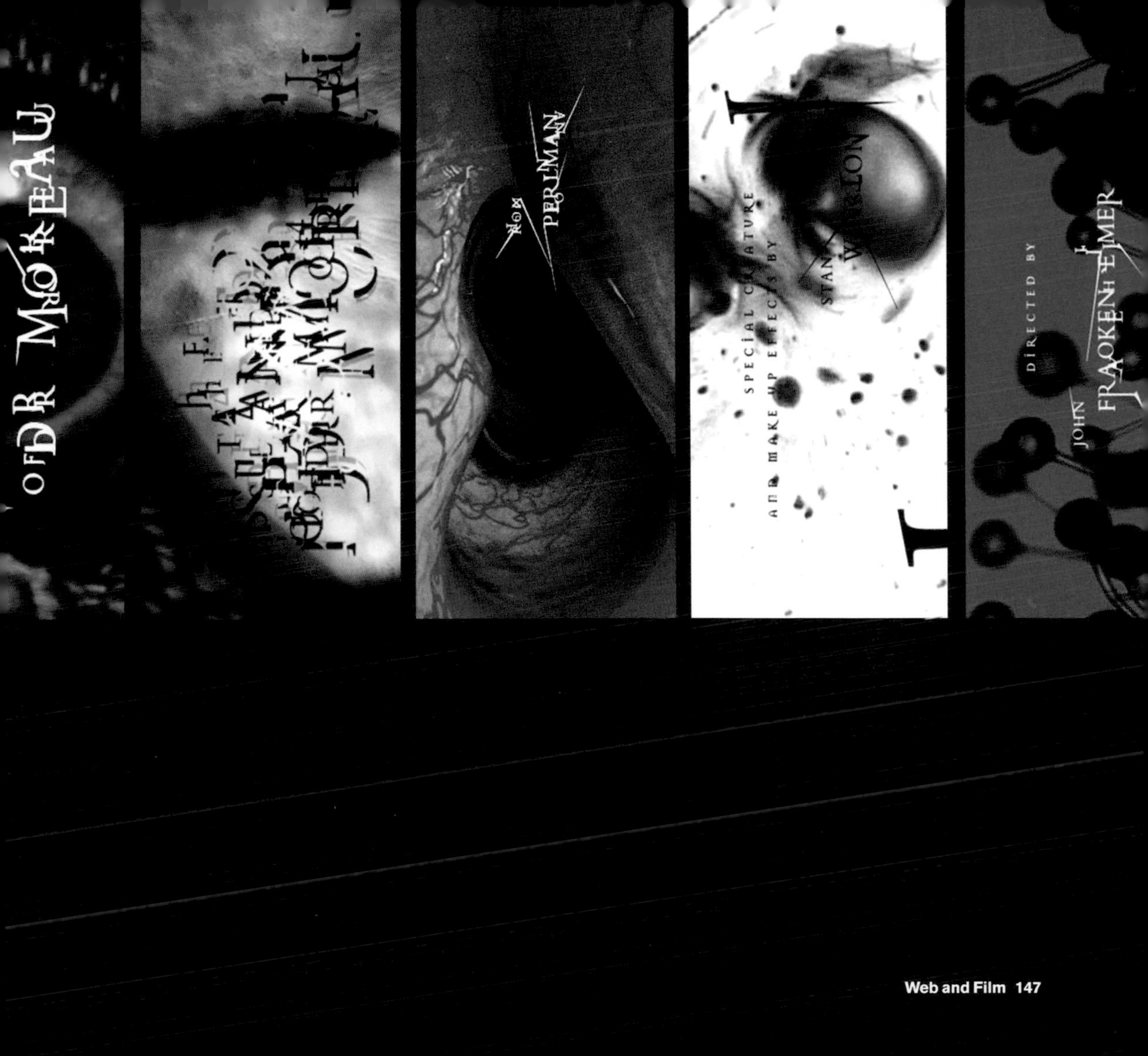
OF DR MOREAU
PERLMAN
DIRECTED BY
JOHN

Portfolios

The portfolios of work that follow have been chosen to illuminate the highly varied ways in which designers work. Some studios are well-known, and have enjoyed extensive international exposure – others have not. Where possible I have featured studios in their early stages of development, so that their principles are young and perhaps closer in age to the student readership of this book. I have also included a selection of studios with women at the helm.

As with examples in previous chapters, this section cannot hope to be representative in any thorough or comprehensive way. Of the myriad designers and design studios, this selection is intended to be viewed as a particular sample – one that highlights two features of practice: how to create an environment which allows the designer to bring together the uncomfortable bedfellows of creativity and business, and how to create design that allows the designers to explore their own interests.

There has been a growing trend over the last 15 years or so of giant conglomerate companies building 'media' empires. The idea is to combine public relations people, market data analysts, advertising agencies, and product and graphic design studios into a vast, interconnected group that can service a client's every marketing and media need. It is very common now for a studio that has reached a certain size and level of maturity to be sold for a huge sum by the founder/owners. In the future this may happen to some of the studios featured here – the allure of increased wealth is great.

However, I am not suggesting that creating good work is impossible within a business run entirely for the benefit of its shareholders. Design magazines and awards annuals prove that a particular kind of ownership of a design studio is not clearly or strictly related to the quality of its design. Conversely, designer-owned studios can churn out work that is kitsch and impervious to the world around it.

For me, within the confines of this book, it is rather a matter of thinking of things from the designer's point of view. Why does a person want to be designing in the first place? To post huge profits for – and take instructions from – shareholders they will never meet? Or to pursue a far more idiosyncratic and personal path? What scale and type of practice best serves the individual?

The idea of giving the same project and brief to ten designers and each one coming back with ten completely different solutions is nothing new. But why is this? Each studio featured here focusses on a specific area of interest with a particular set of ideas. Philippe Apeloig concentrates almost entirely on the communication and branding needs of cultural organisations through the medium of posters. His abiding interest is in letterforms – fragmenting and exploring their shapes and the way they combine into words. Ellen Lupton combines graphic design with her work as one of the medium's most important and influential historians and curators. Number Seventeen work with television networks and combine a love of popular culture with comic surrealism. Each of these designers has found an avenue they feel a need to pursue – one made up of graphic problems they view as personally intriguing, that they solve in a way they find personally satisfying.

Some of the studios and designers on the following pages offer manifestos explaining how they see the world and what motivates them in what they do. In most cases I have drawn my own conclusions from careful examination of their work.

In the previous section, I looked at how impersonal the basic ingredients of graphic design are and how all designers come to their material second-hand. But the plethora of decisions that the designer needs to make in each fresh combination – level of irony, tone of language, exact tone of colour, placing and size of type and so on – renders the result as personal as a fingerprint.

The studios are sequenced in alphabetical order, which is the only reason Atelier Works comes first. I included us because, just as I pass judgement on numerous designers throughout the course of this book, it is only fair that I present myself for the judgement of others.

Atelier Works

It is perhaps best to quote someone writing about Atelier, rather than describe us myself. Hugh Pearman said:

"They know what they're about, these people. They think a lot about who they are and what they are doing. They are among the most self-aware set of designers I have ever come across, conscious of where they stand in design history, who and what their influences are, how they relate to others in the same field. Hearing them dispassionately analysing themselves, you realise that this must be exactly the quality they bring to their clients.

"Their output is certainly not about purveying a house style, an instantly recognisable signature. To do that, they believe, is to restrict yourself. If you become known for a signature style, you will only ever interest people who like that style: you also put yourself at the mercy of changing fashion. And Atelier Works is not about fashion. For all their ranks of computers, their approach seems almost old-fashioned, craft-based."

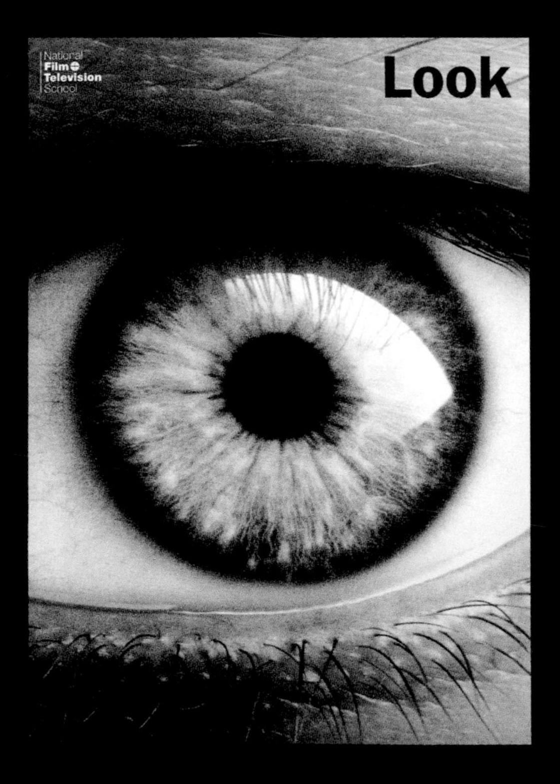

both television and films.
The back cover shows a lens – a mechanical eye. The transformation is from watcher to maker.

Right: Volkswagen corporate Christmas card
Santa on the staff.
(Originally the badge said 'Gift Meister' until it was pointed out that gift in German means poison.)

Right: Exposed
A catalogue for an exhibition of Victorian paintings at the Tate Britain gallery. It has a 'belly-band' protecting the modesty of the woman on the cover. To open the catalogue you have to expose her.

Below: Cut book
Richard Morrison – one of the best, most experienced 'sting' and film-intro makers in Britain – wanted to show some of his collection of photographs of street material: quickly taken shots of defaced signs, torn and overlapped posters and violent graffiti that he uses as a kind of sketchbook of starting points for his work. These pictures are combined with out-takes from four of his typographic film intros. The material can be viewed page by page, showing how Richard evolves and uses the energy of his snapshots in his work. Then, by using the flick book, the type can be viewed as it appears on screen.

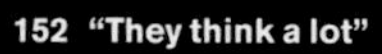

Exposed
The Victorian Nude
TATE
TATE
ARTFUL

Pride in our carpentry skills
For centuries the Master Carpenter has been creating masterpieces such as the magnificent roof of Westminster Hall and countless fine timber-framed houses throughout the country.
Just as a furniture expert will recognise a piece of Hepplewhite, often a Master Carpenter is able to look at timber work and identify the craftsman who produced it. Certain decorated bosses are as distinctive as a signature.
Every Master Carpenter serves an apprenticeship of up to seven years which instils in them great respect for the traditions of the trade. Understandably they treasure their hand tools, often making their own for timber work that is impossible to do by machine. And once made, they hang on to them for life, handing them down the generations from Master to apprentice.
Pride in our skills
1 Boxwood rule A simple but essential piece of equipment for the carpenter. It should be of the highest quality and is a prized possession in the kit of many an older joiner.
2 Centre bits Used for boring across the grain of the wood, metal centre bits are placed in a cranked brace which is revolved by hand.
3 Marking gauge For marking mortice holes and a line parallel to an edge. The stock is locked by a thumb screw often faced with brass to protect against wear. A spur at the end of the stem marks the line.
4 Wooden spokeshave Shapes and finishes the edges of timbers. It has a round sole for concave work and a flat sole for straight and convex work.
5 Chisel The long thin blades are for cutting deep and shallow recesses and for general paring and chamfering. The blades can be rectangular or bevelled to give clearance.
6 Rasp Available with many different textures, this coarse file is used for rough or secondary shaping prior to the final sanded finish.
7 Smoothing plane As its name implies the smoothing plane, which really superseded the axe and the adze, is used chiefly for final smoothing before sanding after initial preparation with a jointer or jack plane.
8 Gouge Also described as curved face chisels, gouges cut and smooth grooves and hollows. Cabinetmakers' gouges have blades with parallel sides whilst carvers' gouges can also be fishtailed.
9 Woodboring augers For boring holes from 1/4 to 1 1/2 inches in diameter both with and across the grain of the wood. The spiral form automatically removes the waste.
10 Tenon saw The tenon saw has triangular-shaped teeth known as peg teeth. It is used for general benchwork, especially when cutting joints. The blade is stiffened with a bar of iron or brass.
HISTORIC PROPERTY RESTORATION LTD
Historic Property Restoration Limited
tel 0117 9721323 fax 0117 9721324
regional offices nationwide
Pride in our leadworking skills
Pipes, drains, gutters and roofing have been the province of the skilled plumber since Roman times. Plumbing is the art of controlling water: taking it where it is needed and then taking it away. For hundreds of years lead was the only metal used and the title "plumber" is taken from plumbum, the Latin for lead. Prior to modern-day safety practices, craftsmen working in lead were given a pint of milk a day to combat the calcium-stripping properties of this ancient metal.
In spite of the use of other materials such as aluminium and copper, lead remains the traditional metal for difficult or ornate roofs such as domes or spires. It is malleable, allowing a plumber with the necessary skill and creativity to boss or mould it without wastage. Applied properly, it lasts the lifetime of a building and reflects the true art of plumbing.
Pride in our skills
1 Measuring tape For the precise measurements vital to the plumber.
2 Plumber's solder Used with a blowlamp to create wiped soldered joints that are as strong as the pipe itself. The solder is heated and when the right quantity and consistency has been applied to the jointing position it is moulded and wiped into shape with a moleskin wiping cloth.
3 Branch gimlet Also known as a gouge or pipe opener. A steel tool with a wooden hand grip, it is used for boring holes in the walls of lead pipes.
4 Hatchet bit soldering iron Made of good-quality smooth forged copper, the end is tapered to a heat-retaining edge which allows the metal to be worked for a longer period. Designed for exposed positions where heat would quickly dissipate or in areas where a naked flame cannot be used.
5 Small boat level A small spirit level used by plumbers to produce the precisely horizontal and vertical work that is essential to their craft.
6 Slate rip For removing split or broken slates. Designed to slide under the slate, the nails are pulled out with the hooked end, allowing the slate to be eased out from under its overlaying neighbours. Refixing is done with a copper strip or tingle.
7 Snips An appropriately named tool for cutting metal.
8 Dresser Ideally made of boxwood, the dresser has a flat beating surface and a round top extending into a handle. It is used for dressing or flattening out the surface of sheet lead.
9 Wooden mallet Normally made from a hardwood such as box, this hammer has a Malacca cane handle and a smooth, lathe-turned head. It is used for bossing, or moulding lead to the required shape.
10 Straight bit soldering irons The forged end tapers to a point for intricate soldering.
GRADE D
HISTORIC PROPERTY RESTORATION LTD
Historic Property Restoration Limited
tel 0117 9721323 fax 0117 9721324
regional offices nationwide

Right: Royal Society of Arts (RSA) annual review
The RSA's own Royal Designers for Industry were commissioned to provide typographic illustrations of the various activities of this venerable institution. One of its central principles is to honour diversity.

Opposite: Tool posters
Historic Property Restoration is the working arm of English Heritage – a workforce of skilled craftsmen who rennovate and restore the historic buildings. Life-size photographs of the craftsmens' tools, many of them specially made, represent their ancient crafts.

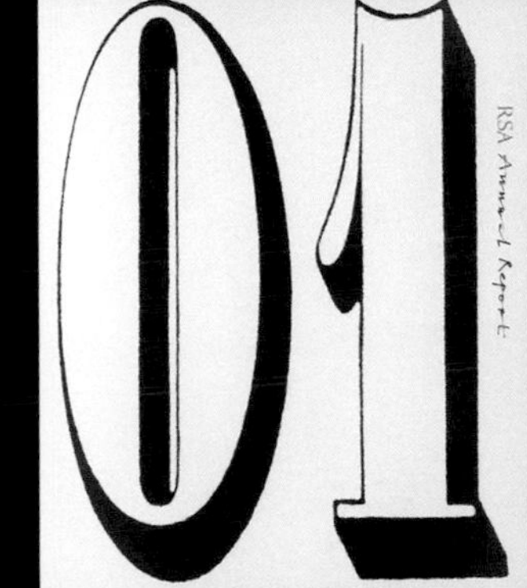

Lectures 2000-2001

LECTURES

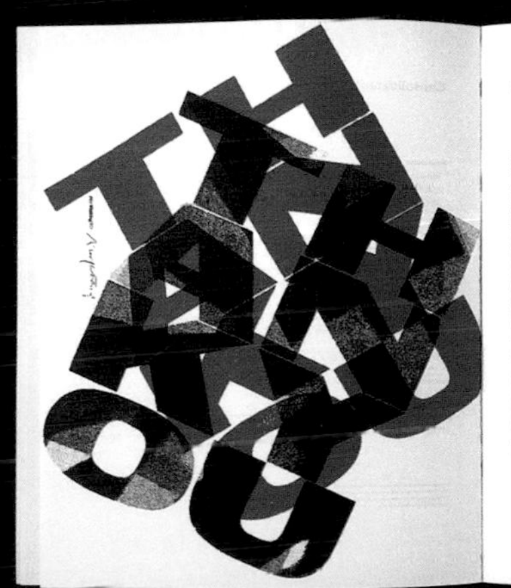

Development

the wine. As the level drops, it sinks down through the die-cut glass.

Opposite:
Sex Life of the Alphabet
Poster for a lecture given by the author – the capital letter 'Q' becomes a metaphor for the sex act.

RSA - Chardonnay - 2000
Vin de Pays du Jardin de la France
Mis en bouteille par les producteurs.
Vinival L'Oucheteau. 44330.
Vallet. France. Produce of France.
12%vol 75cl e

Sex life of the alphabet

A talk by Quentin Newark
of Atelier Works for TypoCircle

at Ammirati Puris Lintas
25 Soho Square London W1
on 27 April at 7.30pm
tickets from patrick.baglee@r-t-s.co.uk

and at Copthorne Hotel
Quayside Newcastle-upon-Tyne
on 6 May at 7.15pm
tickets from Gillian Smith 01482 325503

Philippe Apeloig

Philippe Apeloig writes: “My interest lies more with text than with images. I am fond of neither distraction nor decoration. In my posters, my goal is to obtain a maximum of effects using a minimum of means, in order to guarantee their success as communication. I personally pay a lot of attention to the poise of shapes.

“Typography is the very essence of drawing: a balance between full and empty, light and shadow. It is a discipline halfway between science and art, an exact and arbitrary material, functional and poetic.

“I love modern typography, its experimental, even clumsy nature. It comes alive when it is a little awkward and fragile. In that case, the artist’s sensitivity blossoms and overflows in the most original or radical fashion. Graphic designers who resort to typography as a means of expression define design in its fullest sense as a blend of form and concept. I prefer to leave all the dry and boring rigor to the technicians.

“Of course, graphic design is a form of art. However, the basic objective of the graphic designer is communication. The poster is a popular image which belongs to the urban environment. People pay attention to a poster for less than a minute. So, the visual impact on the public must be strong, and the concept must be predominant.

“To make the ideas come to me, I keep my eyes peeled, I make mental notes of what I see every day in the street, in museums and in books. The ideas crop up later depending on the subject to be handled, the question asked of me and the speed with which I am expected to supply an answer.

“I like it when a poster gives the illusion of movement. An impression of spontaneity should remain, even if it takes meticulous control. Most of the time I start with the text, the typeface, and then move on to the images. I use film-editing techniques, ‘cutting’ my ideas into pieces which I then reassemble in a different order. I work on them until the composition freezes and seems strong enough.”

Left: Coexistence Exhibition organised by the Museum on the Seam, Jerusalem, and a self-portrait of Philippe Apeloig. Photo by Ronald Monk, 2001.

Opposite: Fais ce qu’il te plaît (Do whatever you want) Invitation card for Philippe Apeloig’s lecture at the Galerie Anatome, Paris. Abstract letterforms dissolve into pure form.

les rendez-vous mensuels des rencontres internationales de lure
à la galerie anatome mercredi 16 mai 2001

Clockwise: Au cœur du mot (Inside the word)
Book about Apeloig's work, published by Lars Müller.

Musées s'affiche
Invitation card for the exhibition of Apeloig's work at the Maison Française, New York University.

Au cœur du mot
Poster for the exhibition of Philippe Apeloig's work at the Galerie Anatome, Paris.

Opposite: Celebrating the poster
Poster for a group exhibition at the Eastern Kentucky University.

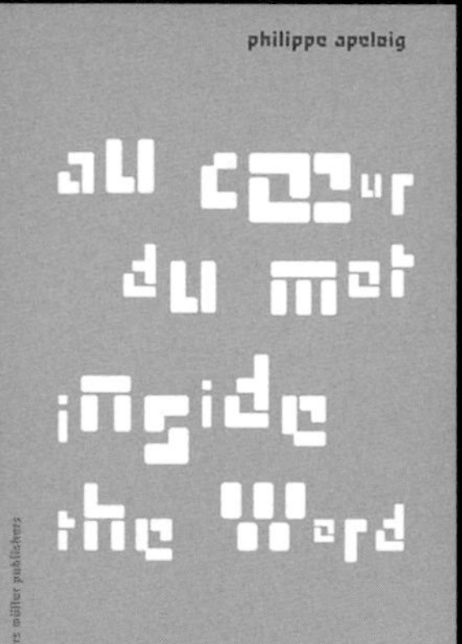

PHILIPPE
APELOIG
LE
MUSÉE
S'AFFICHE
POSTERS
FOR
MUSEUMS
PHILIPPE
APELOIG
LE
MUSÉE
S'AFFICHE
POSTERS
FOR
MUSEUMS

La Maison Française of New York University February 26-March 29, 2001 Monday-Friday 10 am-6 pm

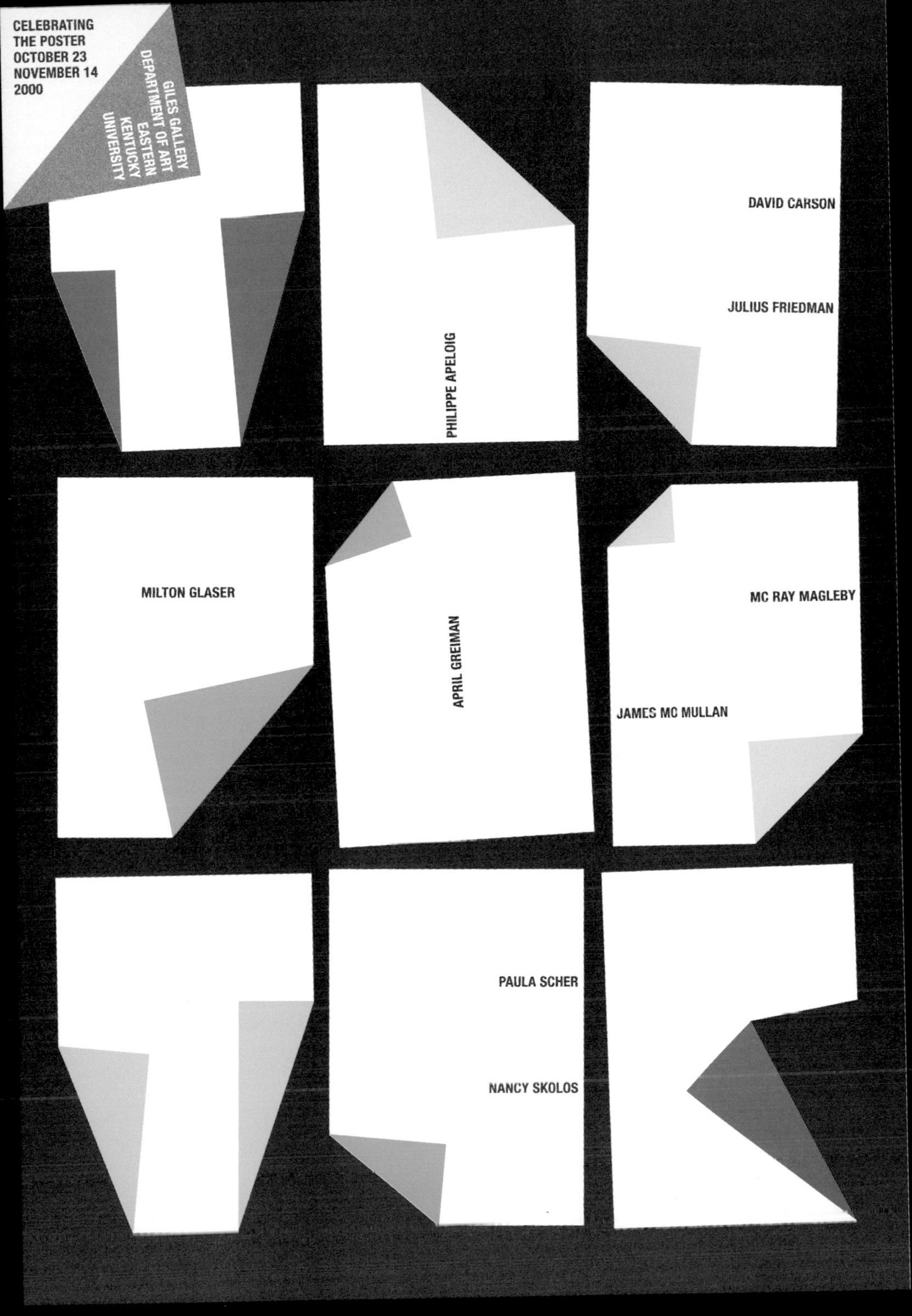
CELEBRATING
THE POSTER
OCTOBER 23
NOVEMBER 14
2000
GILES GALLERY
DEPARTMENT OF ART
EASTERN
KENTUCKY
UNIVERSITY
PHILIPPE APELOIG
DAVID CARSON
JULIUS FRIEDMAN
MILTON GLASER
APRIL GREIMAN
MC RAY MAGLEBY
JAMES MC MULLAN
PAULA SCHER
NANCY SKOLOS

Left to right and opposite: Le regard de Toni Morrison (Toni Morrison's glance)
Variations and final design of a poster for the book festival, La Fête du Livre, Aix-en-Provence 2001. Apeloig searches for the right relationship of type to image.

Fête du Livre
L e R
e g a r
d d e
T o n i
M o r r
i s o n
18-21 octobre
2001
Cité du Livre
Aix-en-Provence

The Anatomy Lesson The Anatomy Less en Zuck er m an N o v e d

Counterlife The Counterl fe The

Deception Decep on Pa tr i m o ny P o r of D e s

Sabbath's Theater Sabbath's T eater G ood re T h e

a communist Married a Com mun s t a t o m y

Goodbye Columbus and Five Short Stories by e Zuck e r m a

When She Was Good When She Was Goo P ort n o u n d T

Goodbye Columbus and Fi ve y 's Com p ai n t n t e r

When She was good The G re a t n m t f e

The Great American Novel Amer ic o of De si r e F a c t

My Life as a Man The Zuca n r P n B ou n o r t i

The Anatomy

Below and opposite:
The Roth Explosion
Poster for La Fête du Livre. The writer Roth's face is portrayed as pure language. Photo by Nancy Crampton.

Right:
Programme Musique
Brochure for the auditorium of the Louvre Museum season. Apeloig avoids the usual music stave and bass clef clichés, instead creating type to reflect a discordant blast of jazz.

Browns

Browns is three young men: Jonathan Ellery, Graham Taylor and Michael Turner. They met and worked together at a bigger studio and then left to form their own for the reason that most designers do – the satisfaction of being masters of their own destiny. The majority of their work is editorial. They manage large amounts of text and pictures in sequence for magazines, annual reports and brochures. Their clients vary widely from cultural organisations and construction firms to pharmaceutical companies and charities. Their editorial skills transfer very readily to their other prolific area of work – photography books, of which there is a rapidly growing stack. Their branding and identity work is also increasing and the Browns studio has swollen to about 12 people.

Their approach often pivots around the communicative power of a photograph. For some projects they do background work, considering various ideas for the picture or sequence, finding the right photographer and then briefing and commissioning. For other briefs, the photographs have already been taken, as in the project shown here. In these instances, the issue is about dealing with preconceived or found material: choosing; balancing; cropping and interfering appropriately with type.

They have a way of dealing with the surreal. The photography they use is often cosmetic and ordinary – straight shots of the subject, with a deep field of vision. But the content plays against this apparent straightforwardness – a bowl of sausage meat becomes a row of dildos; a man mends the head of his robot wife; the scrawny, dead man who is in fact sunbathing. The energy and shock generated by these images was first discovered, or invented, by the Surrealists nearly a century ago. It belongs in dreams, in moments where the ego lets some of the irrationality, sexuality or infantility of the id leak in.

European clichés 2000
The photographer Martin Parr is famous for his cruel and lurid pictures that expose the bizarre and unintended. Browns take the work one step further and force pictures together to create disturbing associations.

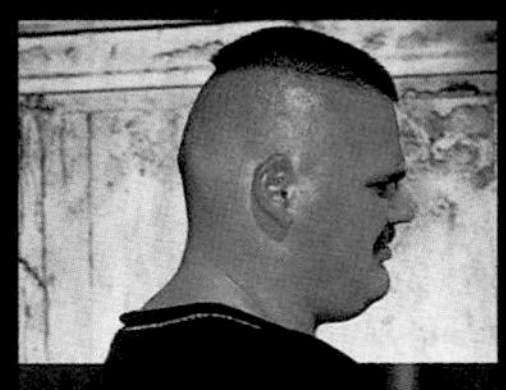

Coney Island
1969 – 1986
Bruce Gilden
Photography by © Bruce Gilden / Magnum
Published by Trebruk
Designed and produced by Browns / London
Printed by Westerham Press

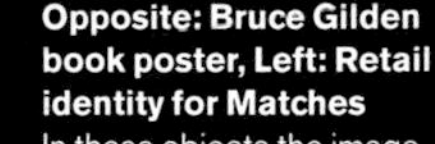

Opposite: Bruce Gilden book poster, Left: Retail identity for Matches
In these objects the image is pronounced and the typography done away with. For Bruce Gilden's poster it is converted into handwriting, and it is absent on the shopping bags altogether. Some designers would feel a need to imprint themselves on the work, competing with the photographer. Browns have more humility, sacrificing their presence in order to make the end result purer and more potent.

Overleaf: Spread from Communicators in Business magazine
Polite typography contrasts with the horror of the picture.

Information overload

Veteran scriptwriter and corporate producer Charles Hewitt fears the citizens of the digital age are approaching a point of critical mass. Photograph by David Stewart.

Cahan Associates

First there was the word. Bill Cahan puts his method like this: "Companies often have a lot to say but don't necessarily know how to say it. As a result, they're not looking for a designer. They're looking for someone who can uncover their story and communicate it. We feel a big part of our job is paring down information to form compelling and accessible messages."

Cahan sees design as message, not as a layout. His starting point is always text. The quality and impact of his writing is astonishing and almost unique in the dreary, predictable arena of American corporate annual reports.

Most studios that produce annual reports do very little with the content the client puts forward. Cahan says: "The content is nasty, boring, impossible to penetrate. It's white papers, analysts' reports, technical documentation... I think that our people have to write it themselves, otherwise they won't understand how to solve the problem... we suffer a lot. It's like a root canal without anaesthesia, trying to get the right word, the right juxtaposition to get your idea across."

An usual feature of how the studio operates is internal competition. Often two or three design teams will produce approaches for the same project. These are presented to the client, and one direction is chosen. The designer whose work is selected then handles the project to the conclusion. One experienced designer points out that this can cause friction – "I have seen a lot of people come and go."

Cahan sells the provocative work of his 15-strong studio like this: "If an annual report isn't entertaining, it isn't informative. If it isn't compelling enough to read, then you've lost the end-user, so you've got to do something that's a little bit different and, at the same time, there needs to be a strategic message."

Stiff cover
The red report for Vivus, the makers of a drug that cures erectile disfunction, uses embarrassment and incongruity for its effect. The copy line on the cover is the last thing you would ever expect to find on an annual report – you can't quite believe what you are reading and you have to open it.

CAUTION:

READING THIS ANNUAL REPORT
MAY CAUSE AN ERECTION

IMPOTENCE IS

OPTIONAL

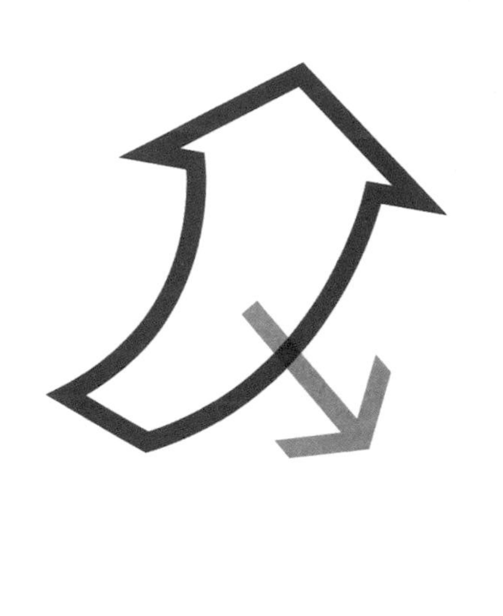

LOCAL

PROBLEM

LOCAL

SOLUTION

In 1997, VIVUS established MUSE® (alprostadil) in the United States as a first line therapy for treatment of erectile dysfunction: MUSE was launched in January of 1997 and by the end of the year, more than 825,000 prescriptions were written and 8 million units sold, thus establishing MUSE in the United States as a leading treatment for erectile dysfunction by urologists and as one of the top 35 most successful first year pharmaceutical products ever.

Local problem, local solution. Experts agree that for many men erectile dysfunction is a local disorder; consequently, the transurethral delivery of treatment provided by MUSE is a novel, local solution to this local problem. MUSE provides the patient, partner and physician a convenient and minimally invasive treatment which explains, in large part, its rapid acceptance and use in 1997.

Alprostadil safety and efficacy. First licensed as a pharmaceutical in 1981, the safety and efficacy of alprostadil as a therapeutic agent is well established. Experimental intracavernosal injection of alprostadil for the treatment of erectile dysfunction began in the late 1980s and culminated with Food and Drug Administration (FDA) clearance of alprostadil for injection therapy of erectile dysfunction in 1995. VIVUS began clinical trials in 1992, and in five short years, successfully demonstrated that alprostadil also can be delivered safely and effectively via the urethra using a small, plastic applicator rather than a needle.

Novel drug delivery. MUSE uses a novel drug delivery system which consists of a single-use, prefilled plastic applicator designed for easy handling, administration and disposal. The small size of the applicator provides both patient and partner with a discreet and easy-to-use treatment option.

Opposite: Vivus report

The pages that follow the cover continue the erectile narrative, and introduce a graphic joke, and then company strategy. By the time you hit extensive text you have a very clear conception of who they are and what they do.

Left: Xilinx report

Xilinx make semiconductor chips. The cover of their 1997 annual report was jammed full of tiny text – information – and had a plastic lens to enlarge and read it. It symbolised the efficient compression of data that the chips achieve. More tiny text inside was broken up by huge road signs carrying key messages.

Founded in 1984, Xilinx is the world's largest supplier of programmable logic solutions providing electronic equipment manufacturers worldwide with faster time to market and increased flexibility. The reduced size and densely packed cover of this annual report symbolizes a Xilinx semiconductor chip, physically demonstrating our focus on increasing density while reducing the size of programmable logic devices. The attached magnifier will help you read about Xilinx leadership in silicon, software, and support. Inside, the report shows how Xilinx has established a new competitive roadmap through the programmable logic landscape.

Dear Fellow Shareholders:

In fiscal 1997, Xilinx recaptured the technological lead and stepped up the pace of innovation in the programmable logic industry. This Annual Report is purposely small. Its reduced size is meant to dramatize how Xilinx uses advanced integrated circuit (IC) technology to increase the density and reduce the size of its devices.

Throughout much of fiscal 1997, a semiconductor-wide inventory correction reduced customer demand. In addition, Xilinx was in the midst of a product transition. Our previously rapid growth slowed. By midyear, we were taking action to get back on track. First, we refocused our R&D resources on our core businesses: SRAM-based field programmable gate arrays (FPGAs) and Flash-based complex programmable logic devices (CPLDs). Second, we dramatically accelerated our adoption of leading-edge semiconductor manufacturing technology in order to increase gate densities, increase device speed, and reduce the cost per device.

These two steps enabled us to sample the industry's first 0.35 micron mixed voltage FPGAs. In addition, we shipped new logic design software and began selling ready-to-use logic cores that reduce time to market for our customers. By our fourth fiscal quarter, revenue growth had returned to historic levels. For the fiscal year as a whole, revenues grew to a record $568 million, up slightly from $561 million in fiscal 1996. Net income was $110 million, or $1.39 per share, up from $102 million, or $1.28 per share, in fiscal 1996.

Accelerating Technology Leadership

Programmable logic companies' process technology has traditionally lagged by a generation or more the IC manufacturing technology used by memory companies. This is no longer the case for Xilinx. Based on the technology roadmap we established in fiscal 1997, we are now among the most aggressive adopters of advanced IC technology in the semiconductor industry. We sampled our first products using 0.35 micron IC process technology in fiscal 1997, and we plan to introduce 0.25 micron in fiscal 1998.*

It took us ten years to increase FPGA density from 1,000 gates to 25,000 gates. Following our current technology roadmap, we believe we will make another exponential leap, from just over 25,000 to 200,000 gates, in about two years, or a quarter of the time required for the last leap.* At the same time, we are leveraging advanced IC process technology to slash product prices. For example, a 10,000-gate Xilinx FPGA that sold for more than $100 in 1994 sells for approximately $10 today.

When transistors on semiconductor devices shrink below 0.5 micron in size, the devices themselves require power supplies lower than the current standard of 5 volts. In fact, each new generation of transistor size will require a correspondingly lower voltage. Xilinx is now the only programmable logic supplier with pin compatibility between devices of different voltages. That means only Xilinx customers can replace a 0.5 micron FPGA with a higher-performance 0.35 micron FPGA without having to redesign the circuit board. Thus Xilinx FPGAs form a bridge between the technological past and future. Our customers can evolve their product designs in stages, selecting the Xilinx FPGAs that give them the best combination of density, speed, power and price.

Delivering Complete Solutions

When Xilinx pioneered FPGAs, we changed the way our customers designed and developed their products. Now we're changing the way logic itself is designed. Looking forward, customers will no longer design large-density FPGAs one gate at a time. They will integrate complex logic designs into their products at the system-level. Xilinx has a superior understanding of the system-level challenges of programmable logic. We offer complete solutions based on that understanding and partner with our customers to guide them through the complexities of submicron IC technology. In addition, as customers design products using FPGAs of 100,000 gates or more, they need more sophisticated design software. They also need pre-implemented cores of logic that help reduce time to market. Xilinx provides both types of software as part of an integrated solution. In such a challenging technological domain, field support becomes critical to assure customers that their logic devices, design software, and logic cores work together flawlessly. Xilinx provides that level of support, around the clock and around the world. The end result is that Xilinx is becoming a strategic, system-level solutions provider for many companies.

At the heart of the Xilinx solutions strategy is our XC4000X family: the highest-density, fastest-speed, and lowest-power FPGAs on the market today. We are also pushing strongly into the market for CPLDs by delivering innovative architectural features at the industry's lowest prices. During product (SEE BACK COVER)

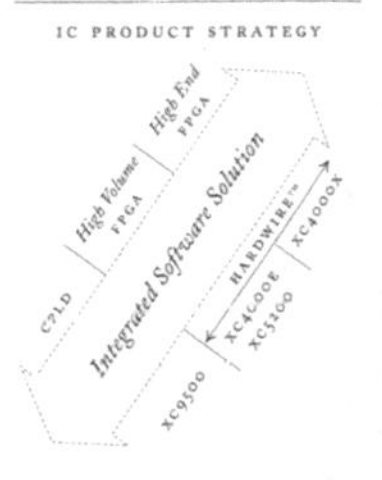

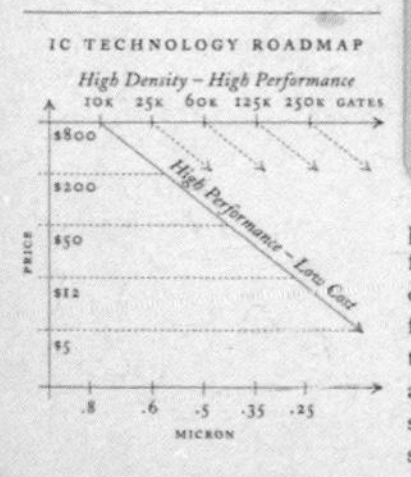

AS XILINX AGGRESSIVELY ADOPTS MORE ADVANCED PROCESS TECHNOLOGIES, THE BENEFITS TO OUR CUSTOMERS ARE TWOFOLD: NOT ONLY CAN WE BE FIRST TO MARKET WITH THE DENSEST, FASTEST AND LOWEST POWER DEVICES, BUT WE CAN MIGRATE OUR EXISTING PRODUCTS TO SMALLER GEOMETRIES, THEREBY DRAMATICALLY REDUCING THE PRICE PER DEVICE.

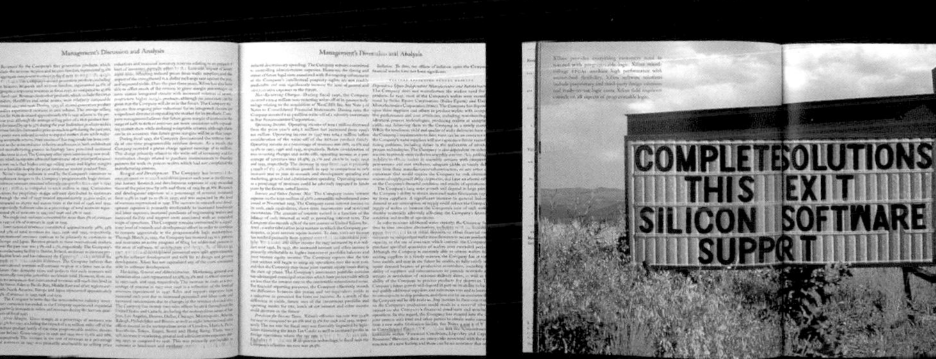

StoraEnso paper promotion
This is a tiny, thick book. Shown full size below, it is 90mm across with a 40mm spine. It rams seemingly disconnected images and words together over 544 pages. There is an explanation at the back, where each of the words is fleshed out. Private is explained so: "12,000 annual reports are produced each year, though less than two per cent of the labor force works at public companies. Should the rest of the working populations care?" To which the quick answer is 'no'. All promotional publications have to find some way of suggesting or recommending a sale, and at least this book contains itself until the last few pages. The bulk of it is an intriguing visual delight.

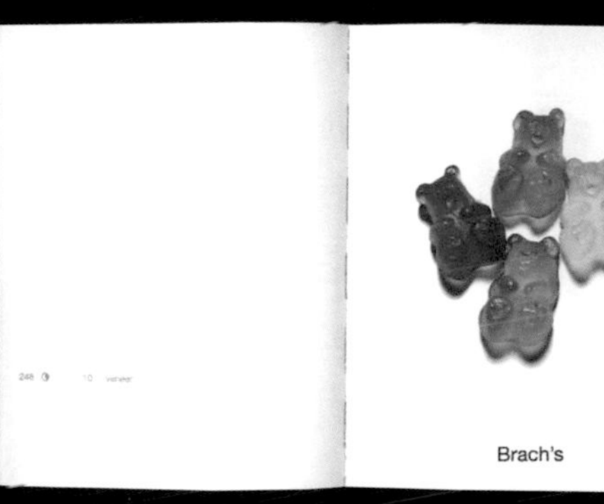

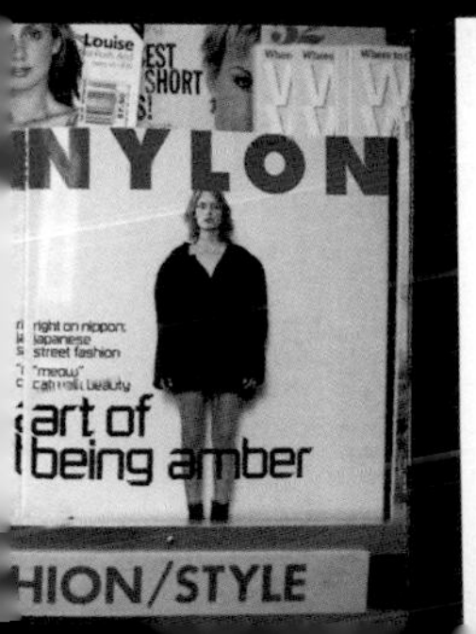

302 13 venture

490 21 color

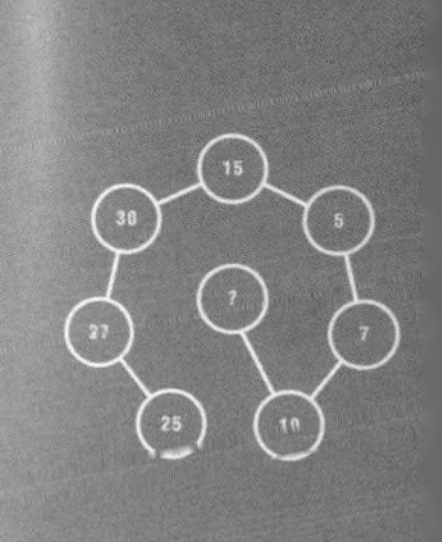

Silicon Valley Bankshares report
This begins with the familiar adage, 'it's not only what you know, it's who you know'. The bank is described by its clients, each of whom is introduced with a rolodex card. This gives a wonderful sense of an informal, practical, human relationship between them. (Although since this is Silicon Valley, surely all the details would be digital? Perhaps not.)

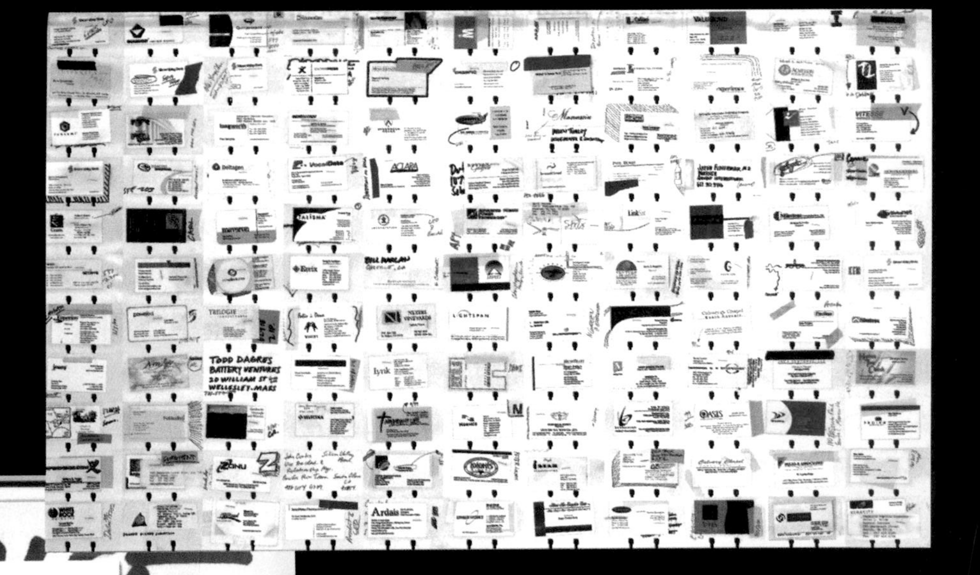

EXTERPRISE

Research Park Plaza
Building One, Suite 300
12401 Research Blvd.
Austin, Texas 78759
Main 512.597.6000
Fax 512.597.6001

Manoj Saxena
President & CEO
msaxena@exterprise.com

They're good at the kind of deals I do.

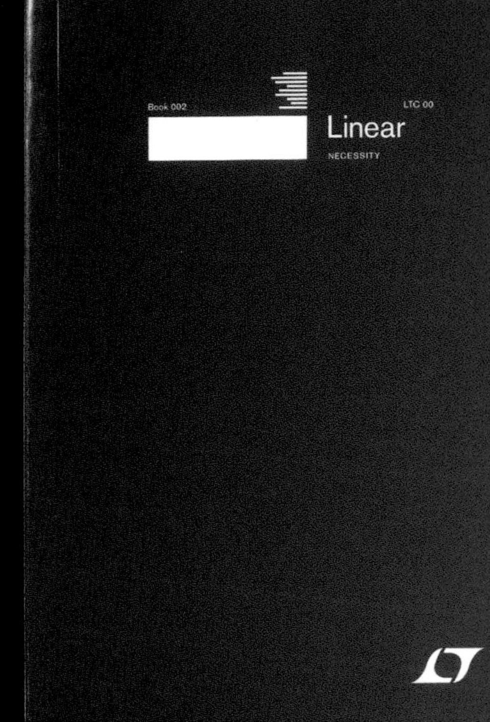

Linear Technology Corporation annual report
The tiny slip-case shown above, 160mm high, contains two books. One, called 'Linear', describes Linear's semiconductor business in a straightforward way, using a narrative text and supportive charts. As it points out, this is linear exposition. The second book, called 'Digital', transcribes digital code from one of Linear's products as a series of numbers and black lines. It is deliberately illegible (compare it to Sagmeister's book for Lou Reed on page 17). The contrast between the two Linear books typifies the worlds that the company has to move between; the linear, sequential world of human communication, and the opaque, simultaneous digital world.

Net Sales

thousands

2000 $ 705,917

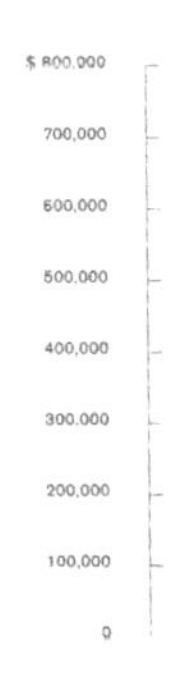

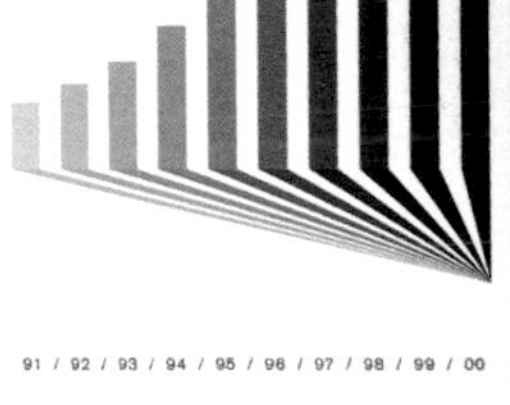

Experimental Jetset

Experimental Jetset is Dutch designers Marieke Stolk, Danny van den Dungen and Erwin Brinkers. There are repeated themes in their work that bear this out, as if each piece of design is a variation on their core beliefs and aesthetic taste. They claim to be influenced by a variety of different cultural fields: punk, Stanley Kubrick, Jean-Luc Godard, Situationism, conspiracy theories and oriental vegetarian cuisine. When considering their influences and how they crop up in their work, it it is no surprise to find that their fascination with random and automatic ways of ordering, surreal juxtaposition and eclectic combinations are all explored with tongue firmly in cheek. They have a sort of manifesto, shown here:

00.
Dutch Dogmatism. Some quick, confusing notes on our approach towards graphic design.

01.
We like to think of our approach towards graphic design as presentative rather than representative. We try to create actual objects that function within specific contexts. Whether these objects are books, installations, invitations, stamps, logotypes or websites is not important, as we approach them all as being very concrete entities.

02.
We don't like to think of graphic design in fashionable terms such as "visual communication", "information architecture" or "experience design". We think all of these terms neglect or deny the physical dimensions of graphic design by confusing the "derivatives" of design (images, experiences, information, content, communication) with the design itself. For us, a piece of design is above all an object, a physical entity. For example, even when a poster is only 1 mm thick, we still consider it an object. The image that is printed on this poster is only a small part of the design – it is the poster as a whole that matters to us.

03.
In other words, we don't create images – we create objects.

04.
As for style, we like to think our way of working is characterised by the way we analyse the context and come up with possible solutions. In that sense we have a real, outdated, hardcore, old-school modernist attitude towards designing: we still think of the design process in terms of "problems" and "solutions". Of course, we realise that the idea of one absolute, objective solution is nonsense considering the relativity and subjectivity of every given context, but that doesn't mean we are not intrigued by this strange tension that exists between the absolute and the relative.

05.
So in short, we try to extract something absolute out of something relative. And then we try to underline its physical dimensions. It may sound abstract, but it's all very concrete in our work.

Below: Maastricht Art Fair catalogue
This consists of 28 pieces of A4 paper, an A2 poster and a clear plastic bag. Every trade fair visitor seems to end up carrying bags filled with promotional material, so this catalogue in its clear plastic bag joins in.

Right: Set of three wristbands
Inspired by pop festival admission tickets. The difference with these is that they are for concerts that never happened, with dates from decades ago. Wearing one will, however, help you create an imaginary sense of what it might have been like – so evocative are the type, names and colours. The wristbands are sold through a catalogue, so if you're wearing one, you may meet someone else wearing one. Two people can then reminisce over a festival that never happened.

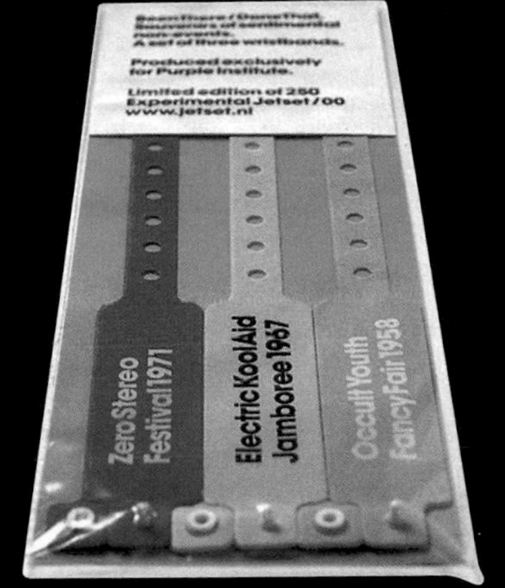

Elysian Fields catalogue
This brief for a group show of artists based on the theme of dreams, was that it should function as a book in its own right, using hundreds of images submitted by the artists. Jetset grouped the images under 'phases' of sleep, and gave them fake pseudo-scientific names like 'panoramism', 'theta twilight', and 'delta deep'. The more or less completed, unrelated images sit happily together, becoming as illogical and unpredictable in their sequence as any dream.

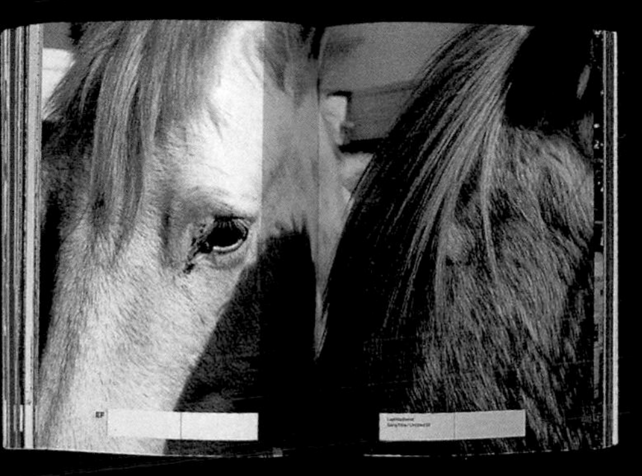

Below: Stamps for the Royal Dutch PTT
These stamps use a powerful and famous graphic device: that of replacing the word love with the image of a heart. In recent times it was made emblematic by Robert Indiana with his LOVE stamps for the US Postal Service, which used a heart instead of the 'o' in love, and then by Milton Glaser with his I LOVE NY logo. Here the Jetset play with the osscilation between word and image by using a hologram. They exploit reference – instead of being used to carry a picture of horses or aircraft, the text on the stamp refers to the stamp itself. They also play with our supposed affection for stamps – do we really love them? Is this idea not generated by the Post Office, which is of course happy to sell more of them?

Opposite: Bag for the Stedelijk Museum
Designed for the Museum shop, this bag contains an art 'item' tightly stitched into the fabric of the bag, which can't be seen until all the stitching is undone. Jetset have unified object, biography (the type is a biography of the artists) and carrier bag into one. They have also added mystery.

I ♥ POSTCARDS

I Love Stamps / Stamps Love Me.
Hologram Stamp for the Royal Dutch PTT (KPN)
Concept & Graphic Design by Experimental Jetset
Printed by Walsall Security Printers UK

Experimental Jetset
Domselaerstraat 7.3
1093 JL Amsterdam

T 31 20 4686036
F 31 20 4686037
E jetset98@xs4all.nl

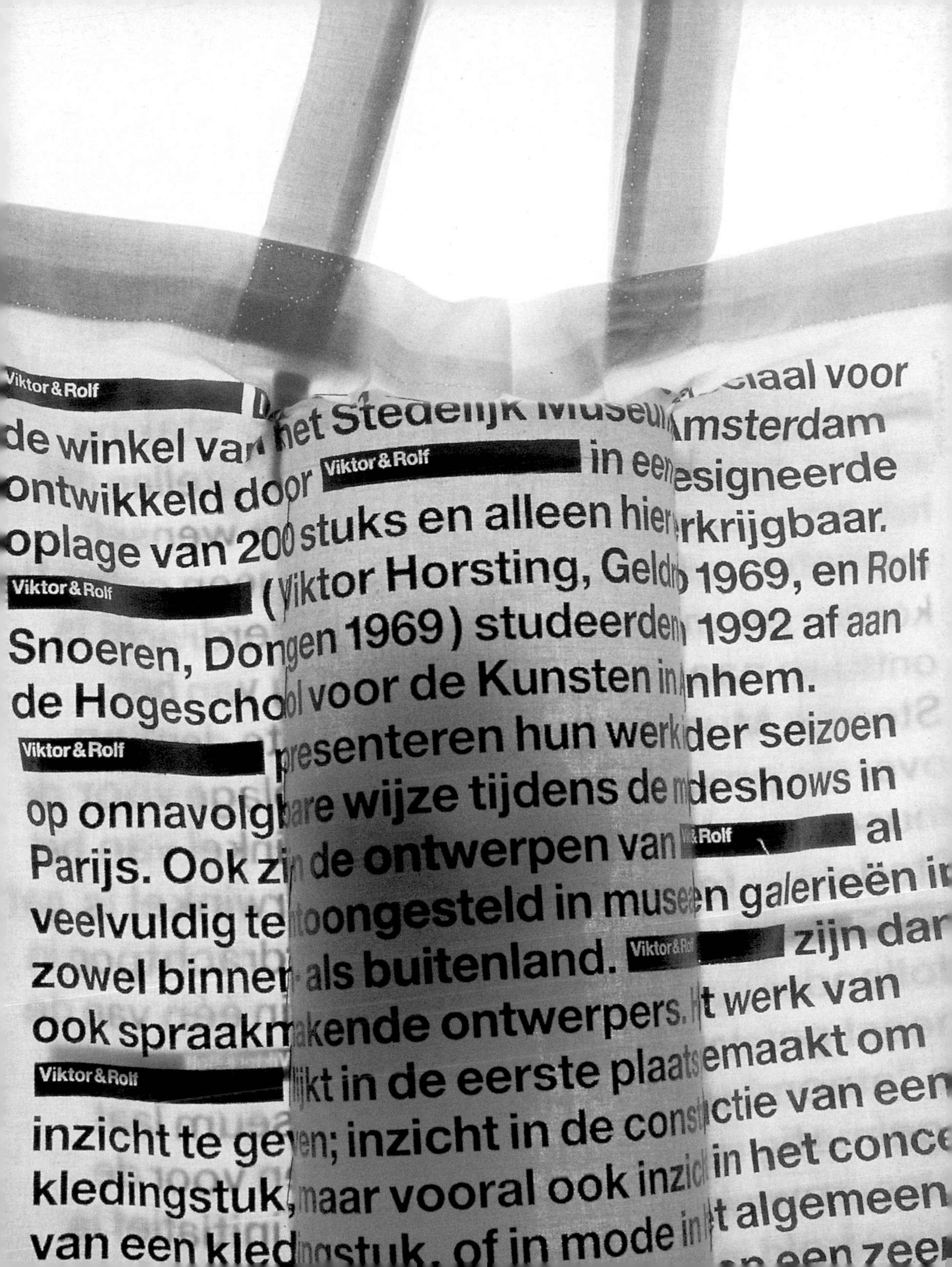

Viktor&Rolf D ... aal voor

de winkel van het Stedelijk Museum Amsterdam

ontwikkeld door Viktor&Rolf in een esigneerde

oplage van 200 stuks en alleen hier erkrijgbaar.

Viktor&Rolf (Viktor Horsting, Geld... 1969, en Rolf

Snoeren, Dongen 1969) studeerden 1992 af aan

de Hogeschool voor de Kunsten in nhem.

Viktor&Rolf presenteren hun werk der seizoen

op onnavolgbare wijze tijdens de deshows in

Parijs. Ook zi de ontwerpen van &Rolf al

veelvuldig tentoongesteld in musen galerieën in

zowel binnen- als buitenland. Viktor&Rol zijn dan

ook spraakmakende ontwerpers. t werk van

Viktor&Rolf lijkt in de eerste plaats emaakt om

inzicht te geven; inzicht in de constctie van een

kledingstuk, maar vooral ook inzic in het conce

van een kledingstuk, of in mode in t algemeen

... een zeer

An architecture catalogue

For this group exhibition, architects were invited to make recommendations on how they would alter the building in which the exhibition was held. To capture the same idea, Jetset sent blank dummies of the catalogue to all the architects, and asked them to customise and modify them. The end result uses a mélange of graphically resolved and polished versions of their ideas.

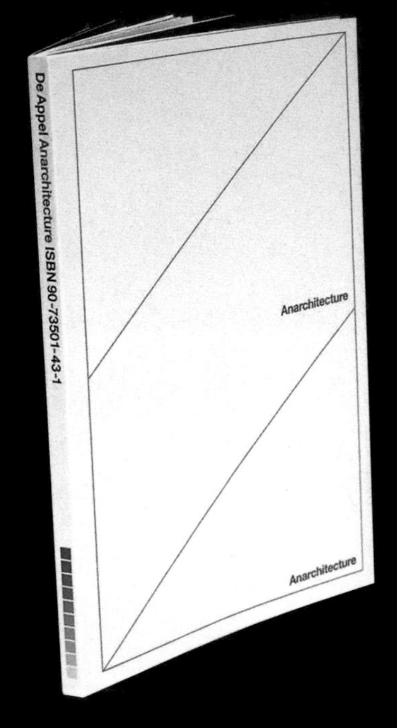

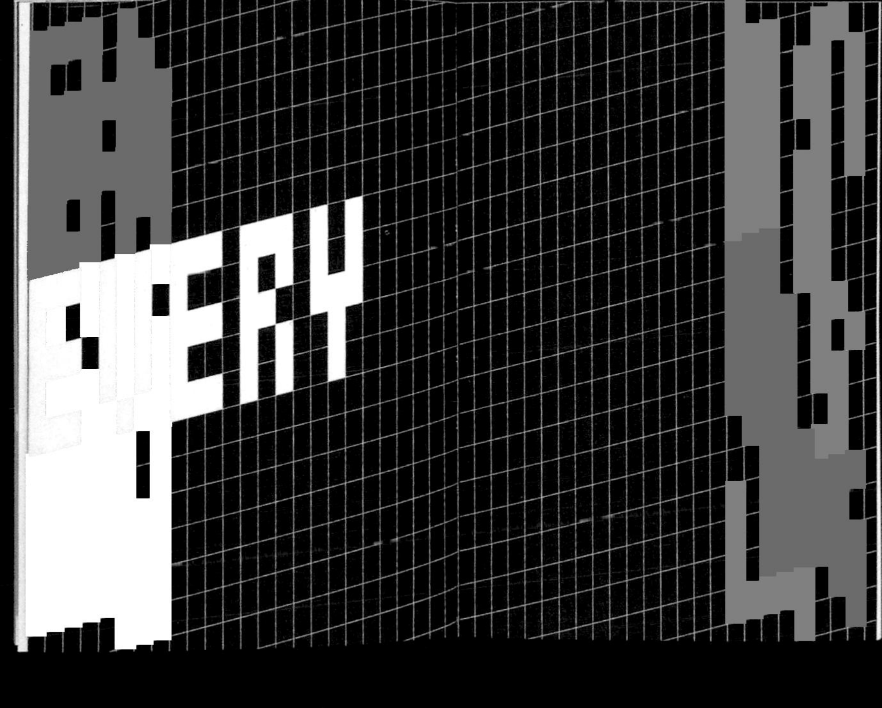

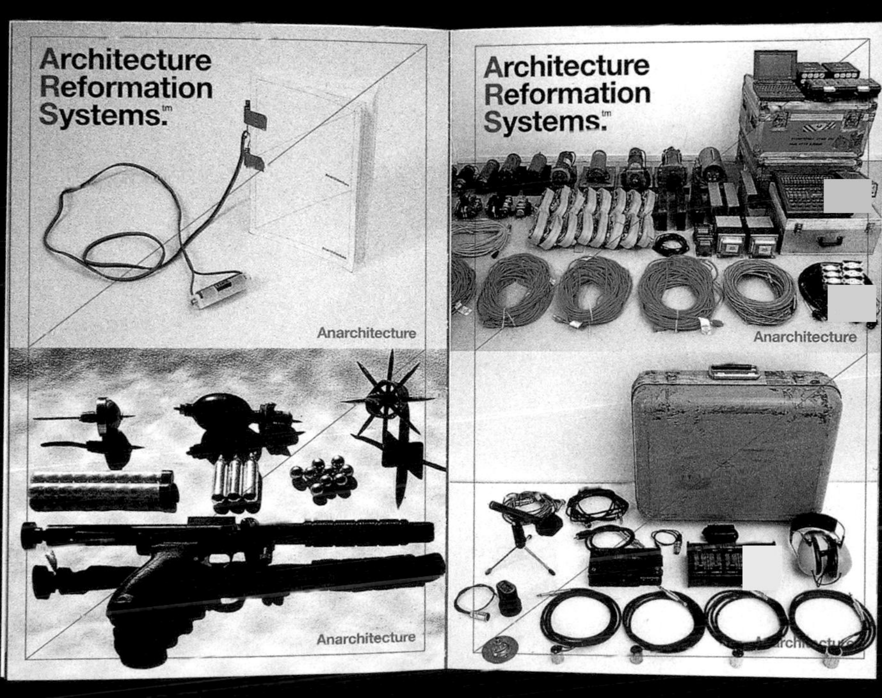
Architecture
Reformation
Systems.tm
Anarchitecture
Anarchitecture
Architecture
Reformation
Systems.tm
Anarchitecture

Rebecca Foster

Foster has taken a path that many designers follow: education, apprenticeship in a series of well-established studios, and then setting up on her own. She has run her own practice for about four years, and does almost everything on her own. She is often compelled by budget constraints to create the illustrations herself (the book covers on this spread, and the table mats and duvet covers overleaf are examples of this). If she drew her own type, rather than using existing typefaces, this process of creation would place her in a direct line of descent from Eric Gill and Milner Gray.

Foster tries to achieve a rich mix of client. Examples shown here: a cultural institution, retailer, publisher, hospital and college. This diversity prevents her from falling into a formulaic and lazy repetition of one particular approach, which is essential if she is to continue finding fresh motivation to massage and manufacture each project with the loving detail that is her stamp.

The underlying approach to all these projects is one of light-touch neo-Modernism. Everything is reduced and boiled down until the message is communicated by just two or three elements: a colour and an icon; a logo and a picture, or a spare drawing and a title. Foster's wry humour pervades her work: little secret drawings hidden in the bookcover flaps for example, and an eternity symbol as a 'g' for a book about recycling. She expects you to think just a little.

ReDesign

Redesign
A logo and dual-language catalogue for an exhibition about sustainability. Note the infinity symbol embedded within the logo.

Opposite: Cookbooks
Foster has tried to create a unified appearance to these books by choosing one typical ingredient from inside each book and rendering it in a similar way. They are resolved with deliberately spare and spacious layouts, unlike most cookery books. They appear like furniture or design publications, a preference that matches the intended readership.

wild food
from land and sea
marco pierre white

eat
2
6raphael
6raphael
6raphael

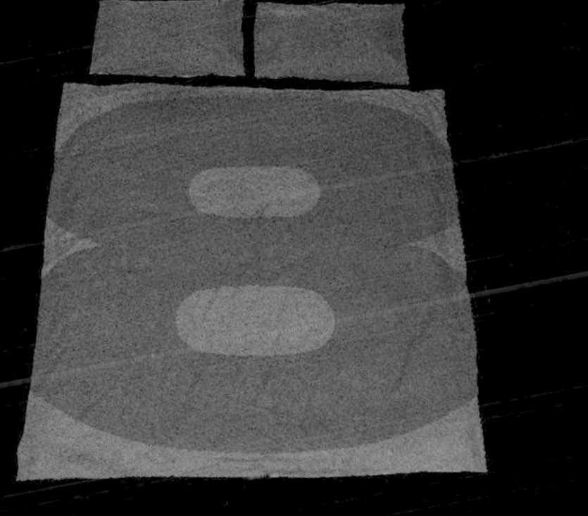

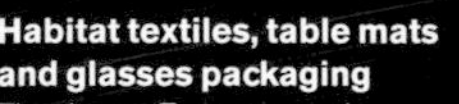

Habitat textiles, table mats and glasses packaging
The theme Foster was given for the textiles and table mats was 'life in the city'. She takes a jumble of graphic emblems from urban life, and gives them a lively feeling with garish, plastic colours. The glasses box shows a series of circles, representing glasses seen from above.

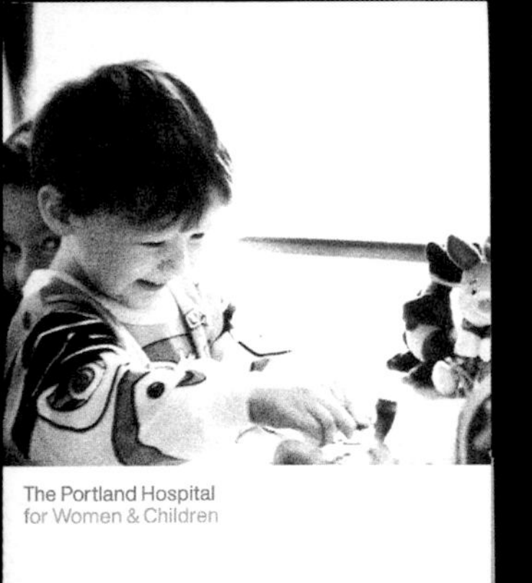
The Portland Hospital
for Women & Children
The Portland Hospital

Jessica
Sandra

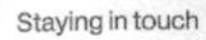
Staying in touch

Postnatal Care
The Portland Hospital
for Women & Children
Gynaecology
The Portland Hospital
for Women & Children
During Your Stay
The Portland Hospital
for Women & Children
Admission Policy
The Portland Hospital
for Women & Children
Audiology
The Portland Hospital
for Women & Children
Physiotherapy
The Portland Hospital
for Women & Children
Imaging
The Portland Hospital
for Women & Children
Fertility
The Portland Hospital
for Women & Children

PRINTMAKING
SCULPTURE

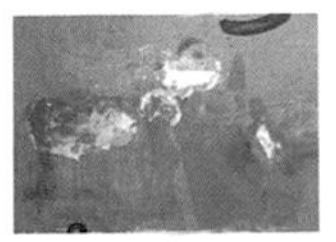

Freya Payne
Bruise, 1996. Printmaking graduate 1994.

David Hockney
A Rake's Progress. The Drinking Scene, 1961–62. Painting graduate 1962, Honorary Doctor.

Tim Mara
Wire Glass and Carrier Bag 1996. Printmaking graduate 1976, Professor of Printmaking 1990–97

Alison Wilding
Assembly, 1991 (detail). Sculpture graduate 1973, current Tutor.

Glynn Williams
Stone Bridge No. 2, 1988. Current Professor of Sculpture

Henry Moore
Draped Seated Woman, 1957–58. Sculpture graduate 192[illegible]

Richard Wentworth
Toy, 1983. Sculpture graduate 1970, current Visiting Professor.

Groovisions

This group are like the wide-eyed 'Chappie' dolls that occur repeatedly in their work – silent and anonymous. The individual designers never take credit for their work. They are never photographed. Groovisions is like a brand, a faceless corporation.*

Groovisions work in much the same territory as H5 – music and the culture that springs from music: bars, clubs and shops. At one level their work is direct. For example, with the project shown here, the basic features of the exhibition – the name, location and dates – can be easily comprehended at a glance. It is at another level, after lengthy contemplation, that the imagery of the work begins to become unsettling. Who are those blank-faced kids? Are they benign or malevolent? Why the loud-speaker/black woman? Why the giant children bestriding a city? Are they playing or destroying?

For me, as a westerner, this blend that might be described as straight-faced bizarre, is very Japanese. Lust for popular culture is quite happily mixed with more distancing and critical aspects of this same culture. The innocent youths are cousins of the manga comic heroes, but here seem used to comment, ever so obliquely, on commodification. In one Groovisions poster, Charles and Ray Eames lie laughing under chair frames they are famous for, but are they actually stapled down and trapped by them?

*I can reveal, from a secret source, that the members of Groovisions are Toru Hara, Hiroshi Ito, Karashima Izumi, Kazuhiro Saito, Kenji Sumioka and Hideyuki Yamano.

Poster for Jam Tokyo-London
A series of roughs and the final design for an exhibition poster. The development speaks for itself, the black 'Chappie' appearing as the most powerful image.

JAM: Tokyo-London
Barbican Gallery
from 10 May to 8 July 2001

Box Office:
020 7638 8891 (bkg fee)
www.barbican.org.uk/JAM

A Japan 2001 event

Sponsored by Shiseido

SHISEIDO

Barbican Centre is owned,
founded and managed by
the Corporation of London

Type and photograph
Clockwise: A boxed catalogue of Groovisions work; pal@pop CD single The Never Ending Rainbows; Saint Etienne album CD The Misadventures of Saint Etienne. Three different projects, each of which uses the same basic technique – sans serif type run over a photograph. It is not always necessary to try to invent ever more novel ways of making basic combinations. If you discover a successful formula, as long as it works for the object in hand, you avoid the risk of failure by using it.

GRV2000
©2000 GROOVISIONS
ISBN4-89369-831-1
16

bis 02
20 soundtrack songs
limited edition
bis 02 the misadventures of saint etienne
the misadventures of
saint etienne

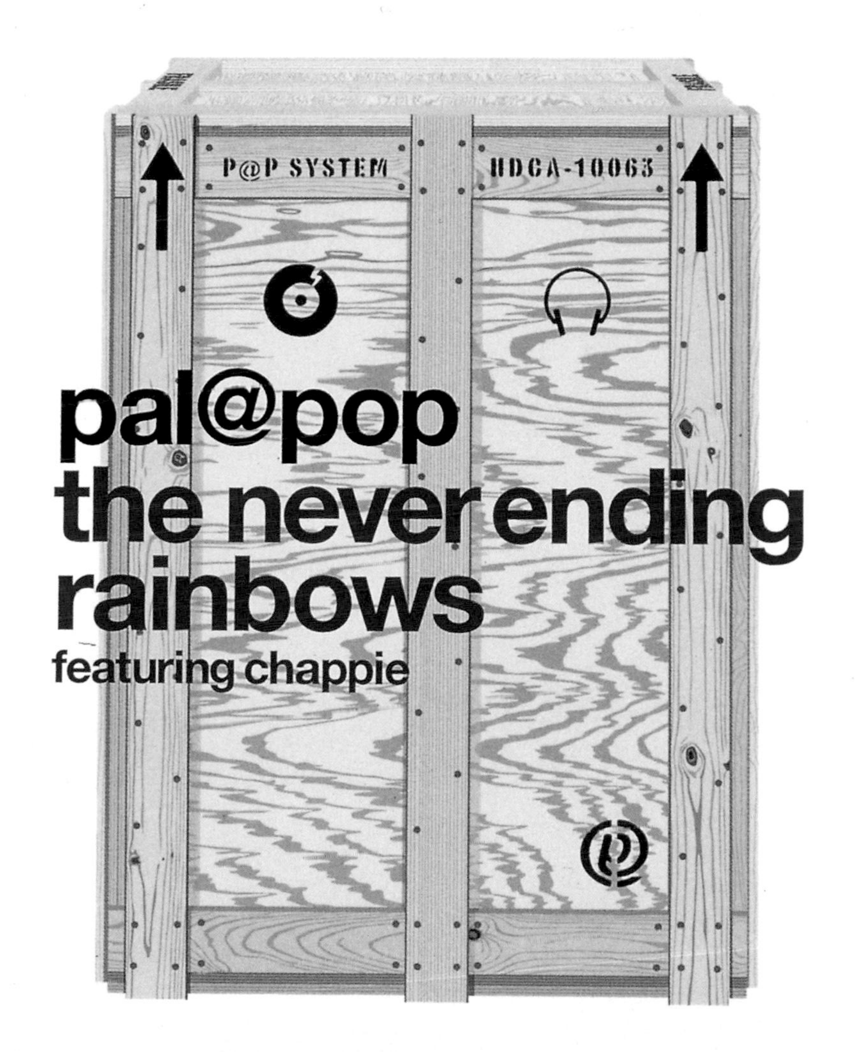
P@P SYSTEM
HDCA-10063
pal@pop
the never ending
rainbows
featuring chappie

Right: CD covers
On a Trip, by Yukihiro Fukutomi and Diary of the Headphonist, by Spanova, a grotesque version of urban life.

Opposite: Eames Design poster
Charles and Ray Eames pinioned by letters.

EAMES DESIGN

CHARLES & RAY EAMES

イームズ・デザイン展

2001.8.10(金)→9.30(日) 東京都美術館 Tokyo Metropolitan Art Museum

●月曜休館 [illegible]9月24日[illegible]は開館、翌9月25日(火)は休館。●開館時間：午前9時〜午後5時（入館は4時30分まで）

主催：東京都美術館、読売新聞社／特別後援：イームズ・オフィス／後援：アメリカ大使館、(社)日本建築[illegible]、(社)日本建築家協会、(社)日本グラフィックデザイナー協会、(社)日本インテリアデザイナー協会、(社)日本インダストリアルデザイナー協会、(社)日本ディスプレイデザイン協会、日本デザイン[illegible]、(財)国際デザイン交流[illegible]／協賛・協力：ハーマンミラージャパン、インター・オフィス、日本アイ・ビー・エム、資生堂、ビームス、日本航空／企画：アプトインターナショナル／構成[illegible]：マイスター、[illegible]アイ／会場デザイン：[illegible]CDA／グラフィック・デザイン：グルーヴィジョンズ

入場料：一般1200円、学生1000円、小・中・高生600円／お問い合わせ：東京都美術館（上野公園内）TEL 03-3823-6921（代表）

【展覧会情報】http://www.eames-design.net

"Eames Office" and the starburst logo are trademarks of Eames Office. www.eamesoffice.com

Rabia Gupta

"As a woman I have never really faced any biases where clients are concerned. More often than not the reaction to me and the work of the studio is that we look more closely at the issues and are often more particular and nit-picking than our male counterparts.

"Of course it helps to go into client meetings dressed down – they might get a shock if I turned up in black leather. (Just kidding.)

"There have been times of deep stress whilst working with printers and production people. Here the issue really is about being given the professional respect a larger, older bearded man would immediately get. But once again, the initial shock of me being a young woman wears off – and once we start talking work it all settles down. I should mention that until two years ago our studio was almost all women, and we loved it. There are eight of us full-time, and three part-time specialists. And now we have had to include a few more lesser mortals [men].

"In Mumbai [formerly Bombay] there are only about five independent design companies, and about 15 freelancers. Ours is probably one of the larger ones. However, the climate is changing, advertising agencies are starting studios up, and Wolff Olins has come over to do a project.

"In India, the concept of design being used strategically as a business aid is still fairly new, and on many occasions I find myself educating people and explaining to them the function and potential of graphic design.

"One of my key aims is to create a portfolio of work that is international in its overall level of sophistication, and in its functional strength, but yet has a distinctly Indian flavour; our use of colour, our textures, our typography. Indian visual culture is unique, it is so complex and multifaceted, I would love for Rabia Gupta Designs to contribute towards defining and putting Indian graphic design on the world map."

Art Club cards
A set of cards promoting a new art gallery: Art Club. Each card energises a quotation with an eclectic range of typefaces and typographic styles. By implication the company has an equally catholic taste in art.

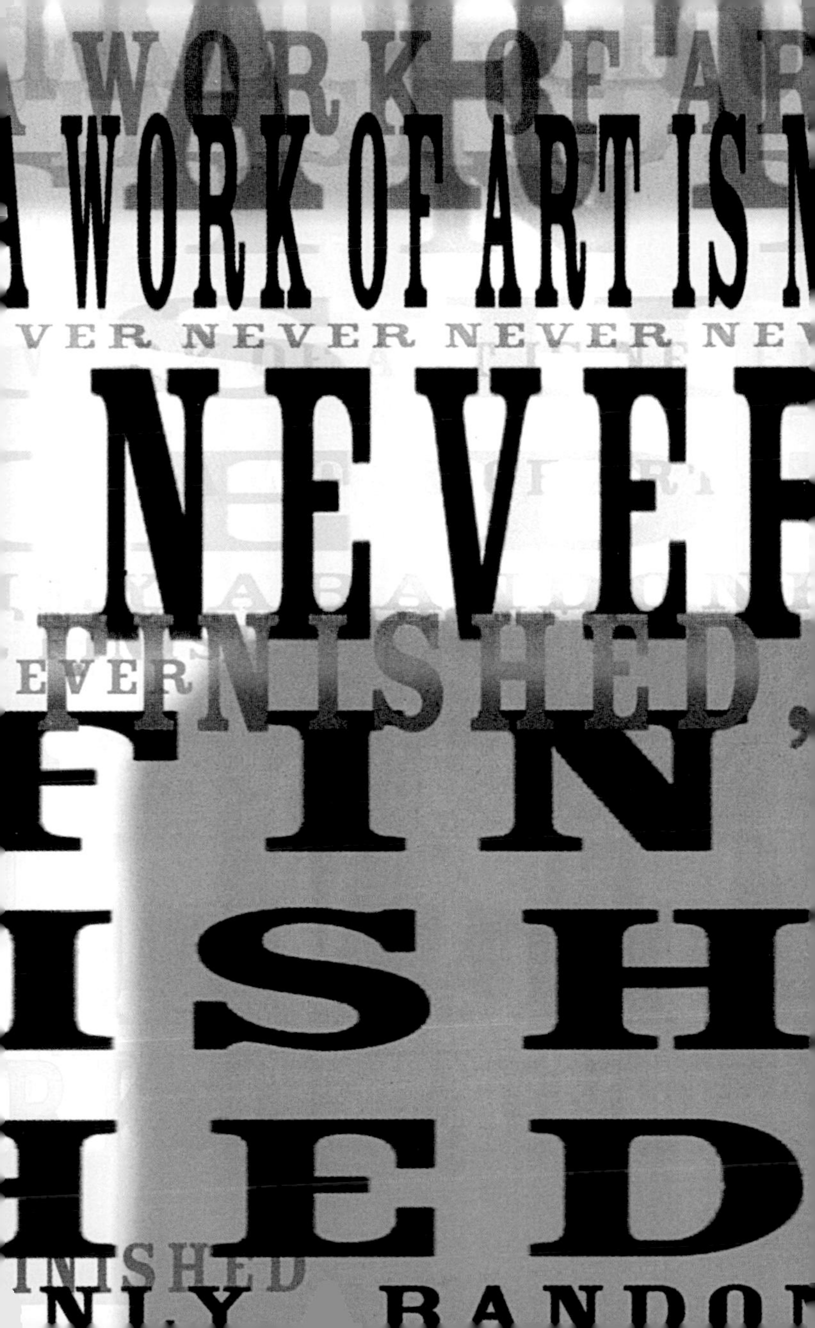
A WORK OF ART IS N
VER NEVER NEVER NEV
NEVE
FINISHED,
EVER
FIN
ISH
IED
INISHED
NLY BANDO

Kalaghoda festival
This festival takes place in a clearly defined rectangle within Mumbai. The logo picks up on this and shows it as a plan, a swirl of vibrant red cutting through the chunk of city. This also recalls the pinwheel fireworks used at every celebration in India. The actual content of the festival – plays, dance, film – is captured on the vertical banners shown here with rich, painterly juxtapositions of type and cropped, fragmented images.

KALA
GHODA
FESTIVAL 2001

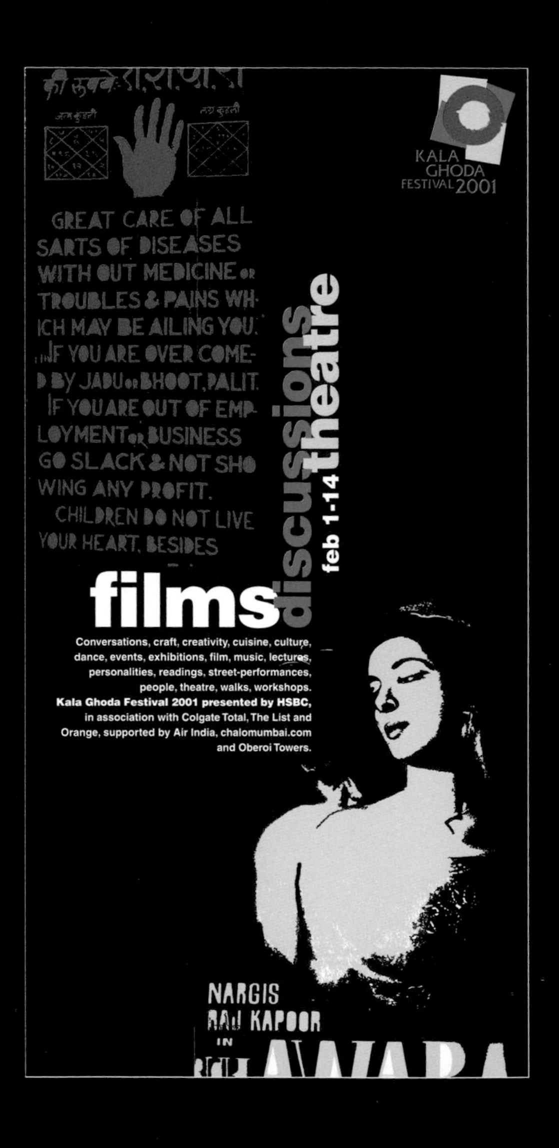

dance

Conversations, craft, creativity, cuisine, culture, dance, events, exhibitions, film, music, lectures, people, theatre, readings, street-performances, walks, workshops, personalities.

Kala Ghoda Festival 2001 presented by HSBC, in association with Colgate Total, The List and Orange, supported by Air India, chalomumbai.com and Oberoi Hotels.

music

performances

feb 1-14

KALA
GHODA
FESTIVAL 2001

heritage

architecture

art

feb 1-14

Conversations, craft, creativity, cuisine, culture, dance, events, exhibitions, film, music, lectures, people, theatre, readings, street-performances, walks, workshops, personalities.

Kala Ghoda Festival 2001 presented by HSBC, in association with Colgate Total, The List and Orange, supported by Air India, chalomumbai.com and Oberoi Hotels.

Sifar means zero, and the singer chose it as a marker of 'many beginnings and endings'. Gupta shows him as setting out on a fantastical journey, a drawn version of the musical journey described through the songs.

Below:
Peace Together logo
This mark was used for a mass peace demonstration following the Pokhran nuclear tests in 1998 by the Indian military. Hundreds of thousands, led by prominent artists, musicians, and writers, joined hands, and sang and listened to speeches. The ambiguous blend of peace dove and hands – not quite clearly resolved as either – flaps over a piece of protest-style lettering.

peace Together '98

"Good money and pretty girls", are the reasons Antoine Bardou-Jacquet gives for directing advertising films and pop music promos. H5 was set up in 1994 by Jacquet and Ludovic Houplain, a friend from ESAG (Ecole Supérieure d'Arts Graphiques). Most of their clients are in the music industry, so much of their graphic work is compressed into the miniature CD format. They describe their approach as "mélanger les genres" (mixing styles), and their sequence of CD covers illustrates this perfectly – each one is a little study of a contemporary graphic idiom.

Access to music clients gave Jacquet and Houplain their first chance to direct a promo, for a single by Alex Gopher called 'The Child'. It was about a couple racing through New York in a taxi to get to the hospital in time for the birth of their baby. The duo married type and movement to create an entire city of swirling, intermeshing typography. The striking freshness and careful execution of this project stood out and made both the film and single very successful. This has led to more offers of short films, which Jacquet is eager to take up. His idea is to build up from these and move towards directing full-length feature films, leaving graphics to the others: Houplain, Hervé de Crécy, Rachel Cazadamont and Yorgo Tloupas.

A basic requirement of H5 laid down by their clients is that the graphic flavour of the CDs be contemporary. H5 borrow the ingredients of fashionable 'supermarket-style' or 'stencil-graffitti' and apply them with aplomb. Their eclectic use of style however, shows no slavish devotion to any particular one. Their real concern is in using the language of each idiom to differentiate their projects and to make each one stand alone: a graphic blast that "comme peut l'être un logo" (acts like a logo).

Selection of CD covers
Left to right: Raw e.p. by Hideo Kobayashi; Latté e.p. by Mocca; Pot Pourri e.p. by Joe Zas; Midnight Funk by Demon; Vintage Low e.p. Brendan Costigane; Wanderungen by Nicholas.

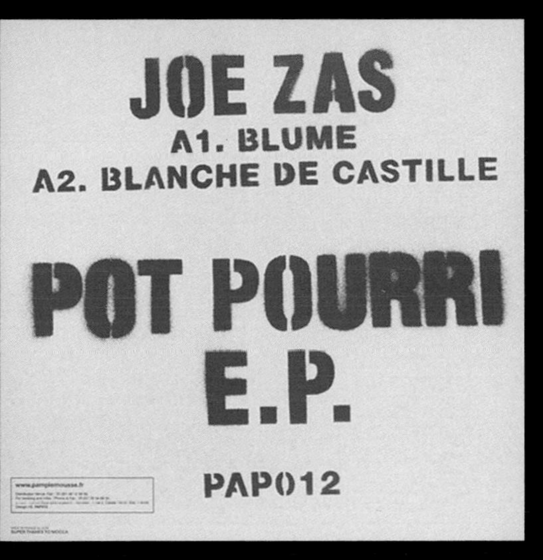

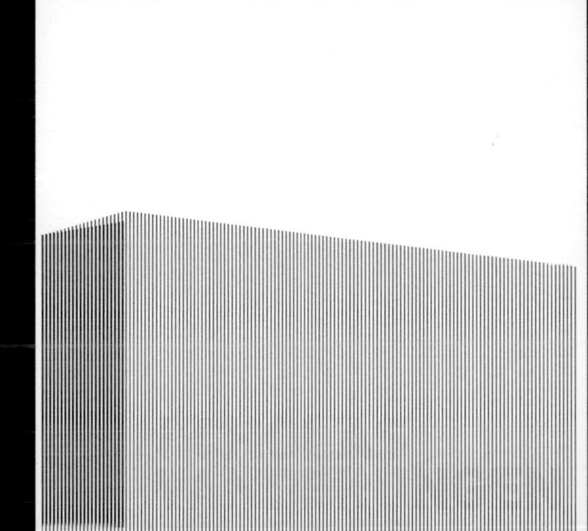

SUPER
DISCOUNT

Promotional film
Made for the Super Furry Animals, and their single Juxtapozed wit'u. The images show a city at night where all the roads and buildings glow with light. The people too, are converted into light, and shimmer as though viewed through a thermal imaging system.

Travelling through a city built of words.

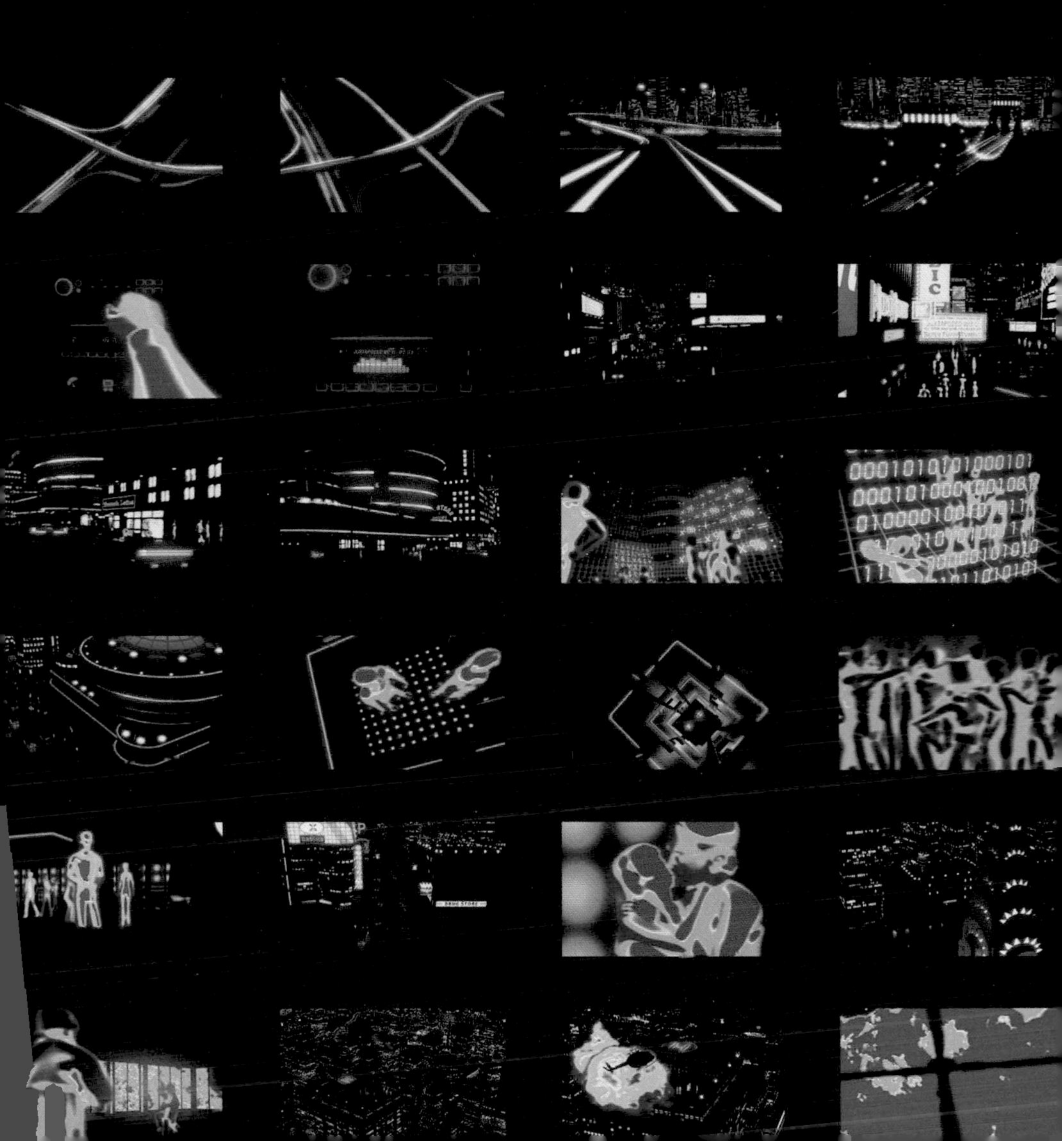

24h adult
sex
SHOW
GIRLS
GIRLS
GIRLS
CAR
PEDESTRIANCROSSING
TAXI
CAR
GENH
OM
USEU
leaf

Zuzana Licko

Licko was born in Bratislava, The Slovak Republic (formerly Czechoslovakia), and emigrated to America. The first typeface she designed was an electronic Greek alphabet for personal use by her father, a biomathematician. She graduated with a degree in graphic communications from the University of California, Berkeley. Licko and her husband, Rudy VanderLans went on to found Emigre magazine in 1984 – a journal that they intended as a test-bed for experimental graphic design. This was the same year that Apple launched the Macintosh computer.

The fonts available for the first Mac were few, of poor quality, and of limited typographic expression. Licko says, "the technology was very primitive, and easy to grasp", so she began designing typefaces. The first few, such as Emperor, were built in the most rudimentary way using individual pixels. As Macintosh increased the sophistication of its software and processing power, Licko developed more nuanced typefaces. The early work – building with individual pixels – is still valuable, as fonts today need low-resolution screen display (these can still be created as pixel letterforms) but high-resolution output (which have more complex form).

The needs of the magazine and the technology available have acted as a framework on Licko. As the magazine has developed, she has been called upon to design new typefaces. Recently Emigre has passed into a new phase, publishing longer articles with less imagery, and the content becoming increasingly concerned with critical theory. Licko has designed typefaces that borrow from 'book' typefaces which have been tested and proven legible over hundreds of years. One such face is Mrs Eaves, Licko's creative reinterpretation of Baskerville. (It is named after John Baskerville's wife, who completed much of his work after he died.) Another new typeface is Filosofia (Italian for philosophy), her tribute to one of the most widely used typefaces in the world, Bodoni.

What sets Licko apart as a typeface designer is a wish to play, and to communicate the pleasure of play – the french-tickler version of Modula is perfect testament to this. This play impulse had its mirror in VanderLans' layouts for the magazine. At its worst this joyous experimentation so incensed some prominent designers, who felt that all design ought to be Modernist – cold and serious – that one accused Emigre (and its typefaces) of being "garbage, lacking depth, refinement, elegance, or a sense of history".

Of course with a little distance we can see that Licko's work is rooted in the continuum, just as any designer's must be. She isn't interested in paying an overt, self-restricting homage to history. For the recent classical typefaces, instead of going for ultra-refined, purist shapes, Licko has deliberately drawn basic letterforms that are bursting with character. And, as an encouragement to play, she has added dozens of extra 'swash' characters and ligatures giving designers as much liberty to personalise and invent as any genericised typeface ever can.

One of the world's best type designers, Matthew Carter, paid Licko this tribute: "Two ideas seem to me to stand behind the originality of Zuzana's work: that the proper study of typography is type, not calligraphy or history, and that legibility is not an intrinsic quality of type but something acquired through use".

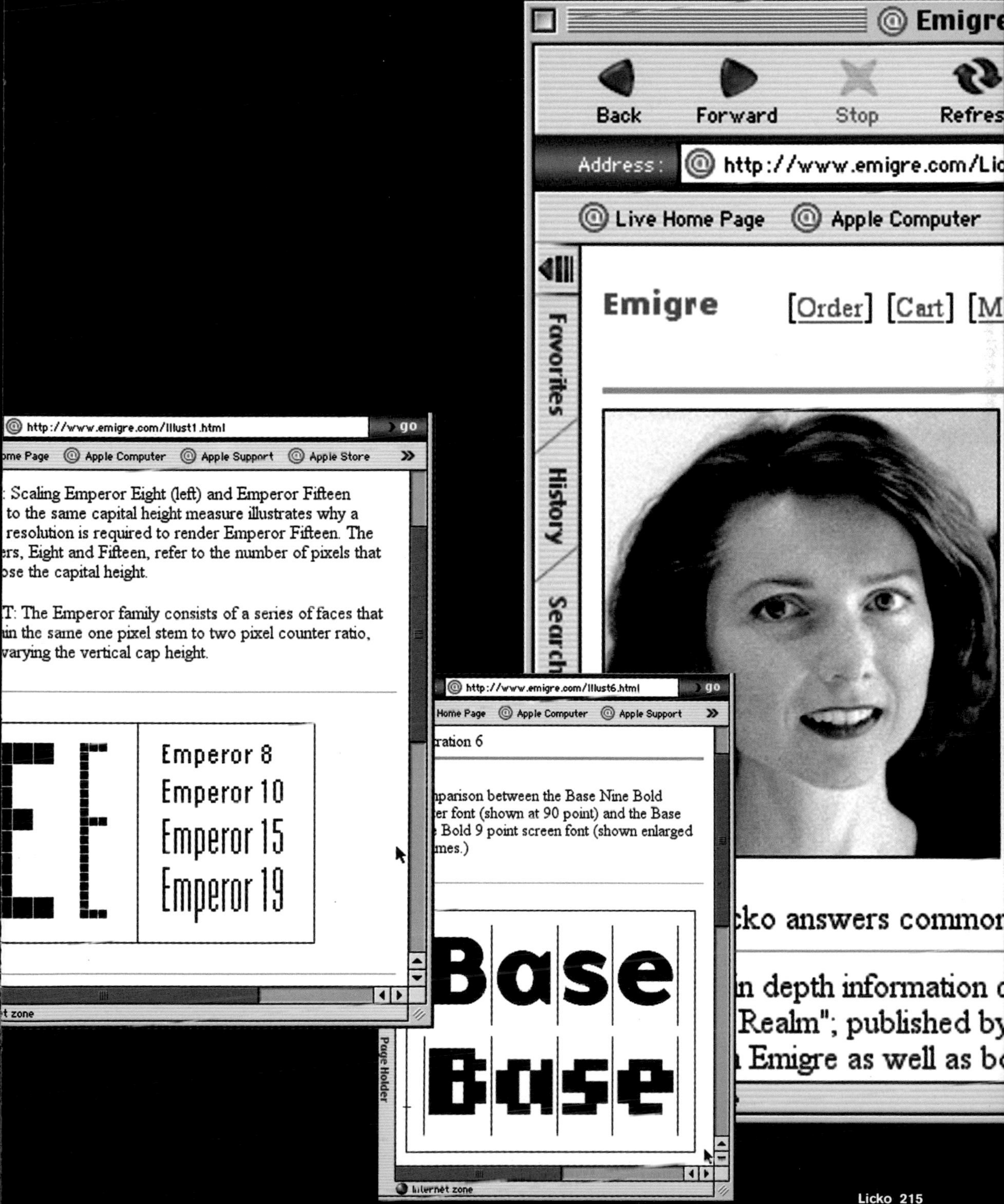
Emigre
Back
Forward
Stop
Refres
Address:
http://www.emigre.com/Lic
Live Home Page
Apple Computer
Favorites
History
Search
Emigre
[Order] [Cart] [M
http://www.emigre.com/Illust1.html
go
ome Page
Apple Computer
Apple Support
Apple Store
: Scaling Emperor Eight (left) and Emperor Fifteen
to the same capital height measure illustrates why a
resolution is required to render Emperor Fifteen. The
ers, Eight and Fifteen, refer to the number of pixels that
ose the capital height.
T: The Emperor family consists of a series of faces that
in the same one pixel stem to two pixel counter ratio,
varying the vertical cap height.
Emperor 8
Emperor 10
Emperor 15
Emperor 19
t zone
http://www.emigre.com/Illust6.html
go
Home Page
Apple Computer
Apple Support
ration 6
nparison between the Base Nine Bold
er font (shown at 90 point) and the Base
Bold 9 point screen font (shown enlarged
mes.)
Base
Base
Page Holder
Internet zone
cko answers commor
n depth information c
Realm"; published by
Emigre as well as bo

Typeface designs
From the ridiculous to the sublime, Licko always invests her fonts with exuberance and strong character. All material from www.emigre.com

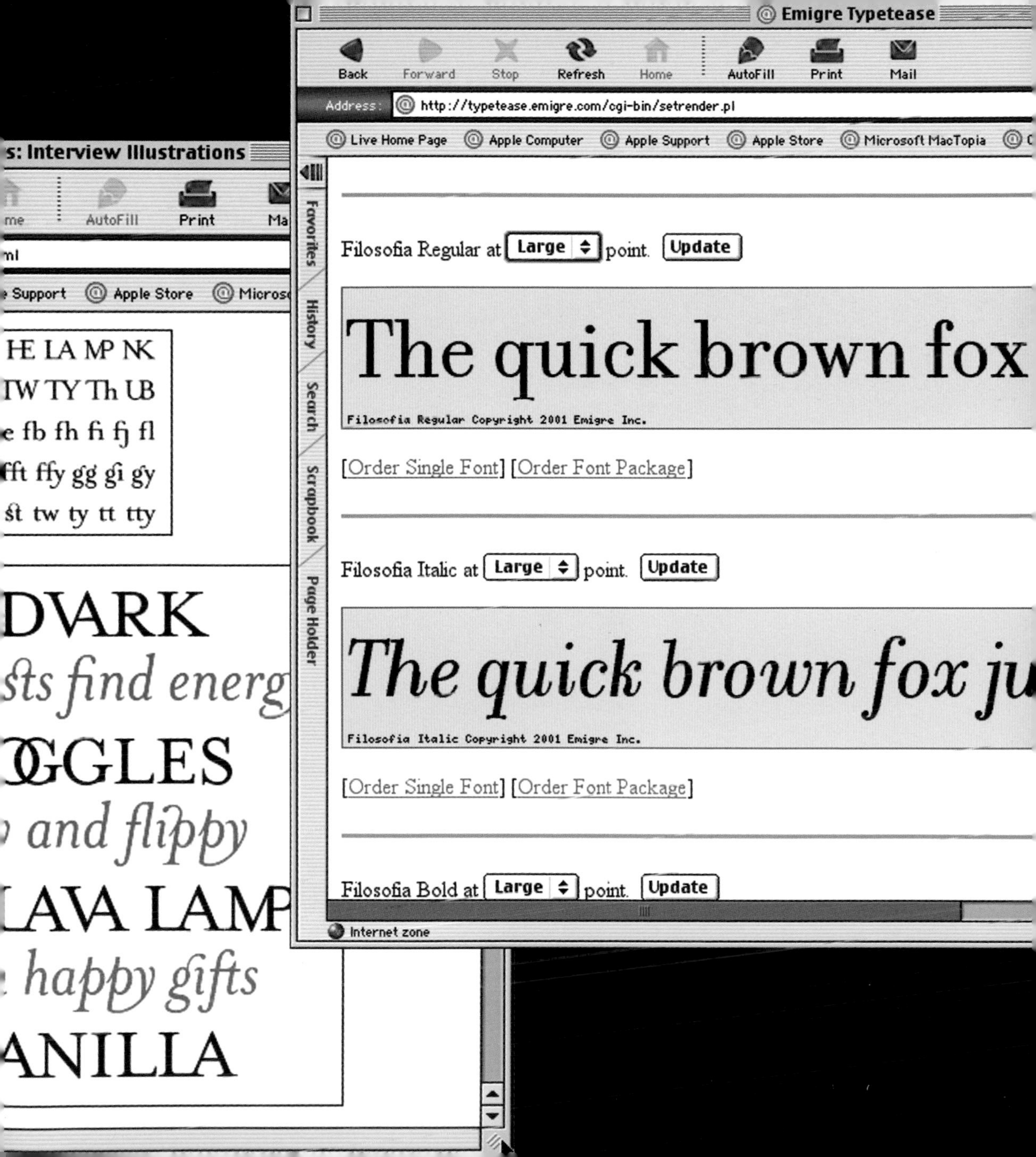

s: Interview Illustrations

me AutoFill Print Ma

ml

e Support Apple Store Micros

HE LA MP NK
TW TY Th UB
e fb fh fi fj fl
fft ffy gg gi gy
st tw ty tt tty

DVARK
sts find energ
OGGLES
and flippy
LAVA LAMP
happy gifts
ANILLA

Emigre Typetease

Back Forward Stop Refresh Home AutoFill Print Mail

Address: http://typetease.emigre.com/cgi-bin/setrender.pl

Live Home Page Apple Computer Apple Support Apple Store Microsoft MacTopia

Favorites History Search Scrapbook Page Holder

Filosofia Regular at Large point. Update

The quick brown fox

Filosofia Regular Copyright 2001 Emigre Inc.

[Order Single Font] [Order Font Package]

Filosofia Italic at Large point. Update

The quick brown fox ju

Filosofia Italic Copyright 2001 Emigre Inc.

[Order Single Font] [Order Font Package]

Filosofia Bold at Large point. Update

Internet zone

Patterns and ceramics
As extensions to her type work, Licko has designed a program that makes patterns from letters. She is currently translating these into textiles (Emigre sell a very stylish set of typographic pyjamas), and ceramics. This is about as far as type has ever been taken.

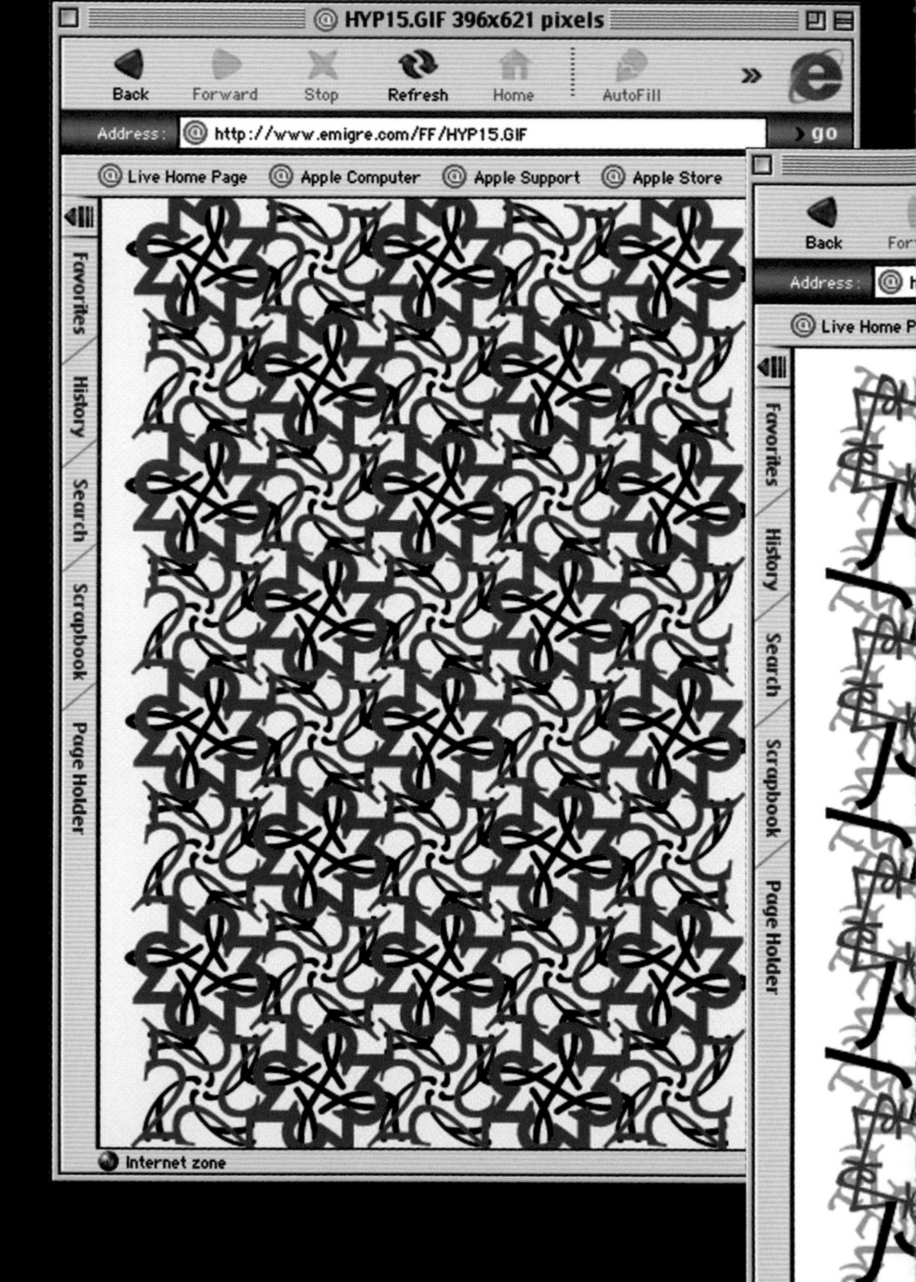

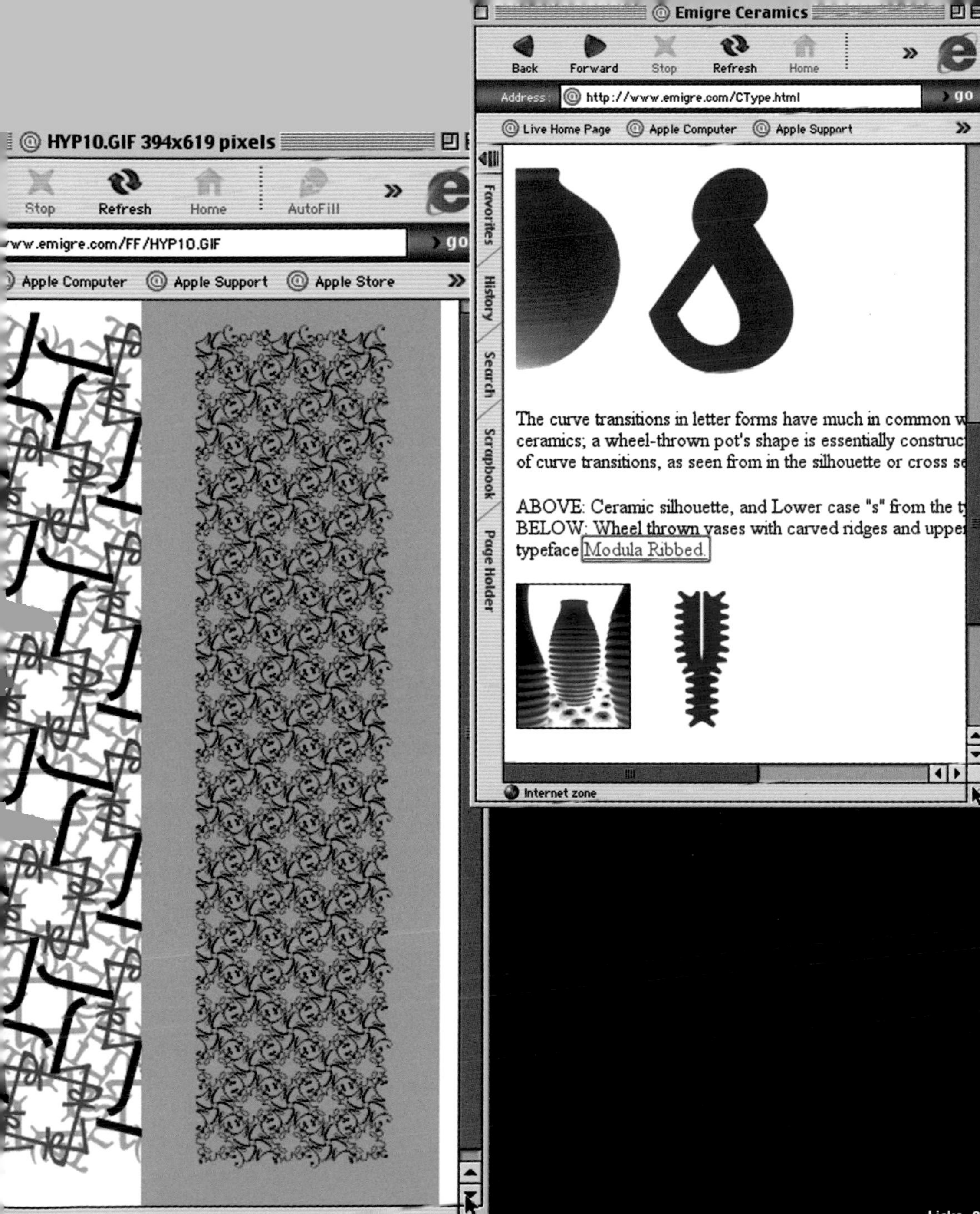
HYP10.GIF 394x619 pixels
Stop
Refresh
Home
AutoFill
ww.emigre.com/FF/HYP10.GIF
go
Apple Computer
Apple Support
Apple Store
Emigre Ceramics
Back
Forward
Stop
Refresh
Home
Address:
http://www.emigre.com/CType.html
go
Live Home Page
Apple Computer
Apple Support
Favorites
History
Search
Scrapbook
Page Holder
The curve transitions in letter forms have much in common w
ceramics; a wheel-thrown pot's shape is essentially construc
of curve transitions, as seen from in the silhouette or cross se
ABOVE: Ceramic silhouette, and Lower case "s" from the ty
BELOW: Wheel thrown vases with carved ridges and upper
typeface Modula Ribbed.
Internet zone

Ellen Lupton

As well as being a very capable graphic designer, Lupton is curator of contemporary design at the Cooper-Hewitt National Design Museum in New York. She has curated over 20 exhibitions, and writes for all the significant design publications – as if this was not enough, she also lectures.

She trained as a designer at Cooper Union in New York, and exercised her interest in design history by taking extra courses. When she was an undergraduate, in the early 1980s, there were no specific design history courses so she effectively compiled her own by selecting various courses on the history of art, art theory, film and philosophy. After graduating she studied with Rosalind Kraus, the notable critic and member of the controversial group of art historians called October.

For some time she ran a studio with her partner, J Abbott Miller, called 'Design/Writing/Research'. The name is a deliberate reversal of the accepted idea that design comes after, and is somehow subservient to, research and writing. Both being designers, Lupton and Miller saw design as intrinsic to the processes of research and writing. Often design was the subject being researched and written about. This is an approach which sees design as far more than simply laying elements on a page and choosing a typeface. This is design in its broadest and most influential sense: design as editing, planning, organising and shaping, design as content, design as culture.

Lupton has edited and written some of the very best and most valuable books on design. Her design, writing and research is always impeccable. She does this, sometimes with Miller, sometimes with other collaborators, sometimes on her own, always to the highest of standards, and always pushing design further. Her book, co-edited with Miller, 'The Bauhaus and Design Theory from Preschool to Post-Modernism', boils down the byzantine complexity of the Bauhaus to ten brief essays over 64 pages which outline the enduring significances and deep influences of the German experiment.

Although Miller has now joined Pentagram, and Lupton concentrates on her role at the Cooper-Hewitt, she says "I still do housework and grocery shopping with Abbott, so I don't miss him".

The Avant-Garde Letterhead
This exhibition tells the story of design's avant-garde through the medium of the letterhead. Built mainly from the collection of one designer, Elaine Lustig Cohen, it was supplemented with work from other sources private and public. Cohen began her collection almost by default when she ran a specialist bookshop in the 1970s, the letterheads – each a beautiful piece of design in its own right – never sold. Eventually she realised that she had amassed some rare pieces of undervalued and overlooked work from some of design's most significant figures: El Lissitsky, László Moholy-Nagy, Kurt Schwitters, Marrinetti and Tristan Tzara. The letterheads often bear very personal and unique letters, signatures, sketches and enclosures. The exhibition, and a related book, organise these pieces into a remarkable survey. Lupton's design of the exhibition focuses on an elegant and clear way of grouping and displaying the content. The elements open to overt expression of style – the materials, the striking colour, the typography – borrow from, and refer you to, the exhibition's content.

F. T. MARINETT
ARA
founded Dada in Switzerland in 1916. Dada qu
THE RING
DUTCH MODERNISM
RG, KURT SCHWITTERS, and other Dada artists interested in the physical quali
lland in 1917. He went to Weimar in 1921 and staged informal lectures at the
etry under the name I. K. BONSET. He met
the Dada artist KURT SCHWITTERS in 1921.
es, including HERBERT
werbe-bau
NWG

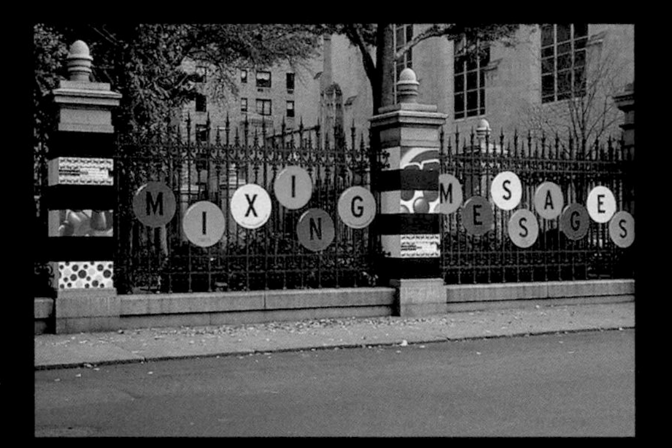

Mixing Messages: Graphic Design in Contemporary Culture
The illustrations here show the sign outside the Cooper-Hewitt, and a suite of exhibition materials, catalogue, invitations, education pack, press pack, and so on. Lupton's explanation for the exhibition is as follows: "On the one hand, design is utterly commonplace, appearing everywhere and produced by anyone. Its past and future are coterminous with human history. On the other hand, design represents a set of refined and narrow interests within a vast web of communications. Viewed from this perspective, design has a brief history and a fragile future.

"This project alternates between these two views. While the more inclusive definition of design appears liberating and democratic at first glance, it can serve to generalise all forms of expression into a value-free flood of signals. In contrast, an overly-narrow definition of design can polarise a diverse array of practices into such categories as design/non-design, professional/non-professional, and mainstream/marginal. These oppositions devalue some practices in relation to others, naming a legitimate centre and an ancillary fringe."

Lupton's design plays with these polarised choices, and casts them as 'popular' and 'refined'. The two sides are then clashed up together, a bit like one of Batman's most notorious opponents, Two-face. The popular is frivolous – candy colours, multiple typefaces and excessive. The refined side uses sans serif type, restrained colours and quieter motifs. The collision graphics, and the title, portray the exhibition as presenting and exploring a cultural schism within design in a light-hearted and playful way.

GRAPHIC DESIGN
IN CONTEMPORARY CULTURE
MIXING MESSAGES
GRAPHIC DESIGN
IN CONTEMPORARY CULTURE
MIXING MESSAGES
GRAPHIC DESIGN IN CONTEMPORARY CULTURE
4
3
2
1
MIXING MESSAGES
The Face of Design
GRAPHIC DESIGN
IN CONTEMPORARY CULTURE
DESIGN KIT
NAME
Dolores
Remedy
Hystrix
Truth
Galliard
NARLY
WHAT EXPRESSIONS DO YOU "READ" IN THESE TYPEFACES?
C.
A typeface is how letters (ABC...) look.
Like our own faces, typefaces show different expressions. Graphic designers use line and shape to create the expression of typefaces.
Cooper-Hewitt
National Design Museum
Smithsonian Institution
Magazine
Fall 1996
First-floor galleries reopen September 17
Mixing Messages: Graphic Design in Contemporary Culture

FREUD
AMERICA
IN THE
WINTER
OF CITIES
the noble savage 4
Yvor Winters On Modern Poets
MY LIFE IN ART
Memoirs of a Revolutionist
The Federalist
Clear Writing
BABY DOLL
ON LOVE
THE PASSOVER ANTHOLOGY
hard candy
please do not touch
Eero Saarinen
Kenzo Tange

Elaine Lustig Cohen: Modern Graphic Designer
A show that explored the work of the wife of famous magazine and book cover designer Alvin Lustig. Whilst Lustig has a firm place in histories of the period as a premier exponent of European Modernism in America in the 1930s and 1940s, Elaine Lustig Cohen, who was almost as prolific, does not. This exhibition was the first devoted to Cohen's whole career. This is a case of curating as a way of correcting, and therefore shaping and creating, history.

Lupton's simple design uses perhaps the most ubiquitous material of 1930s' architectural Modernism – plywood – and lines all the surfaces with it. Cohen's work is then allowed to line the walls and cases unravelling its own story.

Studio Myerscough

This studio is small, with three or four designers at most, organised and knocked into shape by Morag Myerscough. She has a long association with architects and architecture, and seems to have a natural feel for deploying graphics within a space. She has decorated the outsides of buildings with huge hoardings, and inside with sign schemes and exhibitions. She says, "typography used to be steeped in rules but now there are none", which might act as a miniature manifesto. Her work is rarely reductive and well-behaved, often flaunting several typefaces, with overprinting, layers, off-shoots and bits stuck on. Her love of the eclectic is obvious through her use of diverse materials, colours, sources – she creates surfaces and environments where there is a lot to be discovered. Her work is similar to that of Experimental Jetset in that there is a fusing of vernacular and refined modernist cultures. One example is the 'found object', the illuminated bollard sprayed with a graffitto, photographed and then used as a piece of 'found typography' for architectural historian Joe Kerr. Another is the work for Habitat's Christmas packaging. Myerscough borrowed the language of silvery wrapping, quilting, capsules and sample jars from NASA's space programme, and translated it into a refined and ironic set of packages – the night sky and silver being just enough of a link to Christmas.

Opposite: Starting out
The process of generating ideas at the beginning of projects.
Top to bottom: A new name and logo for an interiors store begins with a meeting with the client; various possible names and typestyles; tape diagrams comparing the relative areas of apartments in Tokyo and New York for an exhibition at the Victoria & Albert Museum, London; pinboards with inspiring source material for both projects such as photographs, images, graphic elements, and so on.

ROCK
STYLE
TURN TO THE

26
2
20
28
18
6
16
ANARCHY
LET'S ROCK
BE COOL

Morelands building
A stencilled sign scheme for a rough industrial building converted into offices. Lettering as just another building material.

Packaging for Christmas
For Habitat's Christmas food range, Myerscough raided the vocabulary built by NASA. Spices are sealed in sample jars like moondust.

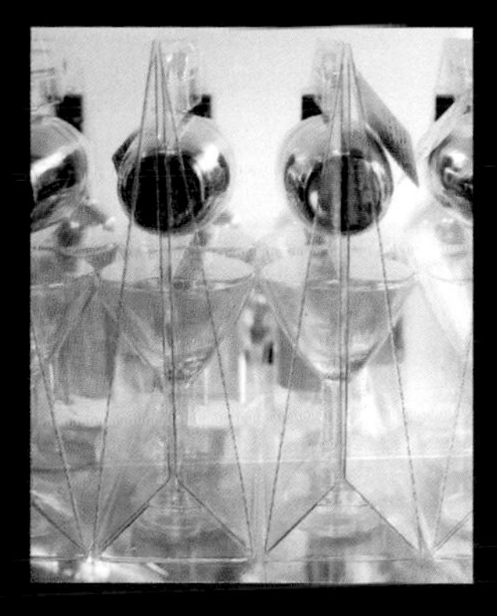

Number Seventeen

Emily Oberman and Bonnie Siegler speak for themselves: “We like things that are moving, both literally and figuratively. We believe that to communicate successfully you have to make an emotional connection with your audience. That connection can be funny or sad or sweet; it just needs to make you feel something. We also like things that actually move. Motion design accounts for the majority of our work, but whether it is for film, television, print, packaging or the web, our work must always be moving.

“We almost always create the content for our clients. We think we bring a certain humanist perspective to even the most complex concepts and this is what connects with the audience. Often we will do that through humour. When you make people laugh, they feel good and then they associate that good feeling with the message you are trying to communicate. It’s a win/win situation because we really like to laugh too. Truthfully, there is almost not a day that passes where we don’t laugh really hard at least once– but not at someone else’s expense, because that would be wrong, very wrong. Unless they trip or their chair makes a farting sound when they sit down.

“We want Number Seventeen to always be the kind of place where work and life blend together. We have been best friends for so long and love what we do so much, that working still counts as recreation. In our office, everyone gets to play. The best idea often comes from someone who is not ‘supposed to’ have the idea or just from trying to make everyone else laugh. In short-ish, we try to do work that moves us and, if we succeed, it will hopefully also move our audience.”

When asked how do you avoid the great pitfall of design: superficiality and the ephemeral, they answer, “what’s wrong with the ephemeral?” This might be their philosophy, cut to a single phrase. This is design shorn of any pretensions, happy to be pop.

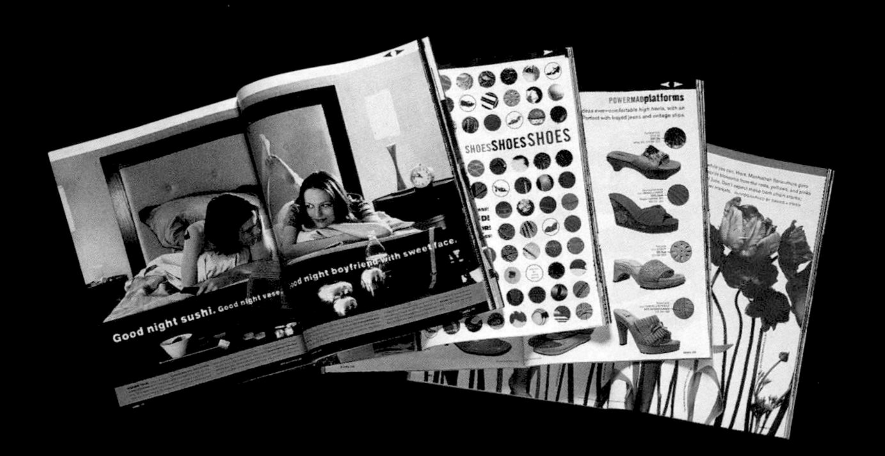

Left: Lucky magazine
Lucky is a Condé Nast magazine about shopping. The design manages to find fresh endless ways of portaying the same obsessions of those that seek retail therapy; rows and rows of products to buy, best bargains, questionnaires and so on.

Opposite: Jane posters
This launch of a new magazine had to avoid dealing with content (none existed), but capture and convey a strong personality. The cards imply hip and sassy with simple changes of the phrase introducing Jane.

HELLO
my voice is
JANE
HELLO
my kitty is
JANE
HELLO
my favorite four letter word is
JANE
HELLO
my encyclopedia is
JANE
HELLO
my court appointed attorney is
JANE
HELLO
my friends call me
JANE
HELLO
my name could have been
JANE
HELLO
my frame of reference is
JANE
HELLO
my mantra is
JANE
HELLO
my authority is
JANE
HELLO
my guide is
JANE
HELLO
my therapist is
JANE
HELLO
my fortune cookie says
JANE
HELLO
you Tarzan, me
JANE
HELLO
my destination is
JANE

Heil Titler!

in COLOR

FINEMAN FILMS FINEMAN FILMS BONNIE SIEGLER EMILY OBERMAN DAVID ISRAEL
"HEIL TITLER" CARMEN QUINONES GILLIAN PINKWATER JOE DESSEREAU PETE CENEDELLA
NUMBER SEVENTEEN MORTY FINEMAN MORTY FINEMAN MORTY FINEMAN

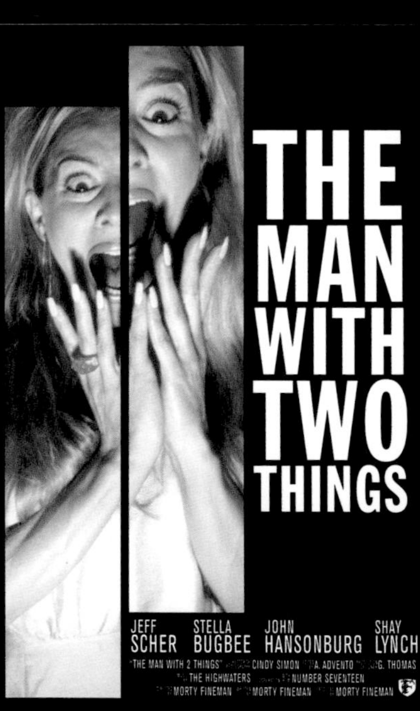

Opposite:
Independent posters
The Independent is a comedy film about a film director who has made 400 terrible B-movies. These are fake posters, used in the film as props, for some of his awful films. Super-kitsch.

Right: The Mercer Hotel
The character of this hotel was cast as 'an invisible servant' (and a gorgeous servant at that) waiting to fulfil any desire or indulgence you might have. The interior designer, Christian Liagré, incorporated this into the rooms, lobbies and bars, using simple but exquisitely beautiful materials. The graphic design follows on but is more overtly witty; brackets hush all the type, and whisper it at you like an experienced gentleman's gentleman might. All the room 'collateral' carries this discreet treatment; the in-room folders, the pads and pencils, the matches, the shampoo bottles, the robes, the do not disturb signs, even the emergency exit sign.

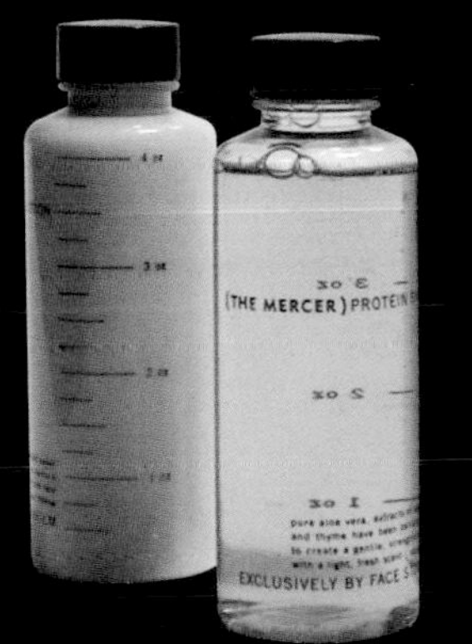

Saturday Night parody commercial
The type mimics the style of bad advertising: the language is overstated, and the letterforms strain for expression. Directed by Jim Signorelli.

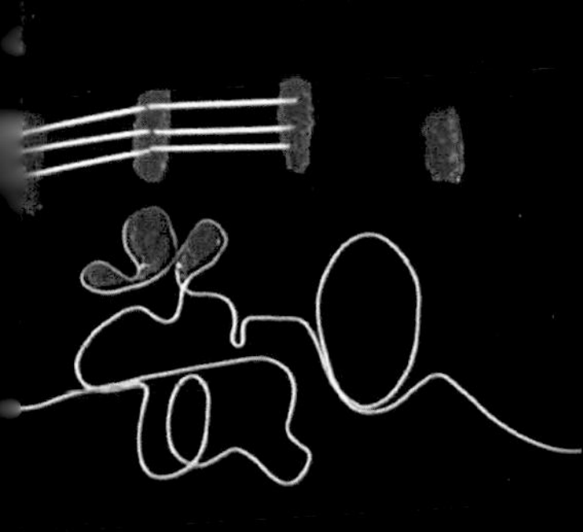

HBO Mealtime Movies, Spaghetti Western
This is an 'interstitial' film, seconds long, introducing the themed programming that follows. It exploits the phrase 'spaghetti western' – a cheap Italian version of the American genre – and takes the words literally. Directed by Jeff Scher.

Rose Design Associates

Rose is a combination of its founders' names: RO for Rebecca Oliver and SE for Simon Elliott. Oliver is administrator and project director, while Elliott runs the studio as creative director, with two or three junior designers and a production manager. Like Experimental Jetset, they see no point in rejecting the sometimes criticised idea of defining the client's needs as 'problem' to which the design is a 'solution'. As far as they are concerned, the client is only partially able to understand their own needs: the client's brief is always an "interpretation" of the situation, and any graphic outcome needs to be underpinned by far greater scrutiny and exploration of the competitors, marketplace, future needs and so on. The style and approach of their work is firmly planted in the European modernist tradition: a clear preference for sans serif typefaces; use of impersonal photography and a seamless fusion of artwork preparation and printing processes. Like many of today's designers they offer a rich and varied set of responses – sometimes spare and asymmetric, sometimes intense. They are often intuitive rather than logical, and not always attempting humour, or always avoiding it.

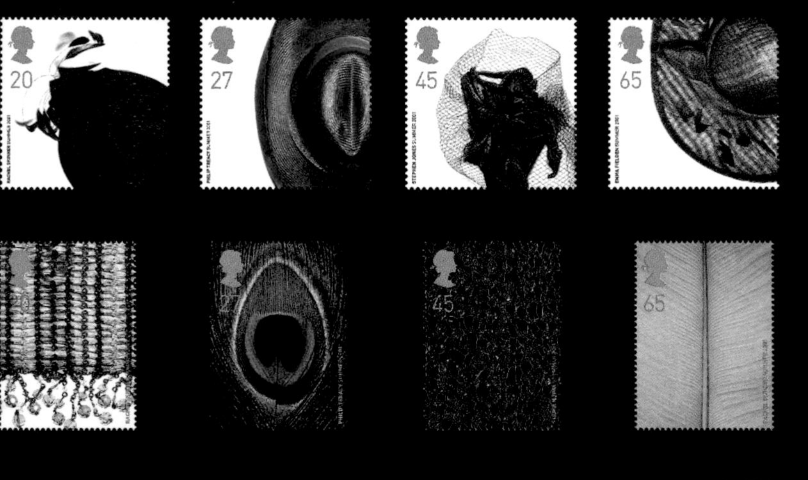

Fabulous Hats stamps
This brief from the Royal Mail asked for designs to show contemporary hats. A series of drafts, left, show three different design approaches. The silhouette route was chosen for two reasons: firstly because the hats on their own look a little unclear, and the details of hat elements do not show the finished hat; and secondly because the Royal Mail do not allow any recognisable person to be depicted on their stamps. The Victoria & Albert Museum was asked to help choose the milliners, and one hat to typify each milliner's work. Rose then asked fashion photographer, Nick Knight, to exploit the properties of each one.

1ST
E
1ST
45
65

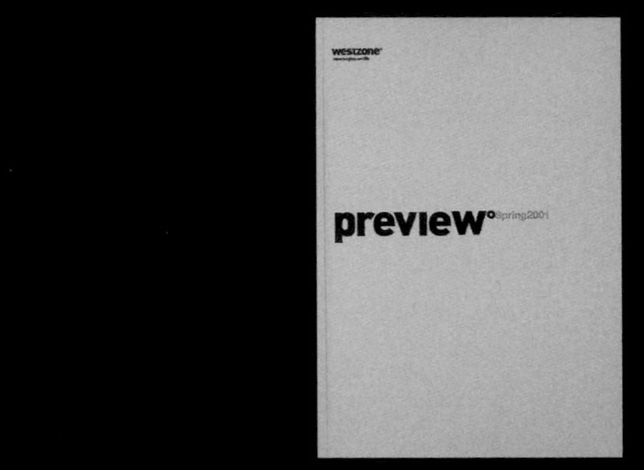

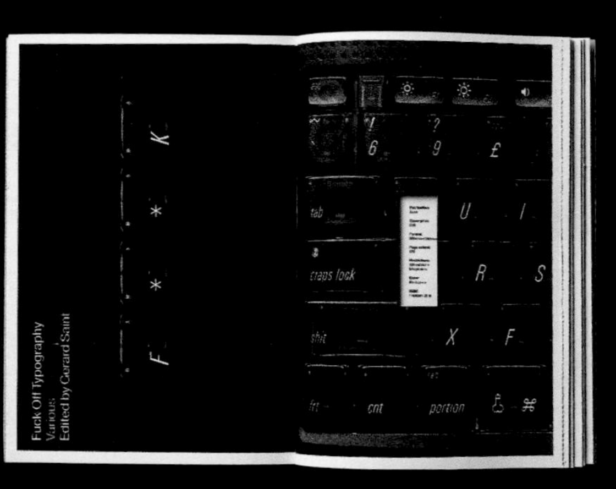

Westzone publishers
This book-sized catalogue for art book publishers Westzone has 'french-folded' pages. Each one is a double page with a perforated outer edge allowing it to be torn open. The incentive to tear the pages apart is that the images are hidden inside. A little cut-out rectangular window then works in two ways: it shows the technical data of the book and also a little truncated section of the image. It's complex, and relies on the reader being able to work out how to use the booklet, as well as having the time and patience to want to play with it. If any readership is going to rise to this challenge, it is art-book readers and dealers. One of the books from the catalogue is shown opposite, and demonstrates perfect judgement in the use of the picture: a startling crop, and elegantly placed typography and logo.

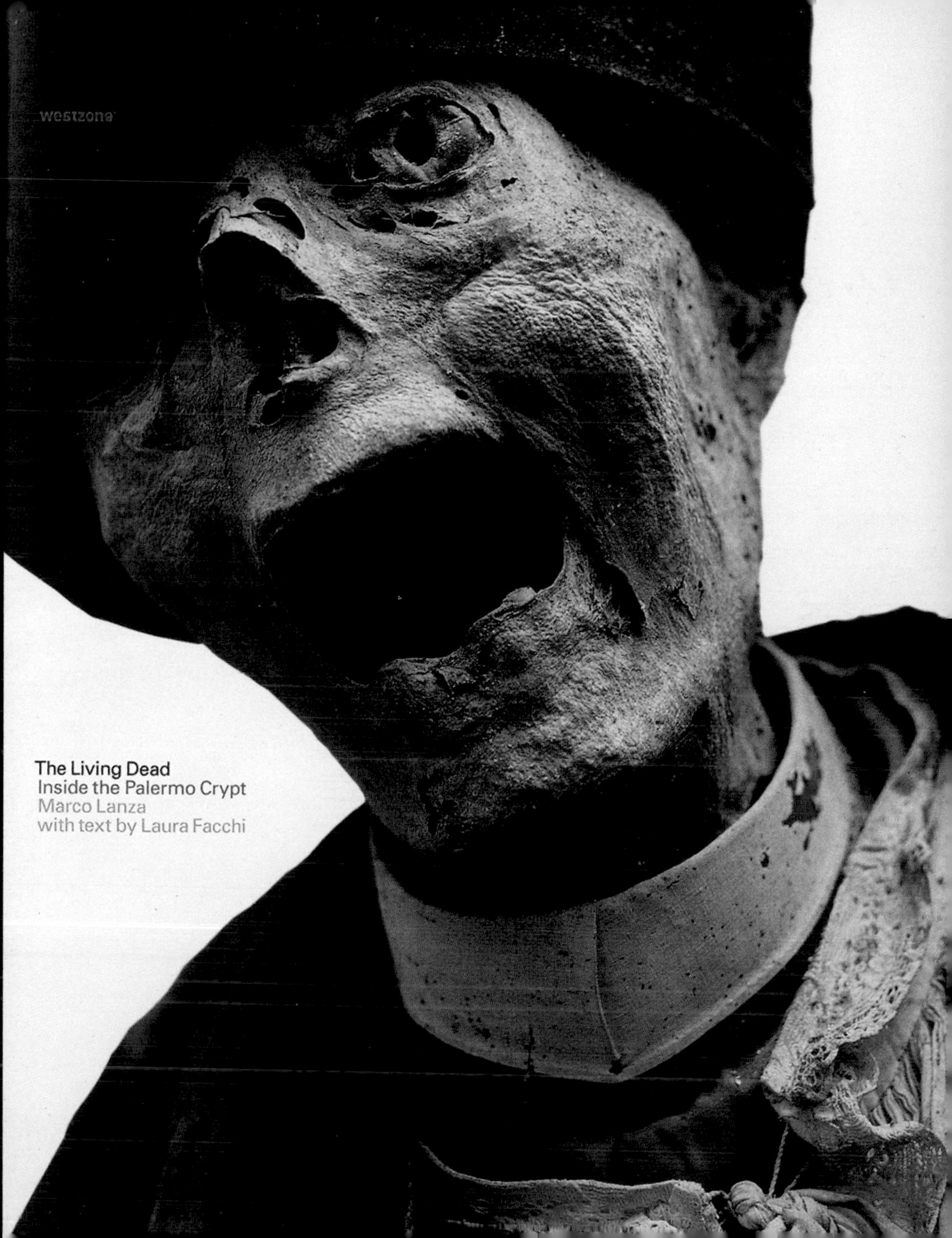

westzone

The Living Dead
Inside the Palermo Crypt
Marco Lanza
with text by Laura Facchi

Gun Nation book
This is a long photo essay by Zed Nelson about America's love affair with the gun. Rose has interpreted its task with this book as one of carefully pacing and paginating Nelson's quietly horrific images. Any overt elements of design, such as captions, make very modest intrusions.

Opposite: Planet Botanic
A 21st-century apothecary, Planet Botanic sells herbal remedies and treatments in a crisp, clinical environment. The emblem that Rose created is a kind of organic rocket – or perhaps a dry reference to the not-quite-of-this world people who use herbal medicine. Whatever, its execution captures exactly enough of the graphic language of pharmaceutical packaging to make it appear professional and trustworthy, as well as playful and warm.

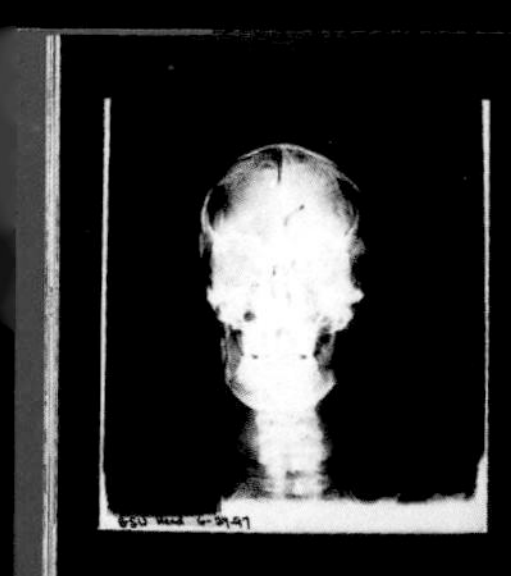

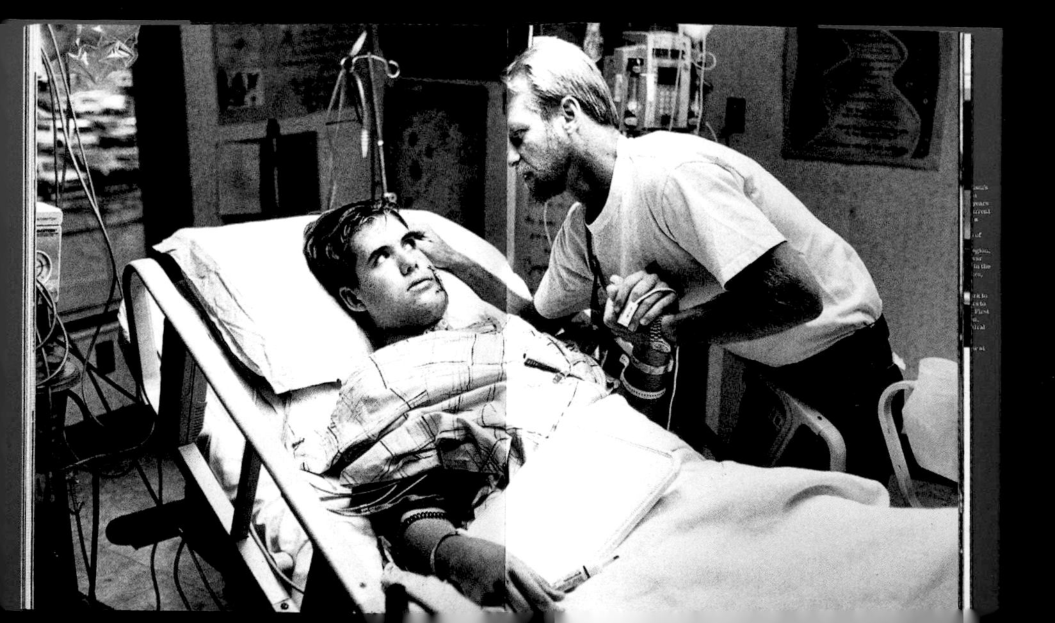

planet botanic™
Herbal
Herbal Cream
Arnica
60ml
Soothing, Healing and anti-inflammatory.
Herbal Cream
Tea Tree
50ml
Herbal Cream
Lavender
Skincare
Homestyle

There can be few signs of a highly evolved design culture more significant than a designer who can make a living entirely from posters for museums and cultural organisations. Sato joins Philippe Apeloig in being able to do full-time projects most designers experience just once or twice in their whole career. He does take on other work, but these spartan posters remain his central interest. His approach is comparable to the Japanese printmakers of the 19th century, each of whom had a distinctive, recognisable personal style. His one or two assistants merely aid him in creating what he calls his "unfettered expressions".

The Japanese have no word for 'design' as distinct from art. These posters are a fusion of these two disciplines. Although they are mechanically printed, they are the product of Sato's astonishingly precise, painstaking and judicious hand.

Opposite: Sato's first poster
Drawn in 1971, this poster epitomises Sato's work. It uses traditional imagery and presents it as fresh and alive. This process of renewal is possible in a culture such as Japan's because people can still read and understand images that date back hundreds of years. This kind of image-making is more difficult in the Western world where ruptures in our societies have resulted in the loss of almost all of the symbolism of the Classical, Christian and feudal traditions. Here Sato uses the carp – emblem of riches and abundance – apparently without any sense of irony. It shimmers in vibrant, fluorescent waves of colour and announces new music.

Below: Night concert
Sato combines a rock (the concert was next to a Shinto shrine) with a moon.

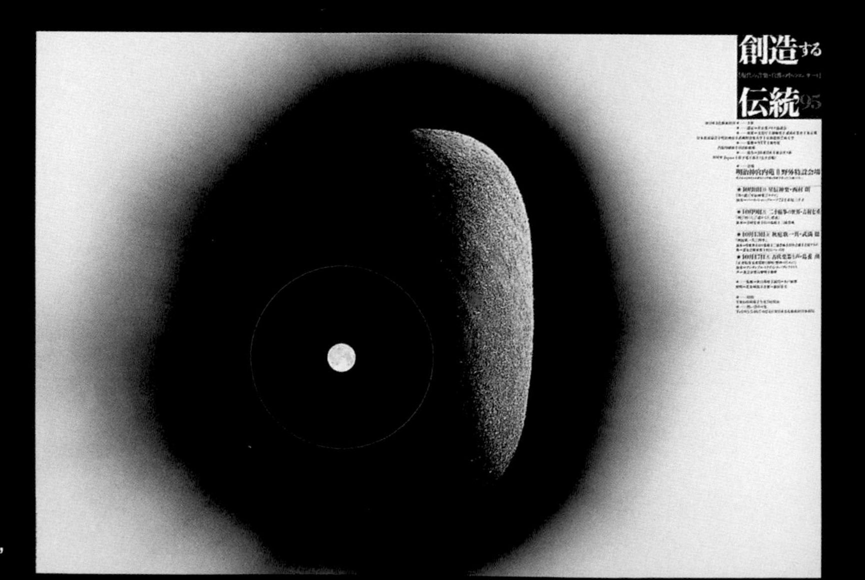

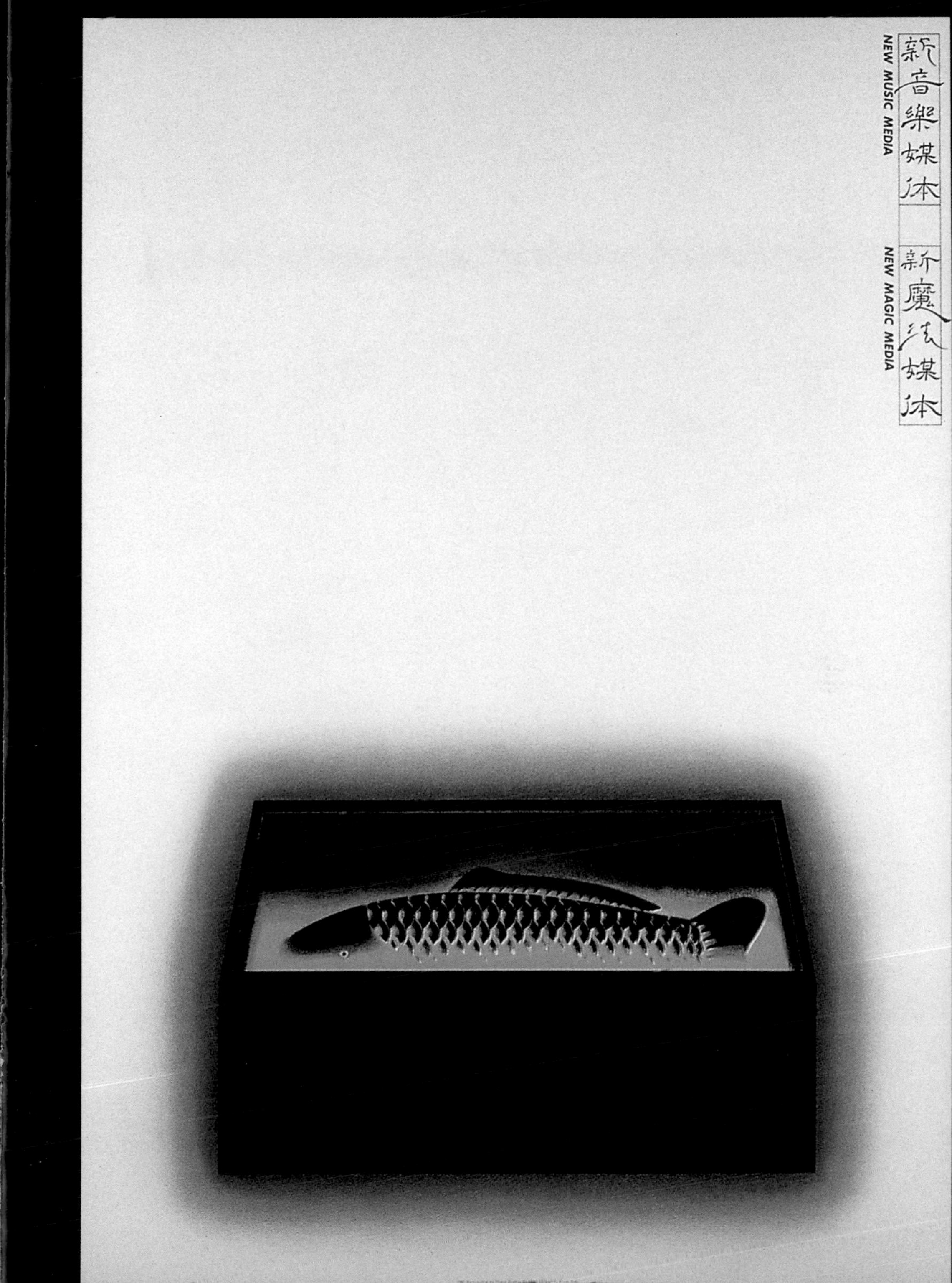
新音樂媒体
NEW MUSIC MEDIA
新魔法媒体
NEW MAGIC MEDIA

Television poster
Comparing the light from the television with the light of the moon.

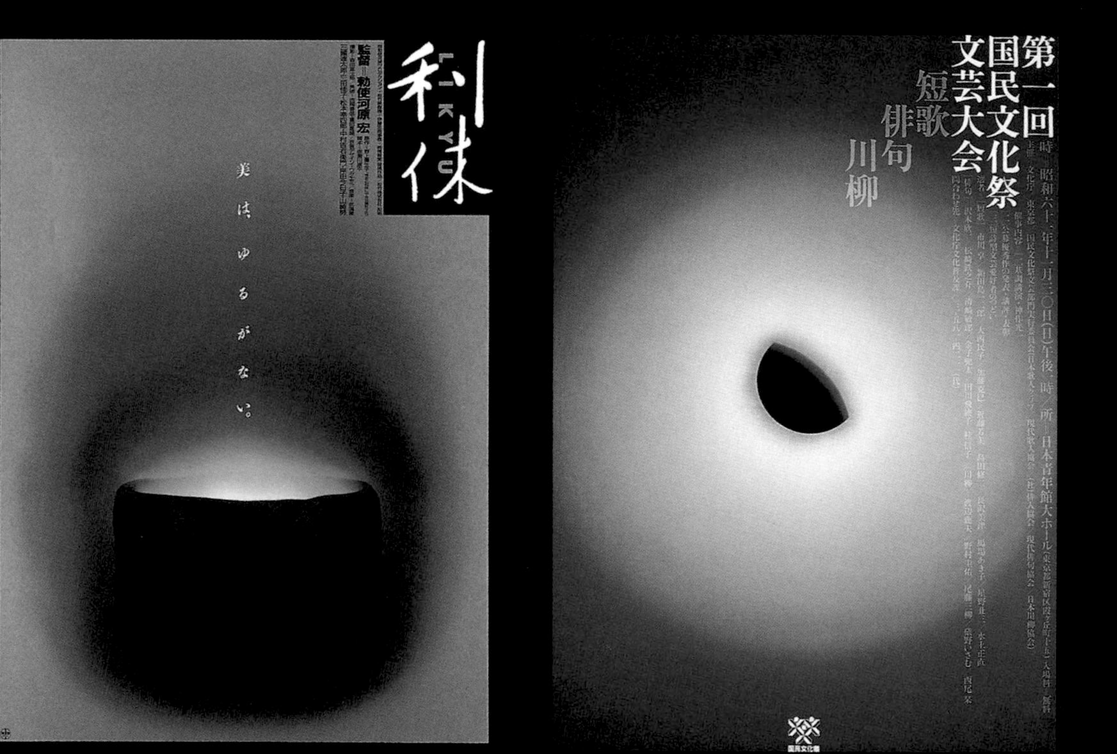

大気の中へ。環境映像テレビジョン
National

Poster for an opera

Announcing a musical in which an alien spaceman and a human fall in love. The roughs and preparatory workings for the poster show the subtle shifts Sato goes through before arriving at a final image. He made the handprint with his own hand, and translated this into a universal, iconic hand with washes of colour on wet Washi (porous Japanese handmade paper). Finally, airbrushing created a finely graded aura.

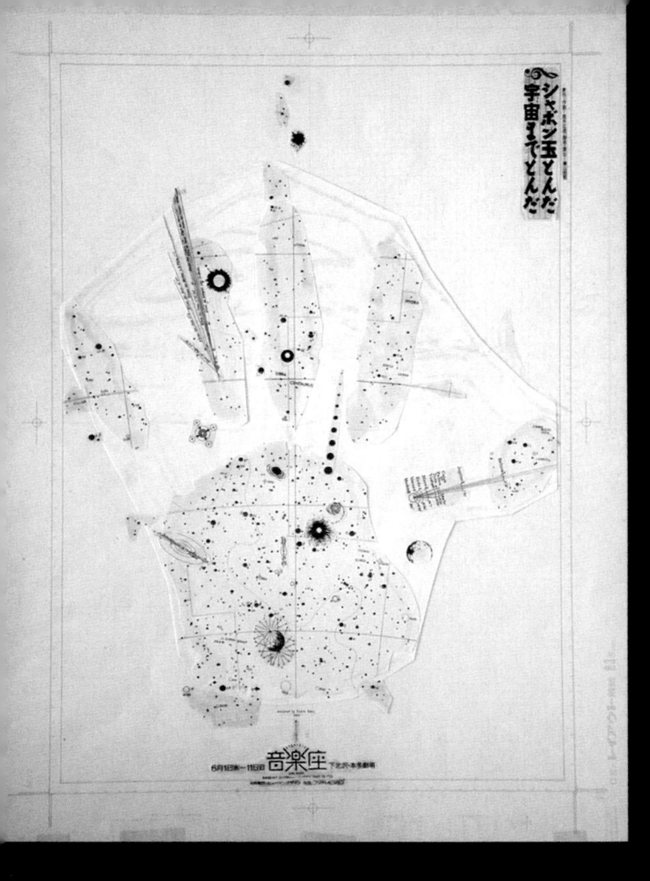

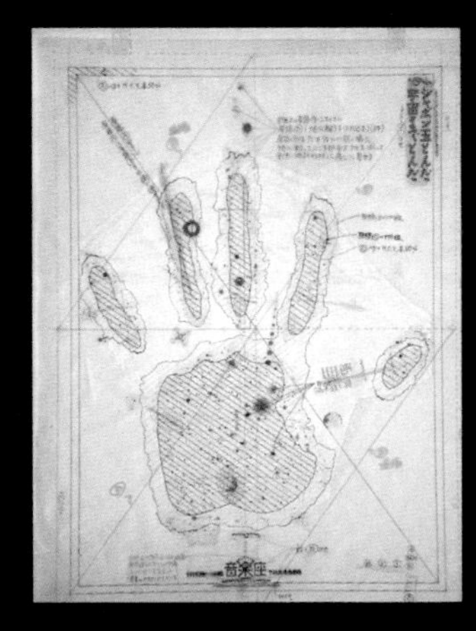

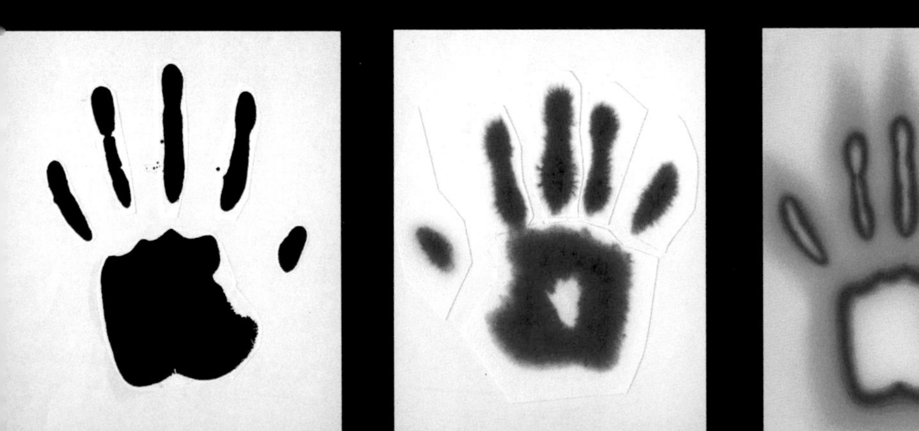

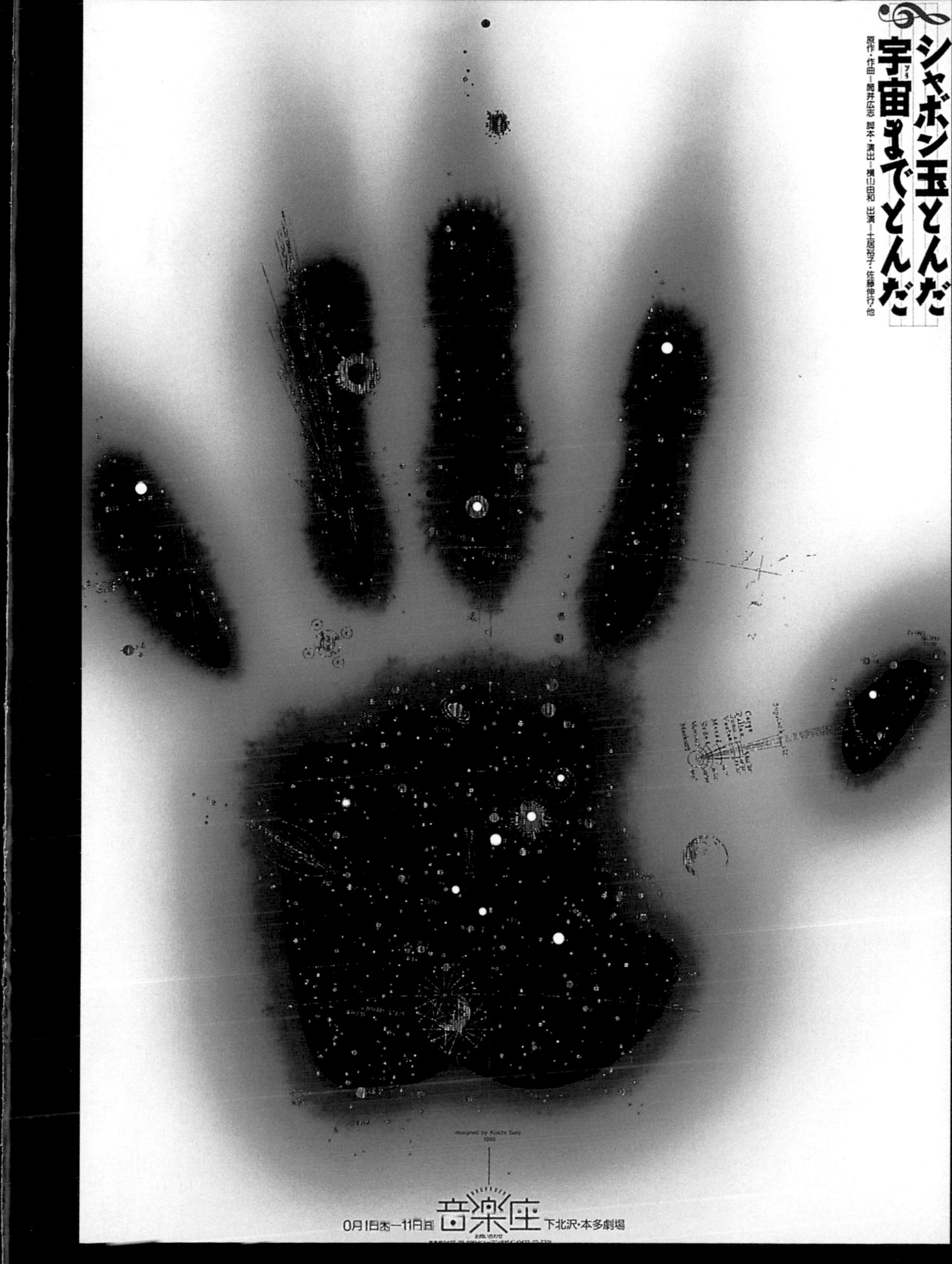

シャボン玉とんだ
宇宙(ソラ)までとんだ
原作・作曲＝筒井広志 脚本・演出＝横山由和 出演＝土居裕子・佐藤伸行・他
designed by Koichi Sato
音楽座
0月1日木—11日日
下北沢・本多劇場

The best books

The emergence of key works in any discipline happens over a long period of time, several decades at least. Much critical and historical work has to flow under the bridge before the central works of criticism can be recognised – so this is necessarily a very personal resumé. I have been careful to choose books that, at the time of writing, are all still in print and readily available. I do not include magazines here. A magazine, by design, is an ongoing project and needs to be engaged with over a long period. No one issue aims at a single, comprehensive, coherent argument. The books below set out to do exactly this.

History

If you have to read just one book about graphic design, then 'Looking Closer 3: Classic Writings on Graphic Design' is the one. Edited by designers and critics Michael Bierut, Jessica Helfand, Steven Heller and Rick Poynor, it is a collection of the most influential essays and articles. It ranges from William Morris in 1893 writing about 'The Ideal Book' to Massimo Vignelli in 1983 with his 'Call for Criticism'. The book manages to touch on all of the significant ideas and issues, and does so by presenting essays that deal with the subject as it arose within design's development. There is much serious and provocative stuff here. Warning for the lazy amongst you: no pictures, all text.

The most thorough history of graphic design is Philip Meggs' 'A History of Graphic Design', which runs to 500 pages. It is illustrated, has a generous page size and is very clear and easy to read. It firmly ties the development of graphic design to the machinery and technology that makes it. Although black-and-white throughout, the range of images is extraordinarily broad – there is no other single book that shows so much material: treasures such as the earliest printing; Chinese prayers dating back to 770 AD; and the Polyglot Bible, with a grid that runs five languages together on every page. It gives a better sense than almost any other book of design's vast scope and impact.

The best short history is Richard Hollis' 'Graphic Design, A Concise History'. This uses miniature black-and-white examples of design inserted into, or beside, the text discussing it – a relationship Hollis is somewhat obsessed with. He starts much later than Meggs and is forced to be briefer in his visits to all the major movements because of the size of the book, but it is therefore quicker to digest. Perfect read for a long journey.

A recent book, 'Graphic Design in the Mechanical Age' by Deborah Rothschild, Ellen Lupton and Darra Goldstein surveys material from just one collection from about 1910 to 1940, but this covers much that is significant in the development of Modernism: Dada, Constructivism, propaganda, photomontage and so on. The quality of the colour reproductions is exquisite, and these are worth intense examination on their own, even without the intelligent text.

Theory

'Decoding Advertisements' by Judith Williamson remains the most thorough analysis of what some designers and critics flippantly refer to as 'visual language' (without ever exploring the implications). This book is unique because it is completely unaffectionate – Williamson is not a designer and is unimpressed by clever picture cropping or sensitive letter spacing. She wants to get at how words and pictures can be used to construct what she calls 'ideological castles' which compel us to behave a certain way. She brings an acerbic mixture of Marxism and Structuralism to bear on a series of adverts from the 1970s, as she examines the design elements in great detail: camera angles; model; lighting; choice of typeface; use of space and so on – in effect the grammar and vocabulary of visual 'language'. Some parts make for difficult reading, especially the denser semiotic material, however it is the most significant theoretical text to date. It is depressing that this book was written in 1978, yet nothing taking on or developing its arguments has appeared since. Strangely enough the book's overtly Marxist politics, which are strongly felt and made the book obscure throughout the 1980s and 1990s, sit comfortably today alongside the arguments of newer politicised critics like Rick Poynor and Naomi Klein.

History and theory

Ellen Lupton and J Abbott Miller's 'Design Writing Research' (also the name of their design studio) examines serious and complex issues like 'deconstruction' with gravity and yet treats the history of punctuation with charm and levity. Eccentric and unafraid of disappearing down cul-de-sacs, this book combines the kind of intensity and thoroughness that can only come from designers passionate about design, yet armed with detailed knowledge and the explicatory ability of fastidious historians. Halfway between a history and a theory, it traces developments to reach theoretical conclusions. Intelligent and very engaging.

Steven Heller is not human, he cannot be! He has written well over 70 books about design, and three or four per year are still appearing. He combines research and writing with a full-time job as a senior art director at the New York Times. Somehow he also fits in teaching at the School of Visual Arts in New York, editing the AIGA Journal of Graphic Design, writing lengthy articles, and organising design conferences. 'Design Literacy, Understanding Graphic Design' co-written with Karen Pomeroy, is an easy and satisfying read. It takes the form of 94 brief and pithy essays, each introducing and examining a significant design piece. Heller's aim with the book was to ensure that "the object (piece of design) is not viewed as a fetish, but as a clue to the thinking of the designer and the working of the design". Each essay is a perfect balance of careful research, setting the design in the context of its making and examination of its visual mechanics – how it uses the elements of graphic design.

Designers

Most books by or about designers need to be read with a pinch of salt. Invariably, the writer is treating her subject with reverence, and withholds a freer, more analytical view of the work. This is particularly the case if the designer is still alive, and doubly the case if the designer is the writer! Very good books do exist however, where the work is of such high quality that however much you are cajoled to admire it, you still can. I offer three examples:

'Tibor' edited by Peter Hall and Michael Bierut, features the work of Tibor Kalman. One essay in the book asks the question, "Does Kalman have an important point to make about design and its relationship to society and politics, or not?" The entire book is an exploration of these contentious issues, showing Kalman's sparkling, clever work culminating in a series of powerful issues of the amazing Colors magazine. The captions are worth particular study, written several years after the creation of the designs they describe, they show how all the participants in a project – client, Kalman, assistant designers – have very different views of how the design came about and who was responsible for it. Unflaggingly stimulating, this book is a concerted effort to see design as something important and transformative.

Paul Rand is highly rated by some: "Every art director and graphic designer in the world should kiss his ass", says George Lois, and denigrated by others as the most significant proponent of an ossified and empty corporate modernism. 'Paul Rand, A Designer's Art' is his exploration of the ideas and areas of interest that shaped his work: the colour black; grids; the meaning and use of trademarks (he designed some of the best in the world); the play instinct and so on. Although the essays are short, they are dense and built on very thorough reading and thinking. The work is stunning, varied and beautifully executed and there is always an unexpected twist. This is design that goes more than halfway to becoming art.

'Sagmeister, Made You Look', written by Peter Hall and Stefan Sagmeister is a tour-de-force. Funny, sweet and honest (he even lists the fees he charged his clients), it is impossible to read this and not fall in love with Sagmeister. The book shows all his work from college to the present (at the time of writing) and is covered in scrawling diary extracts he wrote when working on each piece. Here is an extract: "Just came back from a meeting in Washington. Got introduced to about 30 members of Ben's crew. First impression: overweight, middle-America in polo shirts and supermarket sneakers. Second impression: some of the smartest, most compassionate (and at the same time, most powerful) people I have ever met". If anyone wants to know what a really, really good graphic designer thinks and goes through when he works, then this book will lead the way.

Visual culture

Not specifically about graphic design, but created by one of design's most admired figures, 'The Art of Looking Sideways' by Alan Fletcher is going to be the most cornucopic visual emporium we will see in our lifetimes. Like a gigantic scrapbook it covers every aspect of seeing, wordplay and visual conundrum that one designer is ever likely to encounter.
A snippet from the contents page will give some idea of the extent of its territory: tools; creativity; wit; improvisation; colour; dreaming; sychronicity; mutation; paradigms and automation. A hugely inspiring work.

Glossary

avant-garde
Popular phrase used too promiscuously to have much real meaning left. Once referred to artists, architects and designers who felt that artistic expression could help transform society. The early 20th-century avant-garde is replete with notable figures: Marinetti, Kurt Schwitters, El Lissitzky, Marcel Duchamp. The idea that design can have a revolutionary effect is immensely appealing, since it elevates designers to heroic status. The term avant-garde is now only occasionally used, but replacements appear willy-nilly – 'cutting-edge', 'new', and 'experimental' – regardless of any detectable revolutionary thinking or outcomes.

capitalism
Word dating from the 18th century used to describe the economic and social system that pertains in the Western world, and in varying degrees over most of the rest of the globe. The development of graphic design is inexorably intertwined with capitalism, since most of the features of design stem from market-driven developments: the printing press, the proliferation of different typefaces, computers and the need to differentiate products and companies.

client
Word used to represent the person, organisation or company paying for design work. As such, they are very significant. They choose which designer to use in the first place, and set the framework for the 'content'. They indicate the audience or readership or customers who will receive or purchase the design, and they establish the design's purpose. Many designers wish clients were not necessary, but design would not exist without them.

content
A fugitive word, since it cannot be shown to exist. Generally used to refer to the 'text', and the graphic treatment of the text is called the 'style'. But, of course, you can never have content without it appearing in some form or another, nor style without content. Content is always seen to be important, and style not so.

deconstruction theory
A mode of literary criticism that worries away at the meaning of words. Asked for a succinct definition of deconstruction, its main proponent, Jacques Derrida said "I have no simple and formalisable response to this question. All my essays are attempts to have it out with this formidable question". A number of designers, many influenced by the teaching at Cranbrook and CalArts in America, use phrases and fragments of ideas gleaned from deconstruction in writing or talking about their work. In the long run, it is very positive that designers are now aware of theory, and dense, complex, politically charged theory at that. The relationship between theory and practice needs more reflection: "Theory has opened up a multitude of ways that we can understand our work, but it will not tell anyone how to produce better or more interesting design" (Lorraine Wild).

mainstream
A lazy term, which disintegrates under the mildest examination, usually used in a derogatory sense: the unthinking, tradition-bound rump made up of the majority of ordinary people. It is set up in contrast to what the designer or the critic sees as really mattering: the 'avant-garde', the fresh, the 'cutting edge', the new, the subversive.

Modernism
Used in many different senses. Beginning in the late-19th century, in the worlds of literature and music, Modernism represents a group of wildly experimental and ironic artists like James Joyce and Stravinsky. In architecture and design it began this way, but moved towards what Charles Jencks calls 'univalence': a unified, universal language that could be used all over the globe to usher in a more democratic, fairer and peaceful world. In graphic design it is most strongly typified by the 'Swiss school' of the 1940s and 1950s. The conviction of Modernists is now seen by some designers and critics as aggravating, the style as oppressive and somehow insufficiently capable of allowing 'self-expression'.

politics
Many designers become extremely uncomfortable at the mention of this word. It is complex, not meaning politics in any sense of a political party, but 'generally how you see the world'. Do you think the world is just fine as it is, or does it need radical change? The individual's politics are often affected by who they are: a rich, white, male designer working in London or New York is unlikely to see the need for much change. Politics has made an entry into teaching and writing about design, but in a somewhat covert way. Often, to use the word 'political' is enough to seem 'avant-garde'. Very few designers or critics make their political positions expansively clear. Critic/designer Johanna Drucker argues for "a more rigorous form of criticism, closer in its methods to the literary kind, in which critical positions are clearly stated and defended", to push towards design that is, "more inclusive, more genuinely multicultural, while at the same time maintaining the highest educational, conceptual, and technical standards".

sign
A word from structuralist theory. Something that stands for, refers to, or represents a concept or something in the real world. It can be a word or an image, or both. A new extremely complicated theory has grown up studying the nature of signs, called semiotics. Part science, part linguistics, part literary criticism, Umberto Eco has written the most accessible books explaining semiotics, most recently 'Kant and the Platypus'.

text
Originally used to mean a sequence of words, but now broadly used to mean any structured communication. Therefore any piece of graphic design articulates a 'text', and can be 'read' as a 'text'. This has come about because of the structuralist idea that all words, images, or combinations of the two, are all 'signs'.

Index

Credits

Thanks first to my editors and researcher, Becky Moss, Zara Emerson and Tina Warnock at RotoVision, who all have bottomless patience and sweetness.

Thanks to David Hawkins and Nina Nägel, loyal soldiers in the battle to make this book.

Thanks to all those who have been so generous with all sorts of help, especially Peter Wood, Peter Davenport and Simon Esterson.

Thanks to Ian Chilvers and Patrick Baglee who read proofs and patted my head when I needed it.

Thanks to all those that work with me at Atelier, who all had to put up with messy piles of books and my mood swings for the last six months.

Thanks to Rick Poynor – any perceived criticism or correction of him in this book ought to be taken as a tribute to the centrality of his voluminous writing to any understanding of contemporary design.

Thanks to David Stuart, who casually suggested I try writing (and so is to blame for this book). Thanks to Lynda Relph-Knight, Steve Heller, Patrick Burgoyne and Hans Dieter Reichart who spurred me on by trusting me to write.

Thanks to Derek Birdsall, John McConnell, John Sorrell and Frances Newell, Henry Steiner, Michael Wolff and Ken Garland who each of whom set towering examples to live up to.

Thanks to the magic Alan Fletcher, I owe him an unpayable debt.

Thanks most of all to my wife, Mette, without whom life would barely be worth living.